Global Turning Points

2nd edition

The second edition of this popular and thought-provoking textbook offers an accessible yet sophisticated analysis of the game-changing events and trends that are transforming the world beyond recognition. For the first time in human history more people live in cities than in the countryside, and greater numbers suffer from obesity or being overweight than from hunger. Emerging economies now represent half of the global economy, and during the next few decades, India will become the biggest country in terms of population, China the largest in output, and the United States the richest among the major economies on a per capita income basis. Food and water shortages will likely become humankind's most important challenges. With four new chapters on the rise of the global middle class, the transformative power of technology, institutions and the entrepreneurial spirit, and the trials and tribulations of the financial system, this book provides a thorough introduction to the challenges facing business and society in the twenty-first century.

Mauro F. Guillén is the Director of the Joseph H. Lauder Institute at the University of Pennsylvania, a research-and-teaching program on management and international studies. He is also the Zandman Professor of International Management at the Wharton School. He is the author of nine books and over thirty scholarly papers, and is a former Guggenheim and Fulbright Fellow, and a Member in the Institute for Advanced Study in Princeton. He serves as a member of the Global Agenda Council on Emerging Multinationals at the World Economic Forum, and a trustee of the Fundación Princesa de Asturias.

Emilio Ontiveros is Founder and President of Analistas Financieros Internacionales, S.A., President of Tecnología, Información y Finanzas, and Escuela de Finanzas Aplicadas (subsidiaries of AFI Group, a consultancy). He has served as Professor of Economic and Business Administration at the Universidad Autónoma de Madrid since 1985, where he was Vice Chancellor for four years. He has been Visiting Scholar at the Harvard Royal Complutense College and the Wharton School. He serves, or has served, on the board of directors of several Spanish companies.

Global Turning Points

The Challenges for Business and
Society in the 21st Century

Mauro F. Guillén
Emilio Ontiveros

CAMBRIDGE
UNIVERSITY PRESS

CAMBRIDGE
UNIVERSITY PRESS

University Printing House, Cambridge CB2 8BS, United Kingdom

Cambridge University Press is part of the University of Cambridge.

It furthers the University's mission by disseminating knowledge in the pursuit of education, learning and research at the highest international levels of excellence.

www.cambridge.org
Information on this title: www.cambridge.org/9781316503539

© Mauro F. Guillén and Emilio Ontiveros 2016

First published 2012
Second edition 2016

Printed in the United Kingdom by TJ International Ltd. Padstow Cornwall

A catalog record for this publication is available from the British Library

Library of Congress Cataloging-in-Publication Data
Names: Guillén, Mauro F., author. | Ontiveros Baeza, Emilio, 1948–, author.
Title: Global turning points : the challenges for business and society in the 21st century /
Mauro F. Guillén, Emilio Ontiveros.
Description: Second edition. | Cambridge, United Kingdom : Cambridge University Press, 2016. |
Includes bibliographical references and index.
Identifiers: LCCN 2015037121| ISBN 9781107138681 (Hardback : alk. paper) |
ISBN 9781316503539 (Paperback : alk. paper)
Subjects: LCSH: Economic history–21st century. | Economic forecasting.
Classification: LCC HC59.3 .G85 2016 | DDC 330.9–dc23 LC record available at http://lccn.loc
.gov/2015037121

ISBN 978-1-107-13868-1 Hardback
ISBN 978-1-316-50353-9 Paperback

Contents

List of illustrations   *page* vi
List of tables   viii
Preface   ix

1 Welcome to the twenty-first century   1

2 A global economy out of balance   8

3 The rise of the emerging-market multinationals   24

4 The new demography: aging, migration, and obesity   39

5 From dictatorship to democracy and failed states   59

6 A disparate world: inequality and poverty   76

7 The rise of the global middle class and
   the high-net-worth elite   92

8 The transformative power of technology   108

9 Development, institutions, and entrepreneurship   120

10 The quest for sustainability   136

11 The trials and tribulations of the financial system   149

12 The global powers of the twenty-first century   160

13 Coping with uncertainty and complexity   184

   References   198
   Index   218

Illustrations

Figures

2.1 GDP share of the developed (OECD) versus the emerging and developing economies (non-OECD), 1990–2030   *page* 13

2.2 Proportion of OECD countries with at least two consecutive quarters of GDP decline, by quarter, 1970–2010   16

2.3 Global current account imbalances, 1980–2019 (% of GDP)   18

2.4 Global flows of inward foreign direct investment (FDI) and international mergers and acquisitions (M&As), 1990–2013   18

2.5 Public debt, 1980–2020 (% of GDP)   20

4.1 Total fertility rate and life expectancy at birth, 1950–2100   41

4.2 Population by region (% of world's total), 1950–2100   43

4.3 Age pyramids for selected countries, 1960, 2010, and 2060   45

4.4 Urban population (% of total) and international migrant population (as % of total population)   49

5.1 Global trends in political regimes, 1800–2013   63

5.2 Global trends in armed conflict, 1946–2013   71

5.3 Displaced and refugee populations, 1964–2008   73

5.4 Number of victims in high-casualty terrorist bombings, 1992–2014   74

6.1 Income inequality across countries, weighted by population (Gini Index), 1950–2008   78

7.1 The growth of the global middle class, 1965–2009, with projections to 2030   96

7.2 Distribution of middle-class consumption by country or region, 1965–2009, with projections to 2030   97

7.3 Number of passenger cars and commercial vehicles per 100,000 people, selected countries   99

7.4 Enrollments in tertiary education   100

9.1 Total early-state entrepreneurship, as a percentage of the population aged 18–64, by GDP per capita, 2014   127

9.2 Owner-managers of an established business, as a percentage of the population aged 18–64, by GDP per capita, 2013   128

10.1   World threats to biodiversity   140
10.2   People living under severe water stress   141
10.3   Incremental primary energy demand by fuel and region,
       2008–2035   143
10.4   Global CO_2 emissions   144
10.5   China's share of projected net global increase for
       selected energy indicators   146
12.1   Major economies, 1870–2008   176
12.2   GDP per capita for major economies, 1870–2008   178
13.1   The four institutional gearboxes shaping global
       dynamics in the twenty-first century   193

Map
5.1   State fragility and state failure, 2013   63

Tables

3.1	The 25 largest multinational firms from emerging economies, ranked by foreign assets, 2012	*page* 28
3.2	Cumulative stocks of outward foreign direct investment	30
4.1	World's ten largest cities	47
4.2	Percentage of the population aged 15 or above that is hungry and percentage that is obese, selected countries	50
6.1	Income inequality, selected countries	80
6.2	Trends in real household income by income group, mid 1980s to late 2000s	82
6.3	Women in parliament (% of total seats)	88
7.1	The global middle class in 2009 (actual) and 2030 (forecast)	98
12.1	Population, GDP, and GDP per capita, selected economies, 1–2008	161
12.2	Nye's indicators of power resources, 2012	174
13.1	Major turning points, drivers, and consequences in the twenty-first century	185

Preface

Saying that the world is changing fast has become part of the conventional wisdom. Changes affecting us are not only faster, but more difficult to predict, and of greater economic and political significance. From the economy to politics, and from culture to the environment, the global situation created during the first decade of the twenty-first century is drastically different from the one inherited from the twentieth century. We are overwhelmed by the systemic interactions among economic, business, political, social, demographic, environmental, and geopolitical variables. We are concerned about the consequences of these changes and eager to find new ways of framing and solving the problems they have brought us.

We decided to write this book so as to better understand ourselves the nature and consequences of large-scale changes and to help others understand them. We are interested not just in trends and events but in *turning points*, that is, veritable game changers, inflexions that have transformed human societies as we knew them. The rise of the emerging economies, population aging, urbanization, governmental gridlock and the breakdown of state authority, deepening inequalities, environmental degradation, and the reconfiguration of global power relationships have created a new set of constraints and opportunities that will shape the world for decades to come. In this second, expanded edition we also analyze the rise of the global middle class, the transformative power of technology, the institutions of economic development, and the trials and tribulations of the financial system.

Our main audience is decision makers, from the ordinary citizen who needs to figure out how to balance consumption and saving, or whether to invest more in education or not, to the business leaders and policymakers making big decisions that affect millions of people. We offer them an accessible, yet sophisticated, analysis of major global turning points and future scenarios with an emphasis on actionable issues.

This book is based on years of research and writing on current global issues. Both authors are frequent contributors to public debates in Europe and the United States. We are both academics, but with extensive experience in the private sector as entrepreneurs, consultants, and advisors. In the book we deploy the tools of economics, sociology, and political science to provide an analytical perspective on the big problems and opportunities facing the world in the twenty-first century. We present not just our own points of view but also the different positions among experts on each of the topics discussed in the book. We show a large amount of information on trends and events, including future projections with the goal of ascertaining where the world is at the present day and where it is headed. We also suggest the range of solutions available to us as individuals, citizens, and decision makers, and compare their benefits and costs.

We would like to thank the many business leaders, policymakers, and ordinary citizens we have met over the last few years to discuss the topics covered in this book. They have been a constant source of information and insight. As always, we would also like to thank the people who supported this effort with their hard work, especially Lucía Nogueroles at Analistas Financieros Internacionales. Our families also supported us in other, even more important, ways.

1 Welcome to the twenty-first century

In 2001, two momentous events shook the world. On September 11 a small group of bold terrorists mounted a series of daring attacks on the United States, and on September 17 the World Trade Organization concluded its 15-year-old membership negotiations with China. Although the world's preeminent geopolitical power had been the target of other terrorist attacks during the preceding decade, 9/11 was qualitatively different not only because of the large number of victims but also because it undermined the country's sense of security. Likewise, China's economic and financial rise had been in the making since the 1980s, but it was not until the early 2000s that the world came to the realization that Earth's most populous country would one day also become the largest economy, and that it was already the world's largest exporter and the second largest importer. Chinese exports, trade surpluses, and currency reserves soared, with the US reaching record deficits in its current account. These global imbalances set the stage for the most severe global economic and financial crisis in decades.

Welcome to the twenty-first century. The new centennial is a teenager and it has already developed its own, unique personality. This book deals with the challenges facing us in the new century. It is not one more exercise at projecting past trends into the future, but an analysis of the major global *turning points* confronting us, namely, the game-changing events and trends that are transforming the world beyond recognition. A series of such inflexion points has occurred over the last decade or so – and they will reshape the economic, socio-demographic, political, and geopolitical affairs for decades to come:

- The global economy is out of balance. Most of the large rich economies, with the notable exceptions of Germany and Japan, are running large trade deficits while most emerging economies are enjoying large surpluses. After two decades of intense economic growth, emerging

1

economies now represent about half of global economic activity. Emerging economies are also flexing their financial muscle because they own two thirds of foreign exchange reserves, of which they are accumulating an additional billion dollars *every day*.

- Emerging-market multinational firms are expanding around the world like wildfire. Once a marginal phenomenon, as of 2014 they represented 31 percent of the largest 500 companies in the world, 29 percent of the total number of multinational firms, and 28 percent of new foreign direct investment flows over the previous five years.

- Demographic conditions are changing fast. For the first time in human history, Japan and several Western European countries have inverted age pyramids with more people above age 60 than below age 20. Also for the first time, more people live in cities than in the countryside, and greater numbers suffer from obesity or being overweight than from hunger.

- The political landscape in many parts of the world has taken a turn towards uncertainty, chaos, and anarchy. For the first time since World War II there are more countries in the world affected by state failure than countries ruled by dictators. In general, there is a sharp decline in the legitimacy and capacity of the state in both developed and developing countries.

- We live in an increasingly disparate world. Although income inequality *across* countries has decreased since the turn of the twenty-first century due to the rise of the emerging economies, inequality *within* countries has continued to increase, posing difficult social and political problems in developed and developing countries alike.

- Consumer markets are being transformed by the rise of the global middle class, especially in Brazil, Mexico, China, India, and South-East Asia. Demand for consumer durables and non-durables as well as services will expand rapidly as growth in emerging economies continues to lift people out of poverty. At the top of the social pecking order, the high-net-worth elite will continue to expand and to include more women as a proportion of the total.

- Technology, especially of the mobile kind, continues to revolutionize consumption and lifestyles. Manufacturing and distribution are also being transformed with the advent of artificial intelligence, smart robotics, nanotechnologies, 3D printing, and drones. Meanwhile, bioinformatics and biotechnology promise to overhaul healthcare.

- Economic growth is driven not so much by labor and capital but by institutions, the norms and rules of the game that make it possible for entrepreneurs, companies, suppliers, and financiers to interact on a daily basis. Governments compete with each other to create the best institutional conditions to foster entrepreneurship and innovation.
- Sustainability has become a key priority. Top scientists predict that, without corrective action, climate change will become irreversible at some tipping point during the twenty-first century. By 2030 food prices could be twice as high as in 2012, and half of the world's population could be affected by severe water shortages.
- The financial system continues to give headaches to customers and regulators. A decade after the first signs of trouble emerged, banks and other financial companies have adapted only minimally to the new regulatory environment, the need for greater transparency, and disruptive technological trends.
- The global balance of power is shifting rapidly. During most of the twenty-first century India will be the biggest country in terms of population, China the largest in output, and the United States the richest among the major economies on a per capita income basis.

Some people find it hard to accept that the world order they grew up with might be coming to an end. Others feel that change is so pervasive that one can no longer assume any givens. Both reactions are understandable, precisely because the changes are so massive and they affect so many different aspects of global affairs. There are simply too many moving parts. Complexity is a key future of contemporary global society. Although the risks and the stakes were also high, the Cold War period never gave us a sense of overwhelming insecurity. Even the risk of nuclear war provided the foundation for the doctrine of "mutually assured destruction," which made it possible for the two global superpowers to find an accommodation. The twenty-first century is different. We are at the mercy of the catastrophic disruptions that a malfunctioning component of the increasingly complex global system can bring about. Think about epidemics such as SARS or the swine flu, global financial meltdowns like the one triggered by the subprime crisis in the United States, the European sovereign debt debacle, the riots generated by rising food prices in much of the developing world, or the quake and tsunami in Japan and its widespread consequences for global production and trade. The twenty-first century is the century of complexity.

Perhaps we could easily learn to cope with complexity if it did not come hand in hand with uncertainty. We know how to deal with risk: we can measure it, we can prepare for it, we can anticipate the consequences. But uncertainty is a situation in which we do not understand the variables involved and we lack the tools to quantify them. Uncertainty is difficult to grasp or comprehend. The rise of the global network society has unleashed many different kinds of uncertainties. We are just not sure as to what the effects of droughts, declining fertility rates, or political upheavals will be. We simply have little clue. The twenty-first century is the century of complexity coupled with uncertainty.

Another most intractable feature of the twenty-first century is that most changes appear to be paradoxical. Consider the following examples. The rise of the emerging economies is making it possible for hundreds of millions of people to overcome poverty. However, it also poses stern challenges in terms of job losses in the developed world, competition for energy and natural resources, and global economic and financial governance. We will explore this topic in Chapter 2. Another example is the rise of the emerging-market multinationals, companies that were invisible a few years ago but have suddenly become household names. The paradox about them is that their increasing power and competitiveness is not necessarily based on the possession of technology or marketing skills. They have rewritten the rules of business competition, much to their advantage and at the expense of the traditional multinational firms from Europe, the US, and Japan. We will cover the fascinating rise of the emerging-market multinationals in Chapter 3.

Equally puzzling are the demographic changes that are taking place in the world. The decline in the average number of children born to each woman has proceeded much faster in Europe, East Asia (especially China and Japan), and to a lesser extent North America. Women in those regions now have much better economic, political, and social opportunities available to them. But these societies are aging very quickly. In the meantime, population continues to increase in Africa, South Asia, and the Middle East. It is also ironic that as economic development spreads around the world, we find ourselves in a situation in which there are more people suffering from obesity (about one billion) than from hunger (800 million).

As of the first decade of the twenty-first century, the world has become predominantly urban, with more people living in cities than in the countryside for the first time in human history. Competition for natural resources now affects not only oil and rare minerals but also food and water. We will address the causes and the consequences of these and other demographic turning points in Chapter 4.

If there is an enigma that is likely to haunt us during the twenty-first century, it is why democracy has made great strides as the dominant form of government in the world while at the same time the number of failed states has proliferated. Nearly 50 countries suffer from some degree of state failure, including not only egregious examples such as Chad, Congo, Sudan, Somalia, Iraq, and Afghanistan, but also other threatened states like Mexico, Nigeria, Pakistan, and India. This trend has caused major problems in the global economy and in trade, and made terrorism the dominant form of violent conflict, whereas in the twentieth century conventional wars were. In Chapter 5 we will explain that the confluence of rapid demographic growth, political instability, and natural resources in Africa, the Middle East, and South Asia poses serious threats to global society in the twenty-first century. Another paradoxical trend is the new emphasis on good institutional governance at a the same time that state capacity is diminishing due to the ideology of small government and the fallout from the sovereign debt crisis.

Global inequality and poverty have also come to characterize the twenty-first century in ways that are very different from the recent past. For the first time in two centuries, we are witnessing less inequality *across* countries at the same time that inequality *within* both developed and developing countries is on the increase. Enigmatically, poverty is coming down even in countries in which inequality is on the rise. We will analyze these puzzling turning points in Chapter 6.

While the middle class has contracted in Western Europe and the United States, it is swelling in the emerging world. For the first time in human history, more than half of the world's population will be part of the middle class within a decade. As we will see in Chapter 7, China and India combined will be greater as a middle-class consumer market than Europe and the United States combined. This will enable them to participate in the writing of global market rules, including regulatory matters and product standards. The numbers of high-net-worth individuals are also growing quickly, especially in emerging economies, with the number of female millionaires growing faster than the number of male millionaires.

A main driver of economic vitality in the contemporary world is technology. Mobile technology is transforming consumption and lifestyles, especially among the young. As analyzed in Chapter 8, manufacturing is undergoing a massive revolution due to the implementation of artificial intelligence, smart robotics, nanotechnologies, and 3D printing. Meanwhile, distribution is also becoming automated, and drones may soon deliver goods to homes and offices. Life, and the way we experience life, are changing fast, and so is healthcare, thanks to advances in genetics, biotechnology, and bioinformatics.

Economies are no longer amalgams of capital and labor. Institutions ranging from the educational system to the legal order, and from the stock market to corporate governance, have become key ingredients for economic success. In Chapter 9 we will assess the renewed emphasis on institutions as the foundation for economic growth, entrepreneurship, and innovation. We will also examine the differences between men and women when it comes to founding and managing ventures.

Growth in the emerging economies has come hand in hand with environmental degradation. In developed and developing countries alike, a quest for sustainability is on. The emphasis is not only on energy, but also on green production and consumption of goods and services. Agriculture, construction, and tourism have also become targets of sustainability efforts. Technology and behavioral change are touted as the solutions. Emerging economies are making contributions of their own to global sustainability, as the cases of sugarcane ethanol in Brazil, water management in Thailand, or wind power in China and India attest. Water and food are also becoming scarce commodities. We will examine the challenge of global sustainability in Chapter 10.

Before taking stock of the global balance of power, we will review in Chapter 11 the trials and tribulations of the financial system, a part of the economy that is as indispensable as it is problematic at the present time. Banks and other financial companies are essential to the economy, but they are having enormous trouble adapting to the post-crisis environment, with increased regulatory scrutiny, societal demands for transparency, and a limited ability to adapt to disruptive technological change.

These economic, demographic, and geopolitical turning points are rapidly eroding the dominance of the United States as the leading global power. In April of 2011 the International Monetary Fund shook American public opinion with its prediction that China's economy would be the world's largest by 2016. We will explore in Chapter 12 to what extent historical patterns in the rise and fall of dominant global powers help understand the new situation created in the twenty-first century, one in which not one but several powers may share the global stage.

Finally, in Chapter 13, we will examine the implications of these global turning points for business and for society at large. We seek to identify the challenges and the opportunities that stem from each of them. We will argue that the world needs new approaches to global governance in order to deal with the complexity, uncertainty, and interconnectedness that characterizes the global economy, the international system of states, social dynamics, and geopolitics in the twenty-first century. The world is replete with uncertainty and complexity, and we do not seem to have in place the economic, political, and geopolitical institutions to cope with it all.

The issues summarized – the large and persistent global financial imbalances, the growing lack of competitiveness of rich-country firms relative to the emerging-market multinationals, population aging, urbanization, the obesity epidemic, failed states, terrorism, the unequal distribution of income, environmental degradation, global warming, the looming crisis over food and water, and the lack of global political leadership – present a formidable set of challenges. The potentially negative impact of these issues is exacerbated by the complex ways in which they interact with one another, the uncertainties they generate at all levels, from the local community to the global system, and the speed at which their effects can be felt in an interconnected world. Welcome to the twenty-first century.

2 A global economy out of balance

> **KEY GLOBAL TURNING POINTS**
>
> Emerging economies have come to represent more than half of global economic activity. They account for two thirds of foreign exchange reserves and are accumulating an additional billion dollars *every day*.

From an economic point of view, the transition from the twentieth to the twenty-first century took place in the midst of growing trade and financial interrelationships among countries, and the widespread impact of information and telecommunication technologies. Another important development was an increasing cross-national convergence in policymaking, as a result for the most part of a consensus over the fundamental features of monetary and fiscal policy, the benefits of deregulation, and the importance of letting markets allocate capital, labor, and other resources. The global economy was simply tending towards greater integration under a liberal set of rules (Abdelal 2007; Stiglitz 2002). As Robert Gilpin (1987: 389; 2000) once put it, the late twentieth century resulted in an "increasing interdependence of national economies in trade, finance, and macroeconomic policy." The global economy was moving in the direction of tighter integration in all of its different aspects, from production and distribution to capital and information flows. In this vein, sociologist Manuel Castells (1996: 92) argued that the global economy had become "an economy with the capacity to work as a unit in real time on a planetary scale."

Policymakers were hoping for equal opportunities for all countries that joined this new phase of globalization. Markets were open to everyone in an apparently inclusive way. The frontier of development and well-being was extended to a greater number of economies, all of which were supposedly converging on the living standards of the most advanced countries. Policymakers and analysts also thought that the global economy was eminently governable, and that business cycles were a thing of the past. The sociologist

Roland Robertson (1992: 8) summarized the new mind-set by arguing that globalization encompassed both "the compression of the world and the intensification of consciousness of the world as a whole."

As soon as the new century was ushered in, however, a series of crises turned the global economy upside down: the bursting of the technology bubble, a string of high-profile corporate scandals, and, above all, the global economic and financial crisis triggered by the implosion of the American subprime mortgage market. The "great recession" accentuated a trend towards a two-speed global economy. Despite difficulties in some of them, emerging economies weathered the storm much better than both developing and developed markets, surging ahead economically and financially while the richest and the poorest economies languished and wrestled to cope with high private and public indebtedness.

The first decade of the new century was marked by growing imbalances, which continue to threaten global economic and financial stability. Government debt in the high-income countries has reached levels not seen since the end of World War II, during which the allies borrowed heavily to finance the war effort. The emerging economies have expanded their exports of manufactured goods, mostly to Europe and the United States, while commodity exporters have benefited from rising prices, which has resulted in persistently large trade surpluses in some parts of the world and large deficits in others (see the Box). This trend accelerated considerably after 2001 with China's accession to the World Trade Organization. Lastly, growing trade imbalances have led to a peculiar situation for the first time in global history, namely, the accumulation of large foreign currency reserves in emerging and developing countries, which have become net creditors to the richest countries. Emerging economies have been earning about a billion dollars of additional reserves *every day*, with more than 300 million going to China alone.

Global economic exchange

Countries trade goods, services, and capital with one another. In the process of doing so, some accumulate deficits while others generate surpluses. In the absence of inter-planetary trade, the deficits in some

(cont.)

countries need to be compensated by surpluses of an equivalent magnitude in other countries.

The broadest measure of the economic transactions of a country with the rest of the world is the current account. It comprises the net balance of trade in goods, trade in services, income generated or paid abroad (e.g., dividends on investments), and transfers, such as workers' remittances or foreign aid.

If the current account is in deficit, the country needs to find financing from abroad either in the form of capital transfers or a foreign loan. Countries with a surplus provide the financing and accumulate reserves to the same extent.

During the first decade of the twenty-first century countries such as the US, the UK, much of Continental Europe, and the oil-importing countries in the developing world ran persistently high deficits in their current account, which means that they imported much more than they exported. By contrast, Germany, Japan, China, and a long list of exporters of oil and other commodities accumulated large surpluses.

The growing trade and financial imbalances in the global economy pose serious threats to stability and governance. It is also important to note that, with only a few exceptions, emerging economies are providing the financing for the large current account and government deficits in the high-income countries.

One should keep in mind, however, that the root causes of these growing imbalances do not lie in the shifting structure of international economic exchange alone. "While currency and trade adjustments have a role to play in reducing the problem of imbalances," Pankaj Ghemawat (2011: 169) has cogently argued, "the United States also needs to address the domestic factors that underlie its savings-investment gap." So does most of Western Europe, with the exceptions of Germany, the Netherlands, Denmark, and Switzerland. At the other end of the spectrum, China should stimulate domestic demand as an engine of growth.

Global encounters of the third kind

We inherited from the twentieth century a rich legacy of international cooperation that made it possible for the global community to overcome the destruction and dislocation brought about by World War II. The legendary Bretton Woods agreements of 1944, which came into effect in 1947, facilitated economic and trade growth. For four interminable decades, however, the world remained divided into two competing political–economic blocs. Free markets supplemented by Keynesian policymaking ultimately won the battle over central planning. The momentum was strong enough to overcome the difficult oil crisis of the 1970s, and globalization continued to grow even after the collapse of the orderly system of quasi-fixed exchange rates.

Trade and capital flow liberalization, especially as practiced by the most developed countries, widened the gap between capitalist and centrally planned economies. Economic backwardness combined with an aspiration for political participation and freedoms to produce the momentous breakdown of Communist rule in Eastern Europe and the Soviet Union. We entered the twenty-first century confident in that free markets and democracy had demonstrated their superiority when it came to organizing societies and economies. A triumphant mood took over. The coming into effect of the World Trade Organization in 1995 was perhaps the crowning achievement of decades of tortuous negotiations to create a truly free global trading system. Although the world was also fragmenting into large, continental-sized trade blocs such as the European Union, the North American Free Trade Agreement, and the Mercosur Customs Union, the momentum was one of integration (Mansfield and Milner 1999). Globalism appeared to be consistent with the emergence of regionalism in trade.

Economic and political change coincided with the proliferation of information and telecommunications technologies, which – we now know – also contributed to economic integration and political transformations. Companies learned how to operate in far-flung locations as a unit in real time, investors could move money around the world at a moment's notice, individuals stayed connected no matter their location. Some analysts declared the death of distance (Cairncross 1997). Moore's Law that computing capacity would increase while the cost declined made it possible to boost productivity (Brynjolfsson *et al.* 2002), while the Internet enabled connectivity, and spurred multiple new industries while transforming everything from agriculture to publishing, production to sales, logistics to financial markets, and education to social networking. Outsourcing, offshoring, delocalization, and myriad other forms of spatial reorganization followed suit. Their influence is also noticeable in the process of regional integration, especially in less developed economies (Ontiveros *et al.* 2008). Large American service-sector corporations like Accenture and IBM now have more employees in emerging economies than in the United States. Still, the potential of information and telecommunication technologies is far from being fully realized. The economy, the society, and the political system are all changing as a result of their widespread adoption and use.

We are thus witnessing not a third phase of globalization in the twenty-first century but a qualitatively different globalization of the third kind, a far cry from the late nineteenth century or the post-World War II period. Emerging economies and even many poor countries are increasingly participants in a more interconnected global economic system in which the geographical and functional divisions of labor are changing very fast. In Africa, for instance, just 16 million people had a mobile phone in 2000. By the end of the decade, the number approached 500 million and 70 percent of the population had mobile service coverage. Farmers, small business owners, and consumers in general can communicate and even perform financial transactions easily and at low cost (Aker and Mbiti 2010). Latin America has already reached levels of mobile telephone use equivalent to those of Europe. The new global economy of the twenty-first century, supported by information and telecommunication technologies, could well realize for the first time the promise of a world in which knowledge is dispersed, production technologies and skills are widely shared, and trade and capital movements are truly seamless.

This globalization of the third kind is also characterized by the rise of the emerging economies as prominent global players, namely the BRICs (Brazil, Russia, India, China) and the MINTSs (Mexico, Indonesia, Nigeria, Turkey, South Africa). During the first decade of the twenty-first century, the emerging economies grew at an average annual rate of between 8 and 9 percent, compared to 2 or 3 percent for the most developed countries.

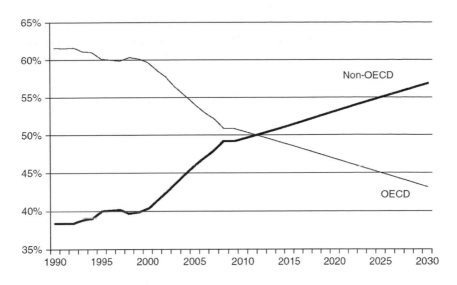

Figure 2.1 GDP share of the developed (OECD) versus the emerging and developing economies (non-OECD), 1990–2030 (% of global GDP in purchasing power parity terms)
Note: Data from 2009 onwards are projections.
Source: OECD.

As a result, the emerging and developing world is now as big economically as the developed world (see Figure 2.1). The emerging economies, however, are not a homogenous bunch. China's growth has been driven by export-oriented manufacturing, with state-owned banks, infrastructure, and natural-resource companies playing an increasingly important role, especially in terms of foreign investments. The Indian economy, by contrast, has prospered on the basis of human capital with technical skills and the opportunities for global outsourcing of business activities. Both economies are increasing their productivity very quickly (Bosworth and Collins 2008).

Not everything is rosy, however, in the emerging world. Economic growth has come hand in hand with rapid urbanization, especially in China. Residential construction and the expansion of private credit continue to make an important contribution to China's growth. The government is rightly concerned with overheating and the need to avoid real estate and financial bubbles from bursting in an uncontrolled way. Brazil experienced similar problems, with a once soaring currency that undermined its international competitiveness while massive capital inflows contributed to a bubble economy that could disinflate if foreign money stampedes out of the country at the first sign of trouble. The three largest emerging economies of China, India, and Brazil also confront a massive challenge in terms of ensuring that the benefits of economic growth reach the most disadvantaged social strata and rural areas.

The increasing global economic and financial integration does not mean that the world is flat, as Thomas Friedman (2005) would have us believe. Numerous analysts have pointed out that the world is "spiky" (Florida 2005) or "semi-globalized" (Ghemawat 2007). The global spread of markets and multinational corporations is incomplete. Different organizational forms of corporate activity continue to exist around the world as state-owned corporations, family firms, and business conglomerates proliferate in some countries but not others. Migration flows are nowhere near the intensity registered in the late nineteenth and early twentieth centuries. Industries such as healthcare, transportation, water, and electricity continue to be highly regulated. The global economy appears to be as diverse as decades ago, although it is decisively more interconnected and interdependent.

The most complex crisis in history

Rather than an inflexion in the economic cycle, the global financial crisis that started in the summer of 2007 represents a major watershed and epitomizes the consequences of the increasingly interconnected nature of the global economy. Its rapid spread across markets – from real estate to the financial sector and the real economy – and across countries speaks to the staggeringly complex web of linkages that has come to characterize global economic and financial activity (Guillén and Suárez 2010; Guillén 2015). The unprecedented nature of the crisis was made evident by the fact that the financial convulsion originated from the world's most sophisticated, innovative, and globally interconnected financial system, whereas previous banking crises tended to involve emerging and developing countries (Laeven and Valencia 2008). The size and global integration of financial operators, their abysmal risk management practices, the failures of financial regulators, and the dubious workings of the rating agencies all contributed to the perfect storm of 2008, when global financial markets nearly melted down, wholesale financing for banks dried up, and a severe credit crunch for consumers and businesses choked economic activity (Reinhardt and Rogoff 2009; Berges *et al.* 2014).

The economic and financial crisis was fueled by global imbalances – the large savings and reserve accumulation in emerging economies coupled with the large deficits of the US, Spain, and other economies – but had its origin in a relatively small corner of the American real estate market. The liquidity crisis that started in the summer of 2007 was triggered by rising doubts about subprime mortgages and the value of the derivative securities associated with them. The original liquidity crisis quickly mutated into a more general crisis of confidence affecting bank lending, corporate investment, and job creation. The crisis quickly put public finances to the test. Deficits soared because of reduced tax revenue, larger unemployment benefit payments, the cost of bailouts, and the attempts to stimulate the economy through fiscal policy (Freedman *et al.* 2009). In addition, governments also relaxed monetary policy, potentially imprinting an inflationary bias into the economy and certainly debasing the currency, especially in the United States (Guillén and Suárez 2010; Guillén 2015). The crisis fundamentally challenged the assumptions and institutions that underpinned the growth of the global economy in the second half of the twentieth century, including the roles of fiscal and monetary policies, the welfare state, and international monetary cooperation. It also shook mainstream assumptions about how actors make economic decisions and interact in the marketplace, leading major economists to refer to "animal spirits" as the best explanation for the financial excesses and the recessionary vicious circle triggered by the meltdown in the financial markets (Akerlof and Shiller 2009).

The financial implosion of 2008 spread much more swiftly and broadly than previous crises like the European currency debacle of 1992, the Mexican "tequila" crisis of 1994–1995, the East Asian "flu" of 1997, and the currency crises in Russia and Brazil in 1998–1999, which were regional in scope and affected only a few economies (Glick and Rose 1999). This time around central banks were forced to intervene quickly to keep credit going through massive injections of liquidity. The Federal Reserve was the most active, as it wrestled to ameliorate the effects of the crisis (Freedman *et al.* 2009). Countries with similar symptoms to the US felt the pain more quickly and severely: high real estate prices, financial

Figure 2.2 Proportion of OECD countries with at least two consecutive quarters of GDP decline, by quarter, 1970–2010
Source: OECD, Economic Outlook (several years).

leverage, and levels of private debt. As Figure 2.2 shows, all OECD member countries suffered from at least two consecutive quarters of GDP decline, something that was utterly unprecedented. This was a crisis afflicting the rich countries, which are deeply in debt and fear for the stability of their currencies, the dollar and the euro, which happen to be the world's major reserve currencies (Beetsma and Giuliodori 2010; Blundell-Wignall and Slovik 2010; Eichengreen 2009).

Particularly severe were the consequences of the global crisis in Europe, which put at risk the most important accomplishment of the whole dynamic of European integration, the monetary union created in 1999. The foundations of the most comprehensive experience in regional integration in the world, and also the oldest, have been seriously compromised by the crisis (Ontiveros and Fernández de Lis 2010; Guillén 2015). It is paradoxical that the indicators of public finances in Europe are no worse than those for the US or Japan. And yet, soaring risk premiums for European bonds indicated that the lack of a fiscal union was not to the liking of investors, who have regarded some government debt as like junk bonds (TrendLab 2011). Thus, it is not so much whether Europe is an "optimal currency area" or not that matters, but rather that the markets expect risk pooling within Europe at some point in the near future.

Further transfers of sovereignty from member states to Brussels and Frankfurt are possible and perhaps advisable in the medium run. But as of the second decade of the twenty-first century Europe confronts the twin problems of political weakness and an economic downturn that pro-cyclical austerity measures are only aggravating. The world economy is also reeling from the effects of the European crisis. After all, the European Union accounts for a third of global GDP and trade. The other victim of the crisis has been the policymaking and academic communities themselves, due to their tardy and incomplete understanding of the basic mechanisms leading to the implosion of financial markets and the great recession that followed (Fernández de Lis and Ontiveros 2009; TrendLab 2011).

Meanwhile, emerging economies were largely spared, although some suffered from the sharp, though temporary, decline in commodity prices during 2008 (IMF 2011). After 2014, a stronger dollar and the slowdown of the global economy posed more formidable challenges to commodity exporters (IMF 2015). The two most conspicuous manifestations of the resilience of emerging economies were their low levels of external debt and the accumulation of foreign reserves. By the end of 2014 China had accumulated 3.7 trillion dollars, Saudi Arabia 698 billion, Russia 356 billion, Brazil 364 billion, and India 345 billion. Thus, emerging economies have become part of the solution to the crisis as the providers of capital to the rich economies, which with the exception of Germany and Japan run large deficits with the rest of the world, in a dramatic illustration of the famous Lucas paradox: the relatively poor funding the rich. Figure 2.3 shows the extent of the current account imbalance between rich and emerging economies, and the fact that its magnitude grew three times bigger during the initial decade of the twenty-first century. Meanwhile, direct investments by multinational corporations, whether in the form of mergers and acquisitions or not, declined sharply as a result of the crisis, as it had done during the 2001–2002 downturn (Figure 2.4).

The crisis also rekindled fears of global protectionism in the form of either tariffs or currency wars, one of the main contributing factors to the Great Depression, famously conceptualized by Joan Robinson as "beggar-thy-neighbor" policies. Given the size of China's trade surplus, much of the attention became focused on the renminbi and the extent of its undervalu-ation relative to the dollar, which represented an effective trade barrier and a source of friction in global economic and financial relationships.

Figure 2.3 Global current account imbalances, 1980–2019 (% of GDP)
Notes: Figures after 2013 are projections.

The difference between the bars above the zero line and those below is due to statistical discrepancy.
Source: IMF, *World Economic Outlook*.

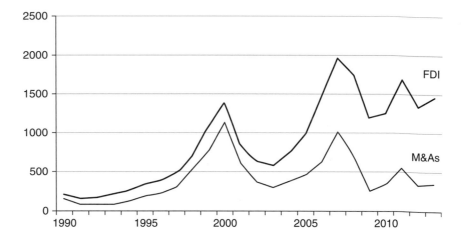

Figure 2.4 Global flows of inward foreign direct investment (FDI) and international mergers and acquisitions (M&As), 1990–2013 (billions of US dollars)
Source: United Nations Conference on Trade and Development.

Financial services after the crisis

It is perhaps too early to fully assess the fallout from the global financial crisis. Probably the most readily apparent consequence is the turning point in terms of financial regulation. After decades of deregulation and a vigorous trend towards self-regulation, governments around the world are opting for increased regulation and closer supervision. Given rampant market failures and the growth of "shadow" banking activities, monetary and financial authorities have no choice but to intervene more heavily than in the past. The attention has been refocused on leverage ratios, capital requirements, and systemic risks. It is important to note that between 1987 and 2007 financial institutions in the G7 countries (the US, Japan, the UK, Germany, France, Italy, and Canada) had increased their leverage threefold, compared to a 50 percent increase in the case of households, 30 percent for non-financial companies, and 25 percent for governments (IMF 2009).

Financial intermediaries have lost during the crisis their most important asset, namely, trust. Their risk-loving investment strategies, in some cases bordering on the illegal, have undermined the confidence that public opinion and policymakers once had. Personal and corporate bankruptcies, unemployment, and falling living standards are some of the consequences of the financial excesses of the first decade of the twenty-first century. We will analyze this issue in depth in Chapter 11 (no irony intended).

Another important consequence of the crisis is the foreseeable end of the era of cheap money for borrowers. Despite the loose monetary policy championed by most of the major central banks, the channeling of credit to businesses and households will continue to be restricted due to the new reserve and liquidity requirements for banks designed to forestall a new crisis. Higher capital adequacy ratios for banks and stiffer regulation will increase borrowing costs for businesses, households, and governments. In particular, as governments in Europe, the US, and Japan struggled to cope with the effects of the crisis, their indebtedness has skyrocketed to levels not seen since the end of World War II (IMF 2010), while many emerging and developing economies reduced their debt burden (see Figure 2.5).

The growing financing needs of the economies facing a problem of competitiveness have not escaped financial markets, which are punishing

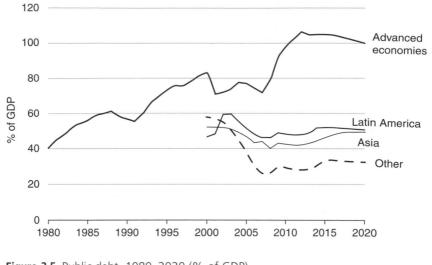

Figure 2.5 Public debt, 1980–2020 (% of GDP)
Note: Figures after 2013 are projections.
Source: IMF.

their governments with ever higher borrowing costs. Skepticism about the viability of pay-as-you-go pension systems and other welfare programs casts further doubt on the future of the rich economies and their decades-old approach to economic growth and social well-being. This problem has reached its climax in Europe, where the structural weaknesses of the single currency add complexity to the problem. But Japan and even the United States are also under scrutiny for their fiscal problems, although in the case of Japan most government debt is owed to domestic households, not international lenders (IMF 2010). Perhaps financial markets will respond to the new financial needs of government in the rich economies by creating more versatile financial instruments with longer terms of up to 100 years.

Changes in the distribution of global economic power

The depth of the crisis in the high-income economies of Europe, Japan, and the United States paralleled by high rates of growth in the emerging economies has accelerated the redistribution of economic and financial power in the world. Uncertainty about the future has taken center stage, volatility has become the norm in financial markets, and a stiff race to control natural resources and energy sources is on. Projections indicated that before the end of the second decade of the twenty-first century China would be the largest economy followed by the United States, India, Brazil, and Japan, with no European economy ranked among the world's top 5, as we will analyze in Chapter 12.

It is generally the case that debtors are in a more precarious position than creditors. Moreover, if creditors see their share of global production increase, it is logical to conclude that their bargaining power and influence are likely on the increase. The G7 continues to be a formidable power club, but it can no longer resolve global economic and financial issues the way it used to. The G20 was born before the crisis, and certainly brings to the table most of the key actors in the new global economy of the twenty-first century. Multilateral agencies such as the IMF and the World Bank are now governed in a way that reflects the growing power of the emerging economies, if imperfectly so.

In the rich economies, the long-term impact of the global economic and financial crisis may include persistently high unemployment, especially among the younger and the older age groups, a heavy debt burden that will force tax increases and a reduction in government services, and years of financial deleveraging and capital expenses as banks and other financial institutions clean up their balance sheets (IMF 2011). These lingering financial problems will erode the growth potential of many advanced economies, especially in Europe, and bring about many changes to the global competitive league.

Joseph Schumpeter once argued that "creative destruction" was the fundamental process underlying the extraordinary capacity of the market economy to deliver better standards of living over the long run. The twenty-first century will certainly witness more Schumpeterian dynamics rather than less, with the main actors and geographies of such creative tensions shifting away from the rich to the emerging economies, thus closing the gap between the two. Although for more than a hundred years the US has been the dominant research and development (R&D) power, its hegemony is on the decline. One should not take innovation in emerging economies lightly. They are no longer churning out cheap T-shirts. China and India educate more than 700,000 engineers annually. Scientific and technological breakthroughs will be more likely to occur in emerging economies as they step up their R&D investments. In just over a decade China has gone from investing virtually nothing in R&D to being the second largest investor in the world. If present trends continue, in another ten years or so China could achieve global technological leadership. For instance, in a high-tech field such as wind power, four of the ten largest turbine manufacturers are Chinese firms, and one is Indian. Chinese firms can easily keep up with the pace of technological change and start being innovators (Breznitz and Murphree 2011). Another emerging technological power is Brazil. Its companies lead the world in technologies for tropical agriculture, biofuels, and deep-sea oil extraction. As innovation shifts geographically, so will financial flows, trade, and migration.

The new global economy of the twenty-first century will need to overcome the many tensions produced by the rise of the emerging world: the appropriation of knowledge and technology, trade frictions, the race for natural resources, and climate change, among others. Income and wealth inequality, a common by-product of economic growth, will also need to be addressed. In 2010 more than 1.4 billion people were classified by the United Nations as living under the poverty line. Global growth will need to be more evenly distributed in order for it to be sustainable.

The global economic and financial crisis has heightened interest in arriving at new formulas for global governance, in an attempt to capitalize on the benefits of globalization while shielding citizens from its frequent ill effects. The crisis has made the failings of capitalism readily apparent. It has also pointed out the need for states to give up some sovereignty in order to manage global problems at the global level. Much attention and effort in the twenty-first century will be devoted to designing a new global economic and financial architecture, one that will surely differ from the one prevalent in the already distant past of the twentieth century.

The twenty-first century will also be the emerging-markets century, given that three quarters of all growth in the global economy is now taking place in Asia, Latin America, the Middle East, and Africa (IMF 2011). As Jim O'Neill, who coined the term BRICs, has argued in his book, *The Growth Map* (2011), the expansion of emerging markets has proceeded at a pace faster than predicted, and it is now extending into other large economies such as Indonesia and Turkey in addition to Brazil, Russia, India, and China.

Although this growth has been fueled by international trade in manufactured goods and in natural resources, domestic consumption in emerging economies is also taking off as a result of rising incomes and the formation of a middle class. It seems that 2015 could be the first year of net capital outflows from emerging markets since 1988. These trends are catapulting to global prominence a new set of companies, the emerging-market multinationals, the subject of the next chapter.

3 The rise of the emerging-market multinationals

> **KEY GLOBAL TURNING POINTS**
> As of 2014 emerging economies and developing countries were home to 31 percent of the largest 500 companies in the world and 35 percent of new foreign direct investment flows.

Running hand in hand with the extraordinary growth of emerging economies at the turn of the twenty-first century, we come across yet another clear sign that the global economy is changing. New multinational firms from countries such as Brazil, Mexico, China, India, Egypt, or Indonesia are expanding around the world, making acquisitions, and gaining market share not only in traditional industries but also in high-technology sectors. This trend has acquired such magnitude that it is rare the household anywhere around the world that does not consume or own a product branded by an emerging-market multinational (Guillén and García-Canal 2009; Van Agtmael 2007).

The figures are tantalizing. While in 1990 about 7.0 percent of all cumulative foreign direct investment in the world was accounted for by the so-called emerging-market multinationals, by the year 2000 the proportion had grown to 11.1 percent, and by 2013 it had almost trebled to 21.1 percent. In that year, emerging and developing economies accounted for 39 percent of new foreign direct investment flows. At the turn of the twenty-first century about 20.8 percent of the 64,592 multinational firms in the world were from emerging or developing countries. By 2010 the proportion had climbed to 29.1 percent of the world's total of 103,786 multinational firms (UNCTAD 2011, 2014). The economic and financial crisis that began in 2007 actually accelerated this phenomenon. While in 2008 there were 78 emerging-market firms on *Fortune* magazine's ranking of the world's largest 500 firms, in 2014 the figure stood at 157, with most of the increase being attributable to the number of Chinese firms, which grew from 29 to 98. A plausible scenario is that by the year 2030 more than half of cumulative foreign direct investment will be accounted for by emerging-market multinationals, and half of the *Fortune* Global 500 firms will be emerging-market multinationals (see the Box).

The main drivers behind this phenomenal growth in investment by the emerging-market multinationals are diverse. These firms invest in order to secure market access, inputs, and strategic assets that they lack, including brands and technologies. Many of them grew big in the domestic market and are now seeking to expand their selling opportunities by making greenfield investments and acquisitions abroad. Some of them pursued a well-defined niche market with global potential. A different trajectory usually characterizes emerging multinationals in infrastructure, energy, and natural resources. Emerging multinationals in infrastructure tend to focus on low-cost and/or high-risk markets as they search for growth opportunities. Those in energy and natural resources tend to be state-owned, and often follow government directives and incentives to secure sources of supply. Thus, there are many different kinds of motivations behind the global expansion of the emerging-market multinationals.

Multinational firms and foreign direct investment

Multinational firms are companies with operations in at least two different countries. They may own foreign manufacturing plants, distribution and storage systems, sales offices, or R&D labs. When they set up a new foreign subsidiary or make an acquisition of a foreign company, they engage in the so-called "foreign direct investment," which differs from foreign portfolio investment in that it is undertaken with the intention of securing operational control.

Multinational firms are very important actors in the global economy. The 500 largest account for about 25 percent of world product and 50 percent of world trade. They receive approximately 80 percent of all payments for technology royalties and fees. No wonder that they frequently get their way in negotiations with governments.

(cont.)

According to the United Nations, in 2010 there were nearly 104,000 multinational firms in the world, of which 30,000 or 29.1 percent were headquartered in emerging economies or developing countries.

The largest multinational firms typically operate in concentrated, capital-intensive industries. They invest abroad in order to exploit their two key advantages, namely, technology and brands. These two advantages are commonly referred to as "intangible assets." By contrast, a majority of emerging-market multinationals started to invest abroad without possessing such intangibles. The reason for their international expansion was, in many cases, precisely to acquire those types of assets.

Taking over major industries

The emerging-market multinationals are not simply large. They have escalated positions in industry rankings to the point of displacing firms from the most advanced economies. For example, the world's largest candy manufacturing company is Arcor of Argentina, while the largest bakery is Bimbo of Mexico, a firm that has taken both the Chinese and the US market by storm and is poised to grow very quickly over the next two decades. CVRD, known as Vale, a Brazilian firm, is the world's third largest mining conglomerate, while Cemex of Mexico is the second largest cement firm, and Tenaris of Argentina the world's leading producer of seamless steel tubes. Embraer of Brazil is the largest manufacturer of regional jets. In China, we come across BYD, the second largest global rechargeable battery maker, and Lenovo, the fourth largest computer brand. Taiwan's Acer is the world's number two. It is quite likely that a number of other Chinese firms in the electronics, automobile, and machinery industries will reach the top five positions within a decade or two. Gazprom of Russia is the world's largest energy company by revenue (excluding oil companies). DP World of Dubai is the world's fourth largest port operator. And in India, Tata Communications is the largest international wholesale voice carrier, Infosys boasts being one of the world's biggest information services companies, while Wipro is one of the top outsourcing services firms.

No matter where you look in the world of the emerging economies, you find large companies getting bigger and more successful year after year.

The largest emerging-market multinationals tend to be active in capital-intensive and/or natural-resource industries. Leading the pack is China (including Hong Kong) with four firms among the world's top 100 ranked by foreign assets, followed by Malaysia and Taiwan with one each (see Table 3.1). These very large emerging-market multinationals tend to be state owned, recently privatized, or family controlled.

The most active emerging-market multinationals to date are those from China ($614 billion in cumulative investment until the end of 2013), Russia (501), Brazil (293), and Taiwan (246). It is important to note that Chinese direct investment is by far the largest because in addition to the $614 billion directly out of the mainland, one must consider a large proportion of the investment from Hong Kong ($1.4 trillion) as indirectly coming from the mainland because many Chinese firms first set up a subsidiary in the Special Administrative Region in order to invest in foreign countries. Emerging and developing countries have invested a total of $5.5 trillion, or 21.1 percent of the world's total (see Table 3.2). It is also instructive to consider these figures relative to the size of each of these economies. The largest ratio of cumulative foreign direct investment stock to GDP is for Taiwan (50.2 percent), followed by Malaysia (43.2), Chile (36.5), South Africa (27.2), Russia (23.4), and the United Arab Emirates (16.1). The ratios for Hong Kong, Ireland, and Panama are very high due to their status as hubs for transit capital.

Emerging-market multinationals have turned acquisitive. For instance, in 2007 Tata Steel of India purchased Britain's Corus Group for $11.2 billion, Tata Motors bought Jaguar and Land Rover for $2.3 billion, Gerdau of Brazil purchased Chaparral Steel in the US for $4.1 billion, Cemex bought Rinker of Australia for $16.5 billion, and SABIC of Saudi Arabia acquired GE Plastics in the US for $11.6 billion. In 2008 Industrial and Commercial Bank of China purchased Standard Bank Group in South Africa for $5.6 billion. In 2010 Bharti Airtel of India purchased Zain Africa of Nigeria for $10.7 billion while Sinopec of China acquired 40 percent of Repsol YPF Brasil for $7.1 billion. Some deals proved hugely controversial, including the 2005 attempt by CNOOC of China to acquire US oil firm Unocal for $18.4 billion, which triggered a nationalist–populist uproar. The US Congress went as far as passing a provision within an energy bill

Table 3.1 The 25 largest multinational firms from emerging economies, ranked by foreign assets, 2012

Rank	Company	Country	Industry	Foreign assets ($m)	TNI[a]
1	Hutchison Whampoa Ltd.	Hong Kong	Diversified	85,721	80.9
2	CITIC Group	China	Diversified	78,602	17.1
3	Hon Hai Precision Industries	Taiwan	Electrical & electronic equipment	65,471	84.3
4	Petronas	Malaysia	Petroleum expl./ref./distr.	49,072	39.2
5	Vale SA	Brazil	Mining & quarrying	45,721	44.5
6	China Ocean Shipping (Group) Company	China	Transport & storage	43,452	48.9
7	China National Offshore Oil Corp	China	Petroleum expl./ref./distr.	34,276	18.6
8	América Móvil SAB de CV	Mexico	Telecommunications	32,008	49.4
9	Lukoil OAO	Russia	Petroleum & natural gas	31,174	42.8
10	Cemex S.A.B. de C.V.	Mexico	Non-metallic mineral products	30,730	80.1
11	Petróleos de Venezuela SA	Venezuela, Bolivarian Republic of	Petroleum expl./ref./distr.	27,462	18.2
12	Samsung Electronics Co., Ltd.	South Korea	Electrical & electronic equipment	26,077	26.9

13	Singapore Telecommunications Ltd.	Singapore	Telecommunications	25,768	63.5
14	Hyundai Motor Company	South Korea	Motor vehicles	25,443	25.6
15	Jardine Matheson Holdings Ltd.	Hong Kong	Diversified	24,284	57.9
16	Sabic-Saudi Basic Industries Corp.	Saudi Arabia	Petroleum expl./ref./distr.	23,540	51.9
17	Gazprom JSC	Russia	Petroleum & natural gas	23,425	24.0
18	Wilmar International Limited	Singapore	Food, beverages, & tobacco	23,088	75.5
19	China Resources Power Holdings Company Ltd.	Hong Kong	Energy	22,938	99.9
20	Tata Motors Ltd.	India	Automobile	21,575	59.2
21	Ooredoo QSC	Qatar	Telecommunications	20,304	82.9
22	Formosa Plastics Group	Taiwan	Chemicals	19,994	20.6
23	New World Development Ltd.	Hong Kong	Diversified	19,857	45.9
24	China National Petroleum Corporation	China	Petroleum expl./ref./distr.	19,284	2.7
25	CapitaLand Ltd.	Singapore	Construction & real estate	18,926	71.1

Note: [a] Transnationality Index, calculated as the average of foreign assets to total assets, foreign sales to total sales, and foreign employment to total employment.

Source: United Nations Conference on Trade and Development, Web table 29, http://unctad.org/en/Pages/DIAE/World%20Investment%20Report/Annex-Tables.aspx (accessed May 10, 2015).

Table 3.2 Cumulative stocks of outward foreign direct investment

Country	$ billion		% of GDP	
	1990	2013	1990	2013
China	4.5	613.6	1.1	6.6
Hong Kong	11.9	1,352.4	15.5	490.4
Taiwan	30.4	245.9	18.4	50.2
India	0.1	119.8	0.0	6.2
Singapore	7.8	497.9	21.2	174.9
South Korea	2.3	219.1	0.9	17.9
Malaysia	0.8	134.0	1.7	43.2
Argentina	6.1	34.1	4.3	7.0
Brazil	41.0	293.3	9.4	13.0
Chile	0.2	101.9	0.5	36.5
Colombia	0.4	39.0	1.0	10.2
Mexico	2.7	143.9	1.0	11.4
Panama	3.9	4.1	73.4	1.9
Peru	0.1	22.9	0.4	5.9
Venezuela	1.2	34.1	2.6	7.0
Russia	. . .	501.2	. . .	23.4
Turkey	1.2	32.8	0.6	4.0
UAE	0.1	63.2	0.0	16.1
Egypt	0.2	6.6	0.4	2.7
South Africa	15.0	95.8	13.4	27.2
Ireland	14.9	502.9	31.2	229.4
Spain	15.7	643.2	3.0	47.4
USA	731.8	6,349.5	12.6	37.5
France	112.4	1,637.1	9.0	59.7
Germany	151.6	1,710.3	8.8	47.1
Italy	60.2	598.4	5.3	28.9
Holland	106.9	1,071.8	35.9	134.4
United Kingdom	229.3	1,884.8	23.1	74.4
Japan	201.4	992.9	6.7	20.1
Developed countries	1948.6	20,765	11.1	47.0
Emerging and developing countries	145.2	5,549	4.1	18.6
World total	2086.8	26,314	9.9	35.6

Note: '. . .' signifies unavailable data.
Source: UNCTAD (2014).

which explicitly condemned the acquisition. A second instance of international friction occurred when DP World of Dubai acquired P&O of Britain in 2006 for $7.0 billion. The target company operated several port terminals in the US, which it had to sell so that the deal could go through. In both cases, concerns about national security were raised.

The sovereign wealth funds

Another controversial type of international investor from emerging economies are sovereign wealth funds, entities that hold assets owned by a government and denominated in a foreign currency. They are managed separately from foreign reserves (used for stabilization and short-term liquidity purposes) with the goal of obtaining a long-term return. Sovereign wealth funds are different from multinational firms in that they do not produce a good or a service. Rather, they invest in debt and equities, though rarely, if ever, taking a controlling stake. While the first sovereign wealth fund was created in 1953, the Kuwait Investment Authority, the term itself was coined at the beginning of the twenty-first century (Rozanov 2005), precisely at the time that they became globally significant.

The main reason for the rise to prominence of sovereign wealth funds is the accumulation of large current account surpluses in countries that export huge amounts of manufactured goods or commodities, such as China, Singapore, Russia, Venezuela, Abu Dhabi, Dubai, and Chile. Although they tend to be very secretive, we know that the largest is the Abu Dhabi Investment Authority, which the Sovereign Wealth Fund Institute estimates has assets worth $773 billion. It is important to note that developed countries are also home to large funds, including Australia, Canada, Norway, Japan, France, the Netherlands, and the United States (Truman 2008, 2010). Taken together, sovereign wealth funds were estimated to manage about $7.1 trillion as of early 2015.

Sovereign wealth funds have recently shifted their investment strategy away from treasuries, bonds, and real estate into equities. In the first decade of the twenty-first century, they took large stakes in companies as diverse as MGM Mirage (9.5 percent), Sainsbury (25), and the London Stock Exchange (28), and smaller shares in oil giants Total (1.6) and British Petroleum (1.0). They became controversial during the global financial crisis that began in 2007 because of some high-profile deals involving troubled financial institutions, including the multi-billion dollar investments in UBS, Citigroup, Morgan Stanley, Merrill Lynch, Barclays, Blackstone, Standard Chartered, and the Carlyle Group. These investments, taken together, amounted to $56.4 billion, the largest being the Government of Singapore Investment Corporation's purchase of 8.6 percent of UBS for $9.8 billion. The crisis, however, did not leave the funds unscathed. One estimate (Setser and Ziemba 2009) put the losses at the Abu Dhabi Investment Authority at $328 billion during 2008 (a 40 percent decline in its value), those at the Kuwait Investment Authority at $228 billion (a 36 percent loss), and the Norwegian Government Pension Fund-Global at $325 billion (a 30 percent decline). In spite of this setback, sovereign wealth funds continue to draw the attention because of the implications for national security and the lack of transparency of many of them. Their size is predicted to grow during the twenty-first century, unless the global economic, trade, and financial imbalances discussed in the previous chapter are reduced.

Are emerging-market multinationals different?

As significant as sovereign wealth funds have become, in the twenty-first century emerging-market multinationals will become even more important. Their sudden irruption onto the global stage raises a number of tantalizing questions. For starters, it is readily apparent that most of them lack the two classic competitive advantages of multinational firms, namely, technology and brands (Hymer 1960). While most of the traditional European, US, and Japanese multinationals invested abroad in order to exploit their proprietary technology and brands, many if not most of the emerging-market multinationals have acquired those intangible assets in the process of, not prior to, going abroad. Thus, the overall question is, what competitive advantages do emerging-market multinationals possess?

One key way in which emerging-market multinationals have broken the mold of the traditional multinational firm is by specializing in the adaptation of existing technology to new market niches as opposed to the creation of new technology, in incremental improvements to existing products, and in the early adoption of new technology. For instance, South Korean and Chinese electronics firms did not pioneer flat panel display technologies, but they have managed to incorporate them into new products and to be more efficient at manufacturing them.

A second way in which they have become competitive abroad is by exploiting "project-execution" capabilities, that is, the ability to conduct feasibility studies, obtain licenses from the state, put together financial packages, secure technology and know-how, set up plants, hire and train the workforce, and establish supply and distribution channels rapidly and efficiently (Amsden and Hikino 1994). In other words, emerging-market multinationals tend to excel at execution.

Networking skills are often cited as a key advantage of emerging-market multinationals. The fact that most of them are either family or government controlled has facilitated their growth and international expansion. For instance, the most common ways for them to operate abroad is through alliances or partial acquisitions, as opposed to the typical pattern of the traditional multinationals which tend to make full acquisitions and set up their own "greenfield" subsidiaries. Full or partial government ownership, although it often raises eyebrows in host countries, is frequently cited as a factor that has made many of them politically savvy (Guillén and García-Canal 2009, 2010), a circumstance that has enabled them to gain a presence in heavily regulated sectors like electricity, oil and gas, transportation, water, and telecommunications. More often than not, they have expanded into other emerging economies or into developing countries, precisely where political advantages may be more useful.

An illustration of this pattern is Chinese and Indian investment in Africa. While European, Japanese, and American firms accounted for 51 percent of foreign investment flows in Africa in 2013, Indian firms accounted for 11 percent, and Chinese firms for about 1 percent, a figure that underestimates the investments because many of them take the form of no-cash infrastructure-for-commodities deals (Chen and Orr 2009; UNCTAD 2015: 34). The largest acquisition to date is the 2006 purchase by China's CNOOC of 45 percent of the Nigerian National Petroleum Corp for $2.7 billion (UNCTAD 2010: 32–37). Chinese firms tend to invest in African countries following a complex pattern in which the Chinese and host-country governments enter into a framework agreement, with China providing the financing through its official export-import bank, the host country awarding a Chinese firm the license to extract natural resources, which are used to pay back the loan, and Chinese construction firms building some kind of infrastructure in exchange for the license. In this way, China gains access to crucial raw materials and energy, while the host country enjoys the new infrastructure (Chen and Orr 2009). This operational pattern of intimate relationships between Chinese state-owned firms and entities, on the one hand, and African governments, on the other, has come under scrutiny in countries such as Angola, Rwanda, or the Sudan because it is not clear the extent to which the local population will benefit from the deals. Moreover, China's presence lends legitimacy to repressive or even genocidal regimes. In many countries, Chinese companies have brought in tens of thousands of workers, raising fears among the local population that they will not benefit from the investments.

The increasing scale, sophistication, and global presence of emerging-market multinationals will surely enable them to allocate more resources to R&D and to build their own brands. Thus, it may be possible for them to develop technological and marketing expertise internally or through acquisitions. In fact, there are many successful precedents. For instance, Samsung Electronics of South Korea (an emerging economy until very recently) is the world's leading consumer electronics firm. Until 1990 it operated as a mere subcontractor to US, European, and Japanese multinationals. Nowadays, it boasts the world's 21st most valuable brand (assessed at $45.5 billion), surpassed only by Nokia in consumer electronics, and has successfully filed for over 72,000 patents with the US Patent & Trademark Office. There are only a handful of companies, or countries for that matter, with a greater number of patents.

To the extent that Samsung Electronics can be thought of as a precedent, the emerging-market multinationals are poised to become technology and marketing powerhouses during the first half of the twenty-first century. In fact, during the first decade alone, residents of emerging markets have jumped from obtaining just 5 percent of new patents granted worldwide to nearly 10 percent. In 2009 as many as 120 firms among the top 1000 R&D spenders were from emerging economies, up from half that number five years earlier. The leading emerging economies were Taiwan (35 firms among the top 1000), South Korea (23), China (21, including Hong Kong), India (12), and Brazil (6). The top three patenting countries were South Korea with 60 percent of the patents obtained by emerging economies, Israel with 11 percent, and China, including Hong Kong, with 6 percent (World Bank 2011b: 77).

Sovereignty, political influence, and geopolitics

The rise of the emerging-market multinationals has intensified a long-running debate about the power and influence of foreign companies in the host countries in which they operate. Multinational corporations have grown so big that their foreign activities often have implications for the stature of the home country in global affairs and for the conduct of foreign policy. The reverse is also possible: the activities of multinational firms can be affected by the foreign policy of the home country. The government can also use the multinationals as tools to achieve diplomatic goals.

The branch of political science known as international relations has attempted to study these issues. Much debate in this field over the last 25 years has focused on who are the key actors in international relations. Realist scholars assert that states are the only actors of importance, while multinational firms, non-governmental organizations (NGOs), international labor union confederations, and multilateral agencies (such as the UN or the IMF) are just instruments of governments or states. By contrast, the proponents of the world-politics paradigm (also referred to as international pluralism) conceive of international relations as the complex interplay among multiple actors who are relatively independent from each other. More recently, other scholars have proposed to look at international relations from a constructivist perspective, one that relegates material interests to the background and highlights shared or negotiated norms for appropriate behavior in the international arena. Thus the constructivist perspective downplays the importance of interest-driven action by states or multinationals, emphasizing instead the role of shared or negotiated norms of appropriate behavior in the international arena (for a review, see Tarrow 2001).

The literature reports ample evidence both of multinationals being used by their own governments to achieve foreign policy objectives and of multinationals using their home governments to obtain certain advantages abroad. There is also mounting evidence that multinationals can and do exert their influence over host countries, a theme superbly conceptualized by Raymond Vernon in his classic book, *Sovereignty at Bay* (1971). The classic example is ITT's role in the fall and demise of the democratically elected President of Chile in 1973 (Gilpin 1987: 231–245; Moran 1977). Thus, there is evidence in favor of the realist, pluralist, and constructivist views.

The rise of the emerging-market multinationals has intensified and transformed these debates, for two reasons. First, many of the countries that are home to the new multinationals are dictatorships or they are less than ideal in their practice of democracy. During the second half of the twentieth century, most multinational firms were headquartered in Western Europe, North America, or Japan, all of them democracies. This in no way meant that they did not engage in corruption or other illicit activities, or that they did not take advantage of repressive labor regimes (Oneal 1992). The increasingly global presence of companies from non-democratic emerging economies is posing serious challenges to the fight for human rights in Africa and Latin America, for instance.

The second important transformation of the debate over sovereignty, political influence, and geopolitics induced by the rise of the emerging-market multinationals has to do with the fact that many of them happen to be state-owned or recently privatized companies. During most of the twentieth century, very few state-owned firms ventured abroad. They used to enjoy a captive domestic market and faced few incentives to take on the risks of foreign expansion. It was only in the wake of privatization, deregulation, and market liberalization that formerly state-controlled firms in Western Europe invested abroad. Although governments in many emerging economies have also engaged in privatization, many of the largest emerging-market multinationals are firms owned by the state in full or in part. For example, among the 100 Global Challengers listed by the Boston Consulting Group in 2009, 31 have the state as a major shareholder (BCG 2009). Of the 36 Chinese companies on the list, 23 were state owned. The other 8 state-owned multinationals came from Brazil, Hungary, Malaysia (2), Russia, and the United Arab Emirates (4). Most of these firms are active in natural resources, energy, oil, or capital-intensive manufacturing. As Ian Bremmer, the President of the Eurasia Group, has observed, "state capitalism is not the reemergence of socialist central planning in a twenty-first-century package. It is a form of bureaucratically engineered capitalism particular to each government that practices it ... For the moment, many of the governments that practice state capitalism have profited from it – both economically and politically" (Bremmer 2010a: 23).

The extent to which state-owned or recently privatized firms from emerging economies will make decisions about foreign investment based on business considerations as opposed to political ones remains to be seen. In strategic and highly regulated industries such as mining, oil, infrastructure, or energy it is hard to believe that state ownership will not matter, at least in terms of how the multinationals operate, as the case of Chinese firms in Africa illustrates (Chen and Orr 2009).

How emerging-market multinationals are changing the world

The rise of the emerging-market multinationals will inevitably change the structure of the global economy. In order to grasp the implications, it is instructive to assess the flows of foreign direct investment at the beginning, the middle, and the end of the twentieth century. On the eve of World War I, the United Kingdom was the world's leading source of foreign direct investment. British companies dominated several consumer goods industries as well as virtually every infrastructure sector. The great expansion of American capitalism after World War II brought about a very different situation by 1967, perhaps the peak of US global economic and financial supremacy. During the 1960s American multinational firms roamed the globe in search of sources of supply, manufacturing sites, and consumer markets. At the turn of the twenty-first century, the situation could not be more different than the one prevailing 50 or 100 years earlier. Instead of there being a dominant country, the US, Europe, Japan, and, increasingly, China run head to head as the leading sources of foreign direct investment. The world is moving quite quickly away from the reality of a hegemonic power and towards a polycentric configuration.

The consequences of this shift are hard to miss. For starters, the centers of managerial decision making are gradually moving away from Paris, London, Frankfurt, New York, Chicago, and Tokyo towards Mexico City, São Paulo, Beijing, Shanghai, Mumbai, Dubai, and a host of other key emerging-market cities. And with them other activities will gravitate towards these new centers of cosmopolitan life, including art collections, music performances, and culinary temples, to name but a few.

Most importantly, new products and services will be designed with emerging-market consumers in mind. Research and development activities will be increasingly located in emerging economies, thus creating high-paying jobs outside of Europe and North America, and perhaps even causing some of those in the old centers of decision making to be sent overseas. As emerging-market multinationals beat their counterparts from the so-called "advanced" economies at their own game, the global economy and the global business community will bear little resemblance to the domination of the business landscape by the European and American multinationals that characterized the twentieth century, challenged only fleetingly by the rise of Japanese firms in the 1980s and 1990s. And to the extent that what's good for an emerging-market multinational is good for its home country, to paraphrase former General Motors CEO and US Secretary of Defense Charles Wilson, the power and influence of emerging countries will likely increase as a result of the enhanced international stature of their companies.

4 The new demography: aging, migration, and obesity

KEY GLOBAL TURNING POINTS

For the first time in human history, several countries have inverted age pyramids with more people above age 60 than below age 20, more people live in cities than in the countryside, and more people suffer from obesity than from hunger.

The twenty-first century is riding a wave of demographic changes that will fundamentally reshape the society and the economy of most countries around the world. Population aging, the shift from the countryside to the city, international migration, lower marriage rates, and the obesity epidemic pose numerous challenges and opportunities. Unlike in previous periods of human history, highly advanced societies with relatively young populations coexist with others experiencing rapid aging. The same diversity in demographic trends is taking place among emerging and developing countries. These trends will make Africa, South Asia, and the Middle East more important demographically, precisely the areas of the world that have proved less stable politically and yet hold most of the world's exhaustible energy and mineral resources. The twenty-first century promises to match its predecessor in terms of producing new demographic trends. "We are taller, heavier, healthier, and longer lived than our ancestors; our bodies are sturdier, less susceptible to disease in early life and slower to wear out. These changes have occurred in all parts of the world and are continuing to occur" (Floud *et al.* 2011: 364).

Demography in the new century

The twentieth century was an eventful one from the demographic point of view. The first quarter was characterized by the final phase of the great transatlantic migration initiated in the late nineteenth century, and was followed by a quarter of demographic stagnation during the Great Depression and World War II, accentuated by war-related mortality. Massive forced migrations in Eastern Europe and the Caucasus followed. The second half of the century was one of rapid population growth due to increasing fertility and declining mortality. The world's population increased from 2.5 billion in 1950 to 6.1 in 2000. In October 2011 the United Nations announced that the seven billionth human being had been born. Contrary to Malthusian doomsday projections about the economic limits to population growth, the percentage of the population suffering from hunger dropped markedly. Another distinctive feature of the second half of the twentieth century was that cross-national migration paled by comparison to the population shift from the countryside to the cities (see the Box).

Demography and demographic predictions

Demography is the statistical study of the size, structure, and distribution of human populations as a result of the dynamics of birth, migration, aging, and death. It is one of the most important branches of science because population structure and change entail major implications for anthropology, economics, geography, politics, epidemiology, finance, marketing, and environmental studies, to name but a few fields. Demographers use data obtained from registries, censuses, and surveys.

While there are many indicators of the main demographic processes, perhaps the most useful and intuitive are the total fertility rate (the number of live births per woman over her reproductive lifetime assuming current age-specific fertility rates), and life expectancy at birth (the number of years that an individual born today is expected to live assuming current mortality rates). It is readily apparent from these definitions that demographic indicators are based on certain assumptions. It is therefore very important to make assumptions explicit when making projections into the future and when interpreting demographic trends.

Figure 4.1 Total fertility rate (children per woman) and life expectancy at birth (years), 1950–2100
Note: Data after 2012 are projections using the medium variant assumption.
Source: United Nations Population Division, *World Population Prospects: The 2012 Revision.*

The twenty-first century is likely to be very different than the second half of the twentieth in that population growth has come to a halt in several regions while others will probably witness further growth. The upper panel of Figure 4.1 shows the evolution of the total fertility rate, measured as the number of children an average woman would have assuming she lives her full reproductive lifetime. For the world as a whole, it came down from nearly 5 children per woman in 1950 to less than 2.5 by 2010. The decline has been most rapid in the more developed parts of the world, from 2.8 to 1.7, meaning that the population is not replacing itself given that a total fertility rate of about 2.1 children per woman is necessary in order to ensure that enough women reach reproductive age.

A related trend has to do with declining marriage rates in Europe, North America, and East Asia. In 2005, and for the first time in US history, there were more women living without than with a spouse. In many parts of China, parents' preferences for boys under the one-child policy have produced a drastic gender imbalance. By the year 2020, 20–30 million Chinese males will not be able to find a Chinese woman to marry within their age group. In parts of Siberia, by contrast, women are so much more numerous due to male migration that they are lobbying for the legalization of polygamy.

In the less developed countries (mostly emerging economies in Asia and Latin America), the decline has also been quite rapid, from 6 children per woman in 1950 to 2.6 by 2010. In the least developed countries, the poorest of them all, total fertility came down from 6.5 to 4.1, still a very high rate. The most important predictor of differences in total fertility rates is women's education. For instance, according to the Population Reference Bureau, at the turn of the twenty-first century Guatemalan women with no education had on average 7.1 children, while those who completed primary education had 5.1, and those with a high school diploma just 2.6. In Kenya the figures were 5.8, 4.8, and 3.5, respectively; in Pakistan 5.7, 4.9, and 3.6; and in the Philippines, 5.0, 5.0, and 3.6. The general increase in women's educational opportunity around the world has been the main trigger of the decline in fertility.

Declining fertility rates mean that population growth will slow down during the twenty-first century. The United Nations Population Division medium estimate of the world's population by the year 2100 is 10.8 billion, while the high estimate is 16.6 billion and the low 6.8 billion. We will examine the implications of population pressure on resources in Chapter 10.

People are also living longer, much longer than during the mid twentieth century. While males were expected to live on average 46.7 years in 1950, by 2010 the figure was 67.1 years. For females, the increase was from

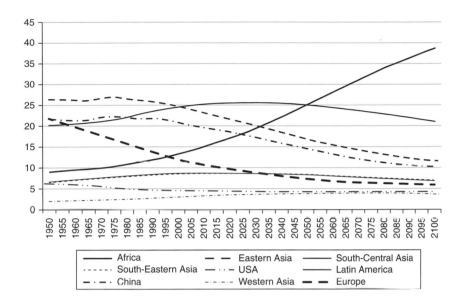

Figure 4.2 Population by region (% of world's total), 1950–2100
Note: Data after 2012 are projections using the medium variant assumption.
Source: United Nations Population Division, *World Population Prospects: The 2012 Revision.*

48.7 to 71.6 years. As the lower panel of Figure 4.1 shows, the increase in life expectancy resulting from better nutrition, hygiene, disease prevention, and healthcare has benefited people in developed and developing countries alike, although an average gap of about 21 years in life expectancy persisted as of 2012.

The different rates at which fertility is coming down in different parts of the world, while mortality rates fall more uniformly, has led demographers to predict very sharp changes in the relative demographic weight of different continents and regions, a development with tantalizing implications from economic, financial, political, and cultural points of view. Figure 4.2 shows that only three regions are projected to increase their share of the world's population during the twenty-first century: Africa, South-Central Asia (including India, Pakistan, and Bangladesh), and Western Asia (i.e., the Middle East), which are among the most unstable politically (see Chapter 5). The shares of South-Eastern Asia, the United States, and Latin America are likely to remain stable, while Europe (including Russia) and Eastern Asia (including China, South Korea, and Japan) will witness a precipitous decline in their relative shares. As a result of these changes, the balance of economic, financial, and geopolitical power in the world is likely to change (Goldstone 2012), as we shall examine in Chapter 12. The two demographic extremes will be Europe, which will decline to less than 8 percent of the world's population by 2050 and less than 6 percent by 2100, and Africa, which will likely be the home to more than 25 percent in 2050 and 38 percent in 2100.

The decline in fertility and the rise in life expectancy has led to "inverted" age pyramids. Figure 4.3 shows the pyramids for several key economies in 1960 and 2010, with the projection for 2060. According to the United Nations Population Division's medium projections, in the year 2000 Germany and Italy had more people of age 60 and above than people below 20. By 2010 Japan, Greece, Portugal, Spain, Austria, Bulgaria, Slovenia, Croatia, Finland, Switzerland, and Sweden had joined the club. By 2025, 46 countries or territories will be in that situation. China and Russia will join in by 2030, the United States by 2035, Brazil by 2040, Mexico and Indonesia by 2050, and India by 2070. Thus, and for the first time in human history, a growing number of countries have inverted age pyramids.

Another important trend continuing from the twentieth century is urbanization. By 2010, and for the first time in human history, more than half of the world's population lived in cities. The United Nations estimates that by the year 2025 there will be nine cities with more than 20 million people each, up from just one (Tokyo) in 2000. Most of the "megacities" will not be in Europe or North America, but in Asia and Latin America (Table 4.1). The biggest city in the world, Tokyo, with 36 million inhabitants, will soon be joined by several other Asian megacities with more than 20 million people each. The rapid increase in urbanization and in the size of megacities will place stress on food, water, and sanitation systems around the world. It is important to keep in mind that urban dwellers have very different lifestyles than rural inhabitants and that cities account for 80 percent of carbon emissions.

People are also predicted to be on the move internationally to a much greater extent than between 1950 and 1990, especially those migrating from developing to developed countries. In particular, both Western Europe and the United States are projected to have international migrant

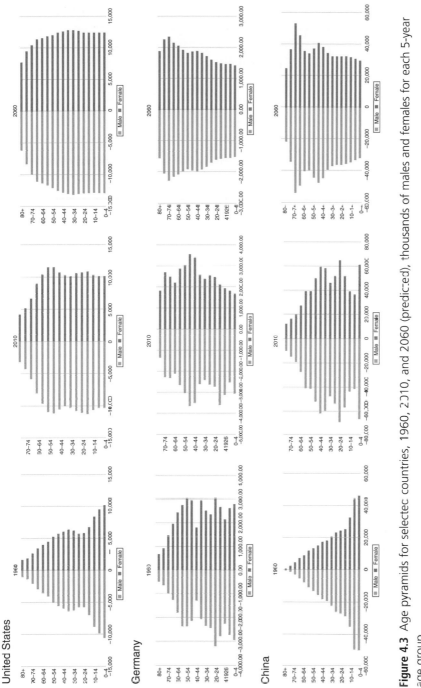

Figure 4.3 Age pyramids for selected countries, 1960, 2010, and 2060 (predicted), thousands of males and females for each 5-year age group

Note: Medium variant assumption.

Source: United Nations Population Division, *World Population Ageing 2013*.

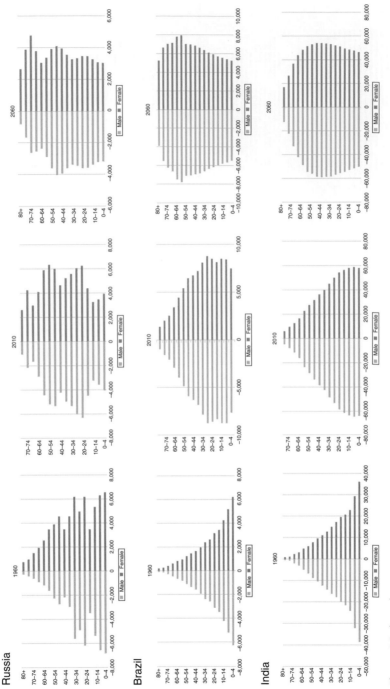

Figure 4.3 (cont.)

Table 4.1 World's ten largest cities

1950		1970		2000		2025	
City	mn	City	mn	City	mn	City	mn
New York[a]	12.3	Tokyo	23.3	Tokyo	34.4	Tokyo	37.1
Tokyo	11.3	New York[a]	16.2	Mexico City	18.0	Delhi	28.6
London	8.4	Osaka-Kobe	9.4	New York[a]	17.8	Mumbai	25.8
Paris	6.5	Mexico City	8.8	São Paulo	17.1	São Paulo	21.6
Moscow	5.4	Los Angeles[b]	8.4	Mumbai	16.1	Dhaka	20.9
Buenos Aires	5.1	Paris	8.4	Delhi	15.7	Mexico City	20.7
Chicago	5.0	Buenos Aires	8.1	Shanghai	13.2	New York[a]	20.6
Kolkata	4.5	São Paulo	7.6	Kolkata	13.1	Kolkata	20.1
Shanghai	4.3	London	7.5	Buenos Aires	11.8	Shanghai	20.0
Osaka-Kobe	4.2	Moscow	7.1	Los Angeles[b]	11.8	Karachi	18.7

Notes:
[a] New York and Newark, New Jersey.
[b] Los Angeles, Long Beach, and Santa Ana.
Source: United Nations Population Division, *World Urbanization Prospects: The 2009 Revision.*

populations representing more than 12 percent of their total population (see the lower panel in Figure 4.4). Immigrants are also disproportionately likely to settle in cities rather than the countryside.

The most significant new demographic development of the twenty-first century, however, is the obesity epidemic, which is engulfing both developed and emerging economies as plenty has led to over-consumption (Floud *et al.* 2011: 365). Estimates indicate that by 2010 there were more people in the world classified as obese or overweight (about one billion) than people suffering from hunger (800 million). Development programs and improvements in agriculture made it possible to reduce the percentage of the world's population that is hungry from 24 percent in 1969–1971 to 13 percent in 2005–2007. Table 4.2 shows the figures for selected countries. Very poor countries in Africa, Latin America, or Asia continue to have relatively high percentages of hungry people and low percentages of obese people. In rapidly growing emerging economies hunger has declined while obesity has grown due to dietary changes induced by increased purchasing power and the more sedentary lifestyles in the cities. China is perhaps the exception in that hunger has declined while obesity has not increased significantly, at least for the time being. In the developed world, with the notable exception of Japan, obesity has become a major health problem. It is interesting to note that poor countries like Algeria, Botswana, South Africa, Cuba, Haiti, Guatemala, Peru, Egypt, Iraq, Morocco, Syria, Tunisia, North Korea, Mongolia, and several Pacific island nations are among the most affected by obesity. Being obese or overweight is a major risk factor for a number of chronic conditions such as diabetes, cardiovascular diseases, cancer, and arthritis. Estimates indicate that as much as 30–40 percent of total healthcare expenditures in the United States, where 44 percent of males and 48 percent of females are affected, can be traced back to obesity.

People often think that the growing problem of obesity will just affect very specific sectors of the economy such as healthcare and pharmaceuticals. The consequences, however, are likely to be felt across the economy, from the clothing, personal care, and consumer electronics industries to automobiles, entertainment, and airlines. "Government statistics estimate that six in every 10 adult women in North America are overweight, while more than one third are obese," observed Euromonitor. "Yet, plus size clothing [size 14 and above] represents less than one fifth of clothing

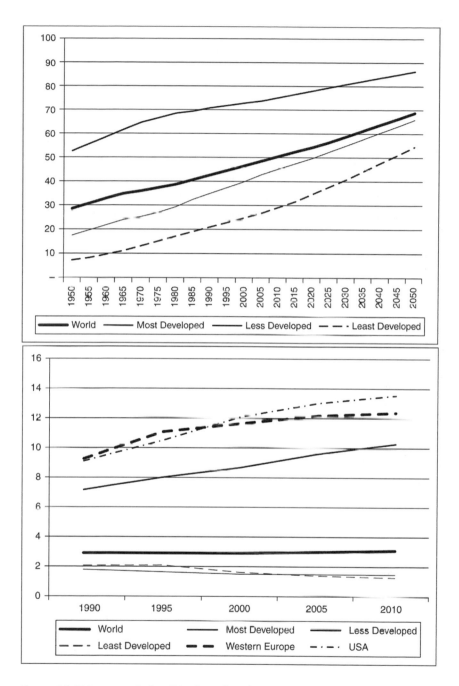

Figure 4.4 Urban population (% of total) and international migrant population (as % of total population)

Source: United Nations Population Division, *World Urbanization Prospects: The 2009 Revision* and *International Migrant Stock: The 2008 Revision*.

Table 4.2 Percentage of the population aged 15 or above that is hungry and percentage that is obese, selected countries

Country	Hungry	Obese Males	Obese Females	Country	Hungry	Obese Males	Obese Females
Algeria	…	6.4	16.2	Belgium	…	14.8	10.7
Botswana	25	6.9	17.7	Denmark	…	12.0	8.3
Ethiopia	41	0.2	0.0	France	…	9.0	7.6
Gambia	19	0.5	3.6	Germany	…	22.9	22.1
Kenya	31	0.1	2.2	Greece	…	30.3	26.4
Nigeria	6	3.0	8.1	Italy	…	14.4	13.7
South Africa	…	7.6	36.8	Poland	…	12.9	18.0
Uganda	21	0.1	1.9	Russia	…	9.6	23.6
Tanzania	34	0.8	3.6	Spain	…	17.3	17.3
Argentina	…	37.4	37.8	Sweden	…	13.3	12.4
Brazil	6	12.4	24.5	Turkey	…	10.8	32.5
Canada	…	25.5	25.7	UK	…	23.7	26.3
Chile	…	24.3	39.1	Bangladesh	27	0.2	0.2
Colombia	10	19.6	26.1	Cambodia	22	0.5	0.4
Cuba	…	20.1	31.5	China	10	4.1	3.6
Guatemala	21	20.5	36.8	India	21	1.7	2.0
Haiti	57	1.3	21.1	Indonesia	13	0.2	3.9
Mexico	…	30.1	41.0	Japan	…	2.3	1.1

Country				Country			
Peru	15	17.7	37.7	Nepal	16	0.3	0.3
USA	...	44.2	48.3	North Korea	33	3.4	12.9
Venezuela	8	29.5	33.0	South Korea	...	8.3	14.6
Afghanistan	...	0.7	2.1	Laos	23	3.3	12.6
Egypt	...	22.0	48.0	Thailand	16	2.6	11.1
Iran	...	10.0	29.5	Malaysia	...	1.7	11.0
Iraq	...	8.3	19.1	Mongolia	26	14.5	36.6
Jordan	...	19.6	37.9	Philippines	15	1.1	5.5
Morocco	...	3.7	23.1	Singapore	...	1.4	2.9
Pakistan	26	1.6	5.0	Vietnam	11	0.0	0.7
Saudi Arabia	...	23.0	36.4	Australia	...	28.4	29.1
Somalia	...	0.6	3.4	Fiji	...	10.7	37.1
Sudan	22	1.5	6.5	New Zealand	...	28.9	39.9
Syria	...	12.4	24.6	Palau	...	35.0	59.4
UAE	...	24.5	42.0	Tonga	...	64.0	78.1
Tunisia	...	7.7	32.6	Samoa	...	42.2	60.9

Note: '...' signifies unavailable data. 'Hungry' is defined by undernourishment, or "the condition of people whose dietary energy consumption is continuously below a minimum dietary energy requirement for maintaining a healthy life and carrying out a light physical activity with an acceptable minimum body-weight for attained-height." Data are for 2005–2007. "Obese" is defined by a Body Mass Index (BMI) equal or greater than 30, expressed as kilograms of weight divided by squared height in meters. Data are for 2010.

Sources: Food and Agriculture Organization, and World Health Organization.

sales." Although the demand for plus-size clothing continues to expand, companies are not redefining their brand and style offerings. "The reluctance to cater better for plus-size women has much to do with fears over image and brand heritage. Conversely, retailers and manufacturers point to low sales as evidence of weak demand" (Euromonitor 2010: 25). Clothing companies that overcome such anxieties stand to gain in market share and profitability.

The economic implications of population aging

While there is widespread agreement as to the causes of population aging, much debate exists about its effects (Johnson 2005; Lloyd-Sherlock 2010; Taylor 2008). It is easy to formulate alarmist projections about the consequences of aging for economic growth and pensions systems. It is equally easy, however, to underestimate their importance. The new demography of the twenty-first century will greatly affect the structure of the global economy, politics, culture, and geopolitics. The growing scarcity of labor in developed countries and its abundance in much of the developing world will likely contribute to both migration and the geographical redistribution of economic activity, with labor-intensive operations being increasingly located in countries with rapid population growth, a process that continues a global trend initiated after World War II. As discussed in Chapter 3, however, the rise of emerging-market multinationals is likely to alter the simple pattern of trade in labor-intensive commodities from the developing to the developed world coupled with trade in capital-intensive goods in the opposite direction. The twenty-first century will not be just about the divide between rich and poor countries. Emerging economies and emerging-market multi-nationals have blurred the distinction.

One of the most important areas of debate concerns the impact of aging on economic growth. At the core of this debate is the question of whether an aging workforce would be more or less productive than a younger one. The conventional argument is that population aging reduces productivity because of more frequent health problems, outdated skills, and cognitive decline. Evidence for these negative effects, however, is ambiguous. A positive effect on productivity is also possible because older workers are more experienced. It is empirically difficult to determine if population aging will fundamentally alter the prospects for economic growth in different parts of the world (Lloyd-Sherlock 2010).

The coming demographic transition in countries with high but rapidly declining fertility rates will pose fewer challenges and probably create a situation in which economic growth can accelerate and become sustainable. One such example is Brazil, which at the turn of the twenty-first century had a relatively young population with few people below age 20 or above age 60. This emerging economy is not only at a sweet point demographically but has recently managed to attain macroeconomic stability, despite recent problems, to develop a sound technological base in industries as important as automobiles, biofuels, and aerospace, and to benefit from the global commodity boom as an exporter of agricultural products, minerals, and oil.

Demographic trends are also likely to affect consumption markets, shifting the center of gravity of the global economy towards Latin America, Asia, and Africa. The changing age structure of the population will alter global demand for durable goods and education towards countries with younger populations, and global demand for healthcare and leisure towards countries experiencing population aging. In addition, many products and services may have to be redesigned so that they are age friendly. Demand for financial services will also shift accordingly, as people's savings and spending behavior differs fundamentally by age, although the evidence is also ambiguous (Lloyd-Sherlock 2010). Lastly, housing prices tend to fall as the population ages, although they do so in a very heterogeneous way given that retirees often buy a second home or move their residence to the sunbelt or closer to where their children live. Not surprisingly, companies and governments are creating study groups like the Global Coalition on Aging to explore the implications.

The impact of population aging on the clothing industry, for instance, will be massive. The global clothing and footwear industry is worth $1.3 trillion a year. In a recent report, a consulting firm stated that "Western Europe's ageing demographics present big challenges for the clothing and footwear sector, most notably in Italy, Germany, Greece and Spain where the under 15 age band currently accounts for less than 15 percent of the population, compared with over 30 percent in key emerging markets such as India and Mexico." Companies in the industry are finding it hard to adapt to the new demographic trends. "Pensioners are also a fast-growing group, but a tougher nut to crack. Typically, they spend less on clothing and footwear than younger age bands (e.g. in Germany) but purchasing power is strong and sophistication high." And in other parts of the world, demographic change is coming hand in hand with social and political change, with major implications for clothing and fashion. "With 39 percent of the [Middle East & Africa] region population under 15 years, there will be a huge influx of new economically-active adult consumers over the next 10 years. In particular, young, fashion-conscious women are identified as a key untapped market" (Euromonitor 2010: 5, 13).

Perhaps the most momentous economic change engendered by the new demographic trends will have to do with the welfare state and its most important programs, namely, education, unemployment, pensions, and healthcare. Higher dependency ratios due to population aging and longer life expectancy in Europe, the United States, and Japan will make it harder to sustain benefits at current levels, although some analyses mention that there are ways in which retirees can be encouraged to work part-time (Lloyd-Sherlock 2010). In Europe, population aging coincided with the onset during the late 1970s of early retirement policies aimed at facilitating industrial restructuring in sectors of the economy subject to low-cost competition (Taylor 2008). In the education sector resources will need to be reallocated away from primary education and into retraining and continuing education for senior citizens, especially if the age of retirement is raised (Taylor 2008). Unemployment insurance and retraining schemes may need to be overhauled if long-term joblessness among the young or among those in specific occupations continues. Old-age pensions funded by "pay-as-you-go" systems – a vintage program of the twentieth century – may have to be replaced by "defined contribution" schemes, and people encouraged or mandated to remain in the labor force longer. Clearly, schemes designed when people lived on average for 50 or 60 years need to be restructured now that life expectancy exceeds 70 or 80 years on average. In the healthcare sector resources will need to be reallocated as the age structure of the population shifts. Some emerging economies – most notably China – will also need to cope with population aging and its consequences for education, unemployment, pension, and healthcare schemes, though without having to restructure preexisting welfare programs.

We will explore in Chapter 10 the global landscape from the point of view of sustainability. Population pressures on energy, food, and water resources have become a priority on the global agenda (Matthew 2012; Waughray 2011). In particular, both demography and climate change are characterized by having a strong momentum, meaning that policies designed to address them must adopt a long-term perspective of 30 or more years.

Another set of implications of aging refers to the world of work and employment. As the population ages and pressures to stay in the labor force mount, jobs themselves will need to be redefined and redesigned so that people in their seventies and even eighties may find work. Labor market regulations, shop-floor organization, and training programs will need to be overhauled. Both policymakers and business managers will have to reexamine the way in which they think about work and about workers. Companies that learn how to incorporate older people as employees could gain a competitive edge in the marketplace, although the existing evidence for such an effect is not fully convincing (Taylor 2008). Another potential trend is that old people excluded from the workforce may pursue entrepreneurship, leveraging their experience and their savings.

The social, cultural, political, and geopolitical consequences

Large demographic swings also bring about social and political change. As population ages, family structures are transformed. The prevalence of childless households, and of families with more grandparents than grandchildren, has increased rapidly in various parts of the world. Older people behave differently, both socially and politically, although it is often hard to predict exactly what the differences are. People in the older age brackets tend to be more interested in politics and to vote more frequently (Lloyd-Sherlock 2010). In many rich countries, they tend to support conservative or right-wing policies to a greater extent. Immigration and urbanization, however, tend to have the opposite effect, thus making it hard to predict the net outcome of major demographic trends. Families with fewer children, especially those with just one, engage in different patterns of social interaction both inside and outside the household. Single-parent households may also become the norm in many parts of the world, with rather unpredictable social and political consequences. Another conflating factor is the rapid growth in telecommunications and social-networking technologies, which probably interacts in complex ways with family size and with the increasing numbers of mothers working outside the household.

One worrisome scenario combining the economic and political consequences of population aging is that the historically few young people who live in Europe and Japan might decide to leave their home country in order to avoid paying for a large cumulative national debt and for their parents' healthcare and defined-benefit pensions, especially given that they will be easily outnumbered at the polls. Migrating to another country with a younger population profile and stronger economic growth would not only offer better job opportunities but also make it possible to avoid the higher taxes associated with debt-servicing, healthcare, and pensions. Voting with their feet could become a preferable and certainly more effective strategy than exercising voice or just staying quiet. If this dynamic acquired a momentum of its own, it could easily become a self-fulfilling prophecy, one that could haunt Europe and Japan for the remainder of the twenty-first century.

In much of the developing world, a different kind of political demographics is emerging. The so-called "youth bulge," situations in which the 15–24-year-old group represents upwards of 30 or 35 percent of the total population, has the potential of reshaping national politics and even geopolitics. As Henrik Urdal (2012: 130) notes, "population growth and a young age structure can be both a blessing and a curse . . . Youth bulges can be regarded as an increased supply of labor that can boost an economy." But he warns that the combination of "youth bulges, poor governance, and failing economic growth can be explosive. This represents a considerable security challenge to many developing countries, particularly in Sub-Saharan Africa, Asia, and parts of the Arab world." Education and employment opportunities are key to defusing this kind of danger, which manifested itself in full force during the Arab Spring of 2011 (Goldstone 2011).

The quantity and quality of the human population also has important implications for military and geopolitical power. Therefore, the changes in the relative size of the population and age distribution across different parts of the world will affect the balance of geopolitical power in the twenty-first century both directly in terms of manpower and indirectly to the extent that demographic dynamism translates into economic growth. Moreover, demographic shifts will also shape attitudes and aspirations, individually and nationally (Howe and Jackson 2012). We will delve into these issues in Chapter 12, paying attention to the different sources of geopolitical dominance, including soft and hard power.

It is clear that the massive demographic changes described in this chapter will shape trends and events in the twenty-first century. While we can use past experience and theoretical models to make predictions as to the nature and magnitude of the economic, social, political, cultural, and geopolitical consequences, it is always hard to envision the future from the vantage point of the present, especially in the case of demography. Above and beyond vital statistics, each generation experiences demographic circumstances in different ways and thus could react in different ways as well. Therefore, one should always take with a grain of salt not only predictions about demographic trends but also, and especially, the consequences and the ultimate meaning of such predictions. For instance, the United Nations medium prediction is that the world's total human population will exceed 10 billion towards the end of the twenty-first century. However, this in no way necessarily means that there will not be enough food, water, energy, and natural resources for everyone to enjoy. Technological change, behavioral aspects related to consumption, and efficiency enhancements in the use of scarce resources can help make ends meet.

Population aging is one example of how important it is to be careful about the implications of demographic changes. It is important to distinguish between cohort and life-course effects, that is, between characteristics intrinsic to a given age group (e.g., those who fought in World War II, the baby-boomers, generation Y, and so on), and changes in behavior over the course of one's lifetime. It is also important to keep in mind that what passes for "old age" is socially and politically constructed, especially by state policies and rules regarding retirement. Debate in this area is often driven by myths such as the joys of retirement, the difficulties of retraining old workers, and so on. The sequential model of education–work–retirement on which many of our policies and expectations are based may need to be revisited in the new century. These and other examples of demographic change illustrate that there is nothing inherently predetermined or inevitable about many of the large-scale trends discussed in this chapter. Quite on the contrary, human agency can shape the consequences of demographic change, turning them into either positive or negative forces. Still, population aging, urbanization, and the obesity epidemic are far more than trends; they are turning points signaling that massive transformations lie ahead of us as we live through the twenty-first century.

5 From dictatorship to democracy and failed states

> **KEY GLOBAL TURNING POINTS**
> For the first time since World War II there are more countries in the
> world affected by state failure than countries ruled by dictators. In
> general, there is a sharp decline in the legitimacy and capacity of the
> state in both developed and developing countries.

Perhaps the most striking way in which the twenty-first century differs from
its predecessor has to do with politics, state fragility, and the nature of violent
conflict. The historian Eric Hobsbawm (1994) argued that the twentieth
century was a "short" one, stretching only between 1914 and 1991, and
was characterized by an epic confrontation between dictatorship and democracy during World War I, the interwar period, World War II, and the Cold
War. In the twenty-first century, by contrast, global political dynamics are
unlikely to be dominated by the extent to which individual freedoms and
political rights are observed. Rather, the problem on everyone's mind will
be failed states, i.e., countries in which central authority has broken down.
The rise of international terrorism, the key form of violent conflict in the
twenty-first century, is related to this breakdown of state authority.

Thus, in many ways the twenty-first century may end up vindicating
Francis Fukuyama's famous "end of history" thesis (1989) in that liberal
democracy and free markets won the battle, although the modern state as
the dominant form of political organization is not uniformly effective
around the world, with major implications for the global economy, global
trade, and the nature of conflict. Samuel Huntington's (1993) premonitory
analysis of the "clash of civilizations" seems to have become awfully
descriptive of the new politics of identity and conflict in the twenty-first
century, in which civil wars are less frequent than during the Cold War
period, interstate wars are even rarer, and the most dangerous and lethal
conflict takes the form of terrorism. Democracy, while formally the

dominant form of government, does not translate into free popular participation and viable opposition in countries such as Russia, Bolivia, Venezuela, Nigeria, and Pakistan, to name but a few, mostly because of the weakness of political and social institutions (Epstein and Converse 2008). Moreover, in spite of the spread of democracy, two billion people continue to live under authoritarian regimes, especially in Africa, the Middle East, South Asia, and East Asia (see the Box).

Political regimes and failed states

There are different types of political regimes, depending on how much room they allow for political participation and opposition. At one end of the spectrum, a *totalitarian* regime (e.g., North Korea) does not allow for any political participation and opposition. At the other end, a *democratic* regime protects a whole range of individual and group political rights. Somewhere in between is the *authoritarian* regime, which allows for some limited forms of participation by certain groups like religious organizations or other civic associations, though the dictator cannot be voted out of power (e.g., Spain under General Franco or South Korea under General Park). Both totalitarian and authoritarian regimes are *dictatorships*. A fourth type is the *sultanistic* regime, in which members of an extended family or clan run political affairs at the expense of formal institutions without appealing to any particular ideology (e.g., Saudi Arabia). Many countries find themselves halfway in between two of these four ideal-types. For instance, China combines features of the totalitarian and the authoritarian type.

A *failed state* is one in which central authority is weak or nonexistent, that is, the government cannot enforce law and order in part or all of the country's territory, cannot provide for minimal public services, and cannot interact with other states as part of the international community. Somalia is frequently mentioned as an example. However, there are degrees of state failure, and as many as 40 or 50 countries around the world are considered to be failed states to a certain extent. Most of them are located in Africa, Latin America, the Middle East, and South and Central Asia (see Map 5.1).

The popular uprisings in North Africa and the Middle East that started in early 2011 represent a stark reminder that democracy has not yet triumphed around the world, and that transitions are only possible when a complex mix of economic, social, political, and geopolitical factors is in place. "The revolutions unfolding across the Middle East represent the breakdown of increasingly corrupt sultanistic regimes," argued Jack Goldstone, a key expert on political revolutions.

Although economies across the region have grown in recent years, the gains have bypassed the majority of the population, being amassed instead by a wealthy few. [Former Egyptian President Hosni] Mubarak and his family reportedly built up a fortune of between $40 billion and $70 billion, and 39 officials and businessmen close to Mubarak's son Gamal are alleged to have made fortunes averaging more than $1 billion each ... Fast-growing and urbanizing populations in the Middle East have been hurt by low wages and by food prices that rose by 32 percent in the last year alone. (Goldstone 2011: 11)

Thus, one of the political challenges of the twenty-first century consists of simultaneously extending democracy to the entire world while making it deeper and more effective in regions and countries that have formally adopted the democratic form of government but do not practice its main precepts (Kapstein and Converse 2008). The most vexing political problem of the twenty-first century, however, has to do with the breakdown of governance and law and order in a growing part of the world, and specifically with failed states, some of which underpin terrorism as the new dominant form of violent conflict.

Four waves of transition from dictatorship to democracy

One of the positive legacies of the twentieth century has to do with the spread of democracy around the world. As of 1900, only parts of Western Europe, some former British colonies such as the United States, and the oligarchical states of Latin America were democracies. In addition, not everyone could vote – women, for instance, had no political rights of their own until decades later. World War I was highly contradictory in its political effects, triggering revolutions that eventually led to totalitarian states like the Soviet Union while giving democracy a chance in Germany and Eastern Europe. However, the rise of fascism in the 1920s and 1930s posed the greatest challenge to democracy, one that would be effectively overcome with World War II. The postwar period was also two-sided. In some parts of the world, most notably Western Europe and some newly independent countries in Africa and Asia, democracy took hold. The cases of Germany, Japan, and India are especially important (Moore 1966). But the Cold War led to the proliferation of both totalitarian communist regimes in Eastern Europe and East Asia, and authoritarian regimes supported by Europe and the United States in an attempt to curb communist takeovers of power in Latin America, Africa, the Middle East, and parts of Asia.

Even before the end of the Cold War, however, a third wave of transitions from dictatorship to democracy took place during the 1970s and 1980s in Southern Europe (e.g., Greece, Portugal, Spain), Latin America (Argentina, Brazil, Chile, and other countries), and East Asia (South Korea, Taiwan). In many of these countries the transition to democracy took place after social and economic development had made strides (Boix 2011; Lipset 1959), a new class of business owners or professionals grew influential (Moore 1966), and labor movements gained strength and demanded political freedoms (Rueschemeyer *et al.* 1992). The fourth wave of democratization properly started in 1989 with the collapse of the Soviet Union and its satellite regimes, with democracy spreading throughout Eastern Europe, the Caucasus, and Central Asia.

Thus, the twentieth century taken as a whole was characterized by the spread of democracy, albeit with notable setbacks. The year 1989 was a milestone, perhaps a culmination, but not an unprecedented turning point. As a result of the four waves of democratization, at the beginning of the twenty-first century there were fewer than 30 countries ruled by dictators while nearly 80 enjoyed democratic freedoms (see Figure 5.1). The first year since World War II in which there were more democracies than dictatorships in the world was 1991. As we shall discuss below, the other legacy of the twentieth century has been failed states and anocracies, whose frequency rose sharply beginning in the mid 1980s. As of the end of 2013, 49 countries suffered from some degree of state failure, forming a long arc of instability stretching from Latin America into Africa, the Middle East, South Asia, and South-East Asia (Map 5.1). An additional 50 countries were anocracies, i.e., situations in which the regime is

Figure 5.1 Global trends in political regimes, 1800–2013
Note: Coded from the Polity scores as "autocracies" (–10 to –6), "anocracies"
(–5 to +5 and the three special values –66, –77, and –88), and "democracies"
(+6 to +10).
Source: Center for Systemic Peace.

Map 5.1 State fragility and state failure, 2013
Source: Center for Systemic Peace.

formally democratic but in practice one individual or clique manipulates the democratic process and runs the country as a dictatorship, as in the cases of Russia or Venezuela. Anocracies tend to be unpredictable, and thus contribute to instability.

It is also important to underline that democracies usually attain better macroeconomic performance than dictatorships in addition to a better record regarding human rights and violent conflict. While a small number of authoritarian regimes have delivered strong economic growth historically (e.g., Spain, Chile, South Korea, Taiwan, China), there are dozens which have mismanaged the economy (Haggard and Kaufman 1995). The evidence, once again, supports Fukuyama's case in that the twentieth century will come down in history as the century that forged a symbiotic relationship between liberal democracy and free markets, one that has raised living standards in many parts of the world. The twentieth century is also responsible for the rise of a rationalistic global culture in which democracy is a major component along with mass schooling, the formal adoption of human and civil rights, the scientific attitude towards problem solving, and the widespread use of technology (Meyer *et al.* 1997), of which information and telecommunications technology has proved to be particularly transformational.

Mobile phones, the Internet, and political mobilization

While the automobile was the key individual or family possession of the twentieth century, the durable good everybody aspired to, the mobile phone is the most desired gadget of the twenty-first century. During the 1990s mobile phones and the Internet took global society by storm. The effects on politics of information and telecommunication technologies, the marriage of mobility and connectivity at decreasing costs, are perhaps as far-reaching as those on business and the economy, and they were felt primarily at the turn of the twenty-first century. For example, mobile phones and the Internet played a key role in the disruptions at the joint IMF–World Bank meetings in Prague in 2000, the demonstrations at the G8 summit in Genoa in 2001, the anti-government popular uprising leading to the removal from office of the President of the Philippines also in 2001, the cover-up of the SARS epidemic in China during 2003, the

Ukrainian Orange Revolution of 2004, the 2004 3/11 terrorist attacks in Madrid, the protests at the Republican convention in New York City in 2004, the anti-Syrian demonstrations in Lebanon in 2005, the anti-Japanese demonstrations in China over the issue of school textbooks also in 2005, the election of Barack Obama in 2008, Iran's "Twitter Revolution" in the wake of the disputed 2009 presidential election, and the posting on the WikiLeaks website of documents pertaining to the wars in Iraq and Afghanistan (Bremmer 2010b). In early 2011, popular protests spread like wildfire from Tunisia to Egypt, Bahrain, Yemen, Libya, Morocco, Syria, and other Arab countries. As of the time of writing, several presidents had been removed from power or were on the verge of being ousted, though it was still unclear if the final outcome of the revolts would be a transition to democracy or not.

Rather than changing minds about key political issues or altering votes at elections, the evidence is that information technologies help mobilize people to act politically, which may or may not result in significant political change. It seems as if the twenty-first century will be quite different from the point of view of political mobilization and its effects. Just before the 2004 general election in Spain, text messaging through mobile phones enabled flash demonstrations and the mobilization of young people, who turned out at the polls in great numbers three days after the 3/11 terrorist bombings. The election removed the conservative party from power and ushered in the opposition socialists, who received 3 million more votes than in the previous election, even though surveys predicted an entirely different outcome, and post-election surveys established that only 0.3 percent of eligible voters changed their vote in response to the attacks (Suárez 2006).

Obama is widely considered to be the first ePresident. Perhaps his biggest feat was to recruit and organize 1.5 million campaign volunteers using the Internet. His campaign posted 1800 videos on YouTube, which taken together received more than 13 million viewings. He amassed 18 million contacts on Facebook. Most importantly, he raised a record $800 million from 4 million individual donors, part of it through the Internet. Two of every three voters between the ages of 10 and 29, who do not tend to vote in large numbers, went for Obama (Kaid 2009). It also seems to be the case that new technologies are rapidly absorbed by political opponents, as the Republican takeover of the House of Representatives in 2010 illustrated.

But as Ian Bremmer, President of the Eurasia Group, cogently argued, new technologies tend to have an immediate impact on democracies. In dictatorships, the protests and demonstrations put the government on the defensive and certainly caused it a public relations crisis, but did not lead to major political change (Bremmer 2010b). Not only can authoritarian or totalitarian regimes repress outbursts of unauthorized political activity, but also there are fewer Internet users in such countries (Guillén and Suárez 2005). Moreover, these regimes control access to, and content on, the Internet through a variety of means, including censorship, firewalls, surveillance, mercenary bloggers, and even virus attacks on unwanted sites. Telecommunications and Internet companies frequently face the dilemma between upholding cherished standards of freedom and caving to political pressure, as exemplified by the cases of Google in China, and Research In Motion (maker of the BlackBerry smart phones) in India, Saudi Arabia, and the United Arab Emirates. Regulation and governance of the Internet is no less of an issue in the rich democracies, where an intense debate over net neutrality erupted in 2005 over guidelines and restrictions implemented by Internet service providers and governments on contents, sites, platforms, equipment, and the modes of communication.

Lastly, information technologies will impact geopolitics in some ways, though not changing the global balance of power. "Although cyberspace may create some power shifts among states by opening limited opportunities for leapfrogging by small states using asymmetrical warfare, it is unlikely to be a game changer," argues Joseph Nye. "The cyberdomain is likely to see an increase in the diffusion of power to nonstate actors and network centrality as a key dimension of power in the twenty-first century" (Nye 2011: 150–151).

"Good governance" and the irony of diminished state legitimacy and capacity

Governance of virtually every aspect of economic, social, and political life – not just the Internet – has become one of the key buzzwords of the twenty-first century. In 2009 the Nobel Prize in Economic Science was shared by an economist and a political scientist who laid the foundations for the formal analysis of governance issues. The topic of governance is raised in many different contexts, ranging from the control of business corporations to the oversight of financial institutions, from the conditions for doing business to the administration of nonprofit organizations, and from the quality of government to the behavior of labor unions and political parties.

Since the 1990s, economists, political scientists, political sociologists, and policymakers have emphasized the importance of good governance and institutional quality (Rodrik 2006). They have compiled numerous databases tracking various characteristics of political regimes across countries since the Napoleonic wars. Other aspects such as the rule of law, the protection of property rights, corporate governance, and the removal of bureaucratic and legal obstacles to entrepreneurship have also received an enormous amount of attention. A bewildering number of organizations launched rankings and indicators of governance and institutional quality during the 1990s, including the World Bank, Transparency International, Freedom House, the Heritage Foundation, the World Economic Forum, the Center for Systemic Peace, and the Fraser Institute, among many others (Munck 2003; World Bank 2010b, 2010c). The assumption underlying these analyses and rankings was that vibrant "economic activity requires good rules," an idea that was first proposed by sociologist Max Weber at the beginning of the twentieth century (Weber 1978: 328–329). Perhaps the most sophisticated and influential elaboration of the argument that good governance, the rule of law, and institutional quality foster economic activity is the one produced by economists (La Porta *et al.* 1998).

The emphasis placed on good governance by multilateral agencies at the turn of the twenty-first century has led to a race by governments around the world to improve their commitment to the rule of law and to institutional quality, at least formally (World Bank 2010b, 2010c). Rankings of countries according to any dimension, especially governance, are always debatable and prone to criticism. However, their effect is unmistakable: in the global economy of the twenty-first century, characterized as it is by free capital flows, governments strive to enhance the rule of law and the quality of institutions so as to attract investors and foster entrepreneurship (Klapper *et al.* 2010).

It has also become clear that some of the rules of "good governance" involve a reduction of the role of the state as a bureaucratic institution regulating the economy. It is ironic that the emphasis on good governance has come hand in hand with a sharp reduction in the legitimacy and capacity of the state, which may constrain its ability to address important social and economic problems. Much of the decline in the legitimacy of the state as an actor in the society and the economy is ideological in its origins, and can be traced back to the Thatcher and Reagan "revolutions" of the 1980s (Evans 1997; Fourcade-Gourinchas and Babb 2002). The privatization of state-owned enterprises – driven by a complex mix of ideological, economic, financial, and pragmatic reasons – pushed back the boundaries of the state even further (Henisz *et al.* 2005; Megginson and Netter 2001).

The other important trend at the turn of the twenty-first century was the loss of financial autonomy of the state in the wake of the increasing influence of financial markets. For some analysts, power not only shifted from the state to financial markets but also within the state from the so-called social ministries (labor, education, health) to the economy ministry and the central bank (Garrett 1998; Polillo and Guillén 2005; Strange 1996). This trend was already underway in the 1980s, but it accelerated with the sharp rise in government indebtedness in the wake of the global economic and financial crisis that started in 2007 (Cottarelli and Schaechter 2010). Unlike during the second half of the twentieth century, government debt became a problem in the developed countries, not the developing world. The long-standing trends of population aging and healthcare cost inflation undermined the financial viability of the welfare state. The crisis provoked bitter political debates and massive fiscal adjustment programs in Western Europe and the United States as governments wrestled to keep up with political and financial-market pressures. The Eurozone also struggled for survival (see Chapter 11). For both ideological and financial reasons, the twenty-first century will be the century of diminished state legitimacy and capacity as a result of a complex mix of ideological, political, economic, and financial cross-pressures.

Failed states

While countries in Europe, the Americas, and East Asia seek to improve their governance scores on the various global rankings – even at the cost of a weakened state apparatus in many respects – the breakdown of state authority has become the dominant political problem in most of Africa, the Middle East, South Asia, and some parts of Latin America. Acute state failure has affected countries as diverse as Haiti, Guinea, Ivory Coast, the

Democratic Republic of Congo, Chad, the Sudan, Ethiopia, Somalia, Yemen, Iraq, Afghanistan, and Myanmar. Others are suffering from diminished state authority, at least in part of their territories, including Mexico, Guatemala, Honduras, El Salvador, Colombia, Bolivia, Mauritania, Niger, Ghana, Togo, Gabon, Nigeria, Pakistan, India, Bangladesh, and Nepal, among many others. All in all, during the first decade of the twenty-first century about 50 countries were suffering from a certain degree of state failure, up from no more than 20 or 25 during the second half of the twentieth century (Map 5.1). Much of the increase was due to the devastating effects of long civil wars, which undermined the institutions of civil society. In some cases the fall of a tyrant created a vacuum of power that civil society was not ready to occupy.

While experts do not agree on the exact degree of state failure for some countries, the overall geography of state failure and the increasing trend over time are unmistakable. And while the breakdown of state authority primarily affects the local population, it has grave consequences for the rest of the world. Failed states tend to become sources of corruption, illegal trade, and regional instability. Those that are strategic because of their natural resources or geographical location can have a disproportionate negative impact on the global economy. Afghanistan, for example, comes across as a landlocked, isolated country whose internal affairs should not have far-reaching implications. However, the country has played and continues to play a key role in the world. For centuries, Afghanistan was at the crossroads of major trade routes, including the Silk Road. The country thus became the target of imperial conquest, from Alexander the Great all the way to the British, Soviet, and American attempts at global supremacy. Perhaps nobody grasped the difficulties involved better than Field Marshall his Grace, The Duke of Wellington, when he observed that "in Afghanistan, a small army would not be able to hold the country, and a large army would starve." Adding to the problem is the fact that between 25 and 40 percent of the opiates in the world, depending on the estimates, comes from Afghanistan.

The most salient case of state failure is Somalia. It is crucial to note that Somalia was never formally colonized, a fact that perhaps contributed to the breakdown of state authority since the breakout of civil war in 1991. Although the conflict has its roots in the Cold War, it is widely regarded as the first war of the twenty-first century, with all of the complex and rapidly shifting alliances among different clans and warring factions. Mogadishu, once known as the "White Pearl of the Indian Ocean," descended into chaos. The United Nations and the United States, by then the only superpower with a chance of making a difference in a faraway place, both failed to curb the violence. As of the end of 2009 as many as 680,000 Somalis, or 6 percent of the population, had sought refuge outside of the country (UN 2010).

Perhaps the best publicized by-product of the breakdown of central authority in Somalia was the rise of piracy, especially after the tsunami of December 2004, which left fishing villages with few viable economic options. As many as 80 or 90 ships were kidnapped during 2008 alone, though patrolling by a multinational coalition subsequently reduced the figure to fewer than 30, according to the US Africa Command. The disruption of global shipping in the Gulf of Aden and the adjacent areas of the Indian Ocean, which are among the busiest maritime routes in the world, encouraged many ships to go around the Cape of Good Hope in order to avoid higher insurance premiums, especially when the price of oil was low. This example shows that, in addition to the hardship inflicted on the local population and the countries receiving the refugees, state failure in Somalia also disrupted the crucial trading route linking the Indian Ocean and the Mediterranean Sea. As of 2015, the Gulf of Guinea is the area with the most piracy attacks.

New forms of violent conflict

Democracies rarely, if ever, wage war against each other. Therefore, the spread of democracy has greatly reduced the occurrence of interstate wars, which have been rare and small in scale since the end of World War II (Figure 5.2). Moreover, nuclear weapons and the doctrine of mutually assured destruction have also mitigated the risk of major interstate confrontations. Large standing armies massed at each other, a mainstay from the 1870s to the 1990s, are not the norm in the twenty-first century, with the exceptions of the Korean peninsula, the Middle East, and the Pakistani–Indian border. China's huge military force of nearly 3 million soldiers seems to be positioned to crush internal dissent rather than to deter or fend off a foreign enemy.

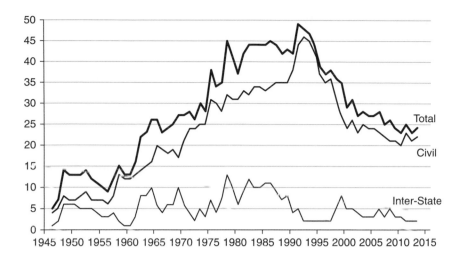

Figure 5.2 Global trends in armed conflict, 1946–2013
Source: Center for Systemic Peace.

According to the historian Niall Ferguson (2006: xli), wars proliferated in the twentieth century because of "ethnic conflict, economic volatility and empires in decline." Of these three root causes, only the latter has disappeared at the onset of the twenty-first century, but it may well make a big difference because violence related to ethnicity and economic problems is manifesting itself in new ways. For another British historian, Eric Hobsbawm, the twentieth century was "an era of religious wars, though the most militant and bloodthirsty of its religions were secular ideologies of nineteenth-century vintage, such as socialism and nationalism, whose god-equivalents were either abstractions or politicians venerated in the manner of divinities." Both secular ideologies and the cult of political personality are on the decline as we leave the twentieth century behind, although "the century ended in a global disorder" (Hobsbawm 1994: 562, 563).

Besides the reduction in the number of interstate conflicts, the nature of war has changed at the turn of the twenty-first century. Armies no longer confront each other over large expanses of territory. The pervasive use of new technology, especially information and telecommunications technology, has transformed the battle-field. The Gulf War of 1990–1991 revealed the first glimpses of the new ways in which the most advanced armies in the world waged war. By the time of the invasion of Afghanistan and Iraq in the early twenty-first century, armies looked more like nimble networks staging highly coordinated attacks. In addition, unmanned drones have been used in combat for the first time. As a result of these trends, the death rate of US soldiers while on active duty in Afghanistan and Iraq was lower than the death rate from automobile accidents and suicides within five years of returning home. Unmanned drones have now become the weapon of choice in low-intensity and anti-terrorism warfare. In a sign of things to come, the US Air Force is now training greater numbers of drone operators than fighter pilots, and rates of post-traumatic stress disorder are actually higher among the former than the latter.

Civil wars, however, proliferated during the so-called Cold War, from fewer than 40 active conflicts during the 1950s to a peak of 160 in 1990. The collapse of the Soviet Union brought the number drastically down to about 70 during the initial years of the twenty-first century (Figure 5.2). Many of these conflicts proved more intractable and lethal than the average interstate war, with some of them lasting several decades. In addition, they oftentimes lead to large displacements of people, who become either internally displaced or international refugees. The twenty-first century has inherited from the 1990s a growing problem of refugee populations (Figure 5.3), which by 2008 stood at over 40 million world-wide. The largest sources of refugee populations are, in decreasing order, Palestinians (4.8 million), Afghanistan (2.9), Iraq (1.8), Somalia (0.7), the Democratic Republic of Congo (0.5), Myanmar (0.4), Colombia (0.4), and the Sudan (0.4). The most important refugee-hosting countries were Pakistan (1.7 million), Iran (1.0), Syria (1.0), Germany (0.6), Jordan (0.4), Kenya (0.3), and Chad (0.3). Most international refugees stay within their region of origin, about one third of them in camps, thus negatively affecting neighboring countries. Three in four refugees live in developing countries (UN 2010). It is important to note that refugees tend to come disproportionately from countries suffering from some degree of state failure, and they also tend to go to other countries with weak authority structures.

The twenty-first century's most distinctive feature as far as violent conflict is concerned is the massive rise in terrorist activity and victims. While during the 1990s the number of deaths from high-casualty terrorist bombings stood at an annual average of 366, beginning with the year 2001 the figure has stayed above 1000 and reached a level as high as 5,276

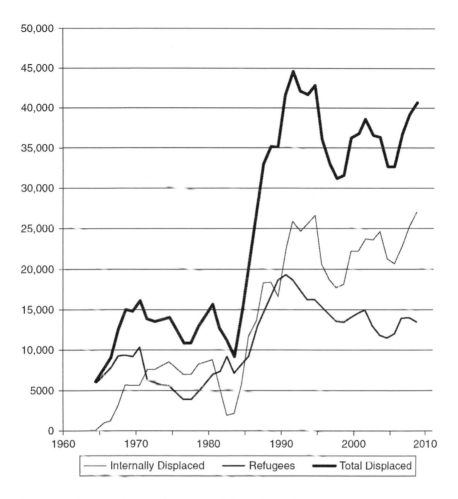

Figure 5.3 Displaced and refugee populations, 1964–2008 (thousands)
Source: Center for Systemic Peace.

in 2007 (Figure 5.4). Even more consequential is the fact that six countries account for nearly 90 percent of the casualties: Iraq, Pakistan, the United States, India, Russia, and Afghanistan, a feature that makes terrorism even more devastating and potentially destabilizing.

Many people associate the spread of terrorism with religious fundamentalism. More broadly, religion has staged a comeback in politics, both globally and locally, and both in well-established democracies such as the United States and in developing countries around the world.

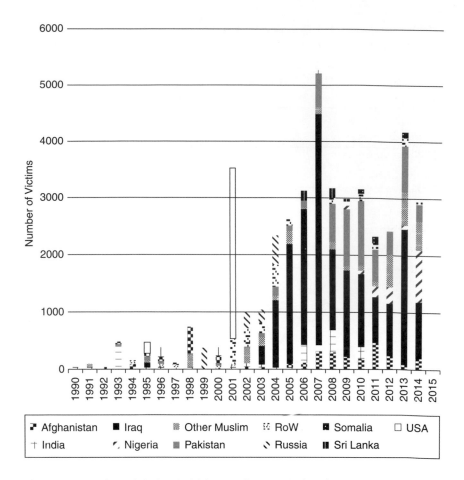

Figure 5.4 Number of victims in high-casualty terrorist bombings, 1992–2014
Source: Center for Systemic Peace.

The importance of this powerful sociopolitical force is highlighted by continuing problems with religious persecution and conflict in the Balkans, the Caucasus, the Middle East, sub-Saharan Africa, China, South Asia, and elsewhere. In Latin America, the rise of evangelical Protestantism could well dislodge the Catholic Church from its centuries-old dominant position in politics and society.

Thus we see that, from a political point of view, the twenty-first century is drastically different from the century that ended with the terrorist attacks on the United States. September 11, 2001 represented a significant turning point in history because the world's remaining superpower and largest economy experienced for the first time a massive terrorist attack staged by perpetrators trained in a country with a failed state and funded by a millionaire living in an oil-rich kingdom ruled by a sultanistic regime. In fact, the rise in international terrorism has come hand in hand with the increase in oil prices. The full consequences of the myriad civil wars of the twentieth century and of the collapse of the Soviet Union became more readily apparent since 2001 with the rise in state fragility in Africa, the Middle East, South Asia, and parts of Latin America.

The twenty-first century started with democracy triumphant and dictatorship in retreat. But it was a beginning marked by the uncertainty and chaos that failed states and terrorism inflicted on global society as a whole. Given that failed states tend to be located in areas rich in natural resources, the twenty-first century presents a new kind of a "resource curse," one that is completely endogenous and much more dangerous than the one encountered during the twentieth century because it affects not just specific countries but the entire global economic and political system. These changes are taking place during a time of diminished state legitimacy and capacity in both developed and developing countries.

6 A disparate world: inequality and poverty

KEY GLOBAL TURNING POINTS

Income inequality *across* countries has decreased since the turn of the twenty-first century. Meanwhile, inequality *within* countries has continued to increase, posing difficult social and political problems in developed and developing countries alike.

One of the most intriguing pieces of news coming out of the World Economic Forum's 2011 meeting in Davos was that yawning economic disparities were identified by the global economic, financial, and business elites gathered at the idyllic Swiss mountain resort town as one of the two most significant global risks facing the world, together with failures in global governance (*The Economist*, January 20, 2011). Such economic disparities manifest themselves in various forms, including poverty and income and wealth inequality. Poverty has been on the decrease for the last few decades thanks to rapid growth in emerging economies, although it has increased in some countries, including both developed and developing ones. The same is generally true of income and wealth inequality. Whether you look at the data within or across countries makes a huge difference, and helps identify yet another turning point into the twenty-first century.

During the last 20 years, the forces commonly associated with globalization have produced – with only a few exceptions – greater income inequality *within* countries (Anand and Segal 2008: 85), something that most economists and experts do not find surprising. The news is elsewhere: inequality *across* countries has decreased since the turn of the twenty-first century, starting to reverse one of the most long-lasting legacies of the Industrial Revolution (Hillebrand 2008). According to a recent World Bank study, "after 20 years of mean-income divergence, GDPs per capita of the countries of the world have begun a process of convergence since 2001. This is due to the pick-up of growth in Africa, post-communist countries and

Latin America. It is unclear how the global crisis will affect this process" (Milanovic 2009: 14). When taking into account the different population sizes of countries, one observes that inequality across countries has been declining since at least the early 1990s due to the China growth effect. Excluding China from the calculations, population-weighted inequality across countries started to come down in the year 2001 thanks to the high growth rates in other emerging economies, from Brazil to India and from Turkey to sub-Saharan Africa (Milanovic 2009; see also Firebaugh 2000). Figure 6.1 displays the evolution of these two indicators from 1950 to 2008.

Inequality

Inequality is a multidimensional concept. Many people think that income inequality is its most important aspect because, after all, income can be spent on all manner of goods and services. Another key aspect, however, has to do with differences in wealth, which turn out to be greater than those in income. The United Nations has advanced a global agenda, called the Millennium Goals, which seeks to reduce global inequality along a number of dimensions, including nutrition, education, gender, health, and environmental sustainability as well as poverty.

Income inequality, however, is an attractive concept because of its implications for other dimensions of inequality and also for its relevance to consumption, business, politics, and geopolitics. Like other forms of inequality, it can be measured within and across countries, rural–urban strata, and gender or race categories.

The most widely used way of measuring income or wealth inequality is through the Gini coefficient, which ranges between zero (when income is evenly distributed across the population) to 100 (all income accrues to one individual or household in a population of infinite size).

The calculation of the Gini coefficient is not intuitive, however. It involves dividing the area above the so-called Lorenz curve describing the actual distribution of income (or wealth) by the total area underneath the 45-degree line of perfect equality. Detailed data on the distribution of income are required. They may come from household surveys or from the national accounts. The quality, coverage, and frequency of the data are common problems when comparing inequality across countries or over time.

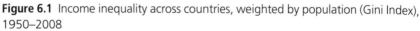

Figure 6.1 Income inequality across countries, weighted by population (Gini Index), 1950–2008

Note: The calculations are based on 140 countries in 1950–1989 and 159 countries in 1990–2008. The difference is due to the breakup of Czechoslovakia, Yugoslavia, and the Soviet Union into independent countries.

Source: Angus Maddison, *Historical Statistics of the World Economy: 1–2008 AD.* www.ggdc.net/maddison (accessed August 20, 2011).

We do not know for sure whether overall global income inequality is on the rise or the decline. Empirical studies differ widely in their findings (Anand and Segal 2008; Hillebrand 2008). But we do know that the contributions of within-country and across-countries inequality have shifted. While at the end of the twentieth century about half of global income inequality had to do with differences across countries and the other half, depending on the study, with its distribution within countries (Anand and Segal 2008: 85), the twenty-first century will likely be characterized by more inequality within than across countries, an effect attributable to two main shifts. First, if emerging and developing countries continue to grow faster than developed countries, as has been the case on average from the mid 1990s to 2011, global inequality across countries will tend to decline.

The second main shift has to do with the likely continued increase in within country inequality. A recent IMF (2007a: 49–50) study concluded that "technological progress alone explains most of the 0.45 percent average annual increase in the Gini coefficient from the early 1980s" to the mid 2000s, which measures income inequality within countries. The IMF used the stock of information and telecommunications technology as the key indicator. "Trade and financial globalization and financial deepening contributed a further 0.1 percent a year each … offset by almost equivalent reductions in the Gini coefficient from increased access to education and a shift of employment away from agriculture." New technology tends to favor skilled workers, thus exacerbating the so-called "skills gap." According to the IMF (2007a: 49), the increase in income inequality due to the diffusion of information and telecommunications technologies has affected both developed and developing countries, although the effect has been far smaller in Latin America than in Asia. It is important to note that globalization has had very different effects on inequality: "Trade globalization has exerted an equalizing impact, whereas financial globalization [and foreign direct investment in particular] has been associated with widening income disparities" (IMF 2007a: 50).

Table 6.1 summarizes the available evidence on the recent evolution of income inequality. Given that the data were drawn from different sources, comparisons need to be made carefully. Between the mid 1990s and the mid 2000s inequality within countries has increased in most countries, with the notable exceptions of Brazil, Russia, Mexico, Nigeria, the Philippines, Turkey, and Spain. Most importantly, in the two most populous countries, China and India, there has been a sharp increase in inequality. Data for China indicate that most of the increase is attributable to yawning disparities within urban areas, and between rural and urban areas. Inequality in rural areas has remained constant or decreased slightly (Chen et al. 2010: 20). For India, no national index exists, but we also observe over time growing income inequality within cities, and between cities and

Table 6.1 Income inequality, selected countries

	Gini coefficient	
	0 = perfect equality	
	100 = maximum inequality	
	Mid 1990s	Most recent
Within countries:		
Brazil	59.1	52.7
Russia	45.2	42.2
India	32.9	33.9
China	38.2	47.8
Egypt	30.1	33.0
Philippines	42.6	39.2
Nigeria	51.1	46.8
Kenya	42.1	47.1
Turkey	44.8	42.2
Mexico	55.2	47.5
OECD countries:		
Japan	24.3	32.1
France	29.7	32.9
Germany	30.2	30.6
Poland	26.9	34.1
Spain	36.4	34.2
Sweden	25.2	25.5
United Kingdom	35.6	35.9
United States	45.0	47.7

Source: World Bank, All the Ginis Database (accessed May 16, 2015).

the countryside (Cain *et al.* 2008: 5). Thus, the increase in inequality within the two countries with the largest populations as well as several developed ones (e.g., Germany, Sweden, and the United States) overshadows the decrease in other, smaller countries. Much of the widening income gap has to do with stagnating wages, which represent 75 percent of household income.

Inequality has risen even in countries traditionally thought to be egalitarian, like Germany, Denmark, and Sweden, where the top 10 percent now receives five times as much income as the bottom 10 percent. In many advanced economies the multiple has reached 10 (e.g., Italy, Japan, Korea, and the United Kingdom), and even 14 (Israel and USA). Latin America stands out as an especially unequal part of the world. In Chile and Mexico the multiple is 25, and in Brazil as high as 50. Among OECD countries, the multiple has grown from the mid 1980s to the late 2000s in Australia, Austria, Canada, the Czech Republic, Denmark, Finland, Germany, Hungary, Israel, Luxembourg, Mexico, the Netherlands, New Zealand, Norway, Sweden, the UK, and the US (Table 6.2; see also OECD 2011c). Interestingly, redistributive policies are more likely to be enacted when the income disparities between the poor and the middle class are smaller relative to the difference between the middle class and the rich (Lupu and Pontusson 2011).

Inequality, of course, is a multidimensional problem. Most studies find that wealth inequality is greater than income inequality, and that it is on the increase within countries as well. While in the year 2000 the top 10 percent of households in the world owned 85 percent of the wealth, they accounted for 67 percent of the income (Davies et al. 2009: 1122). Across countries, we observe a decrease in inequality in terms of education, knowledge, and other human development variables, except for life expectancy, due mostly to the impact of the AIDS epidemic in sub-Saharan Africa (Crow et al. 2009; McGillivray and Markova 2010). Nobel Prize winner Amartya Sen (1992) has forcefully argued that one should adopt a "capabilities" view of inequality encompassing entitlements, relationships, desired outcomes, and freedoms as key components. It is hard to obtain data, though, on such a comprehensive set of variables for a reasonably large sample of countries.

The increasingly unequal income distribution is not only socially undesirable but also a potential brake on economic growth and a factor that can fuel financial crises, like the one initiated in 2007 (Kumhof and Ranciere 2010). The conclusion is clear: unequal distribution of income and wealth, indeed, is not profitable, from any point of view. Moreover, support of economic and financial globalization among the public is faltering precisely because many view it as contributing to inequality.

Table 6.2 Trends in real household income by income group, mid 1980s to late 2000s

Countries	Average annual change (%)			
	Total population	Bottom decile (A)	Top decile (B)	Difference (B)–(A)
Australia	3.6	3.0	4.5	1.5
Austria	1.3	0.6	1.1	0.5
Belgium	1.1	1.7	1.2	−0.5
Canada	1.1	0.9	1.6	0.7
Chile	1.7	2.4	1.2	−1.2
Czech Republic	2.7	1.8	3.0	1.2
Denmark	1.0	0.7	1.5	0.8
Finland	1.7	1.2	2.5	1.3
France	1.2	1.6	1.3	−0.3
Germany	0.9	0.1	1.6	1.5
Greece	2.1	3.4	1.8	−1.6
Hungary	0.6	0.4	0.6	0.2
Ireland	3.6	3.9	2.5	−1.4
Israel	1.7	−1.1	2.4	3.5
Italy	0.8	0.2	1.1	0.9
Japan	0.3	−0.5	0.3	0.8
Luxembourg	2.2	1.5	2.9	1.4
Mexico	1.4	0.8	1.7	0.9
Netherlands	1.4	0.5	1.6	1.1
New Zealand	1.5	1.1	2.5	1.4
Norway	2.3	1.4	2.7	1.3
Portugal	2.0	3.6	1.1	−2.5
Spain	3.1	3.9	2.5	−1.4
Sweden	1.8	0.4	2.4	2.0
Turkey	0.5	0.8	0.1	−0.7
United Kingdom	2.1	0.9	2.5	1.6

	Average annual change (%)			
Countries	Total population	Bottom decile (A)	Top decile (B)	Difference (B)–(A)
United States	1.3	0.5	1.9	1.4
OECD-27	1.7	1.3	1.9	0.6

Note: Income refers to disposable household income, corrected for household size and deflated by the consumer price index (CPI). Average annual changes are calculated over the period from 1985 to 2008, with a number of exceptions: 1983 was the earliest year for Austria, Belgium, and Sweden; 1984 for France, Italy, Mexico, and the United States; 1986 for Finland, Luxembourg, and Norway; 1987 for Ireland; 1988 for Greece; 1991 for Hungary; 1992 for the Czech Republic; and 1995 for Australia and Portugal. The latest year for Chile was 2009; for Denmark, Hungary, and Turkey it was 2007; and for Japan 2006. Changes exclude the years 2000 to 2004 for Austria, Belgium, Ireland, Portugal, and Spain for which surveys were not comparable.
Sources: OECD Database on Household Income Distribution and Poverty. For Israel: http://dx.doi.org/10.1787/888932315602 (accessed January 2, 2012).

The paradox of growing inequality and declining poverty

Poverty is another concept that comes up frequently in discussions of inequality, although the two dimensions are not perfectly correlated with each other. In fact, poverty has come down around the world during the last 25 years while within-country inequality has tended to go up. Poverty has to do with pronounced deprivation. Drawing the poverty line at one dollar a day, there were between 1.1 and nearly 1.5 billion poor people in the world back in 1980, a figure that came down to less than one billion by 2005, of which 427 million were in sub-Saharan Africa, 163 million in India, 131 million in China, 161 million in the rest of Asia, 56 million in Latin America, and 27 million in North Africa and the Middle East. Thus, the proportion of the population of non-OECD countries living in poverty has declined from 35–44 percent to less than 20 percent (Hillebrand 2008: 729–731).

Interestingly, some studies find that the prevalence of poverty now-adays would be even lower if within-country income distributions had not worsened between 1980 and 2005. Hillebrand (2008: 731) estimated that if income inequality had not changed, China would have no poor people today, and India 95 million as opposed to 163 million. As mentioned above, inequality between the cities and the countryside has skyrocketed in both China and India as a result of rapid, but uneven, economic growth. Numbers like these throw the famous statement by Deng Xiaoping into new light: "Let some people get rich first." However, these and other estimates published by scholars, experts, and international organizations use relatively faulty data and make strong assumptions. For instance, there are complex relationships among inequality, economic growth, and poverty, many of which policymakers cannot anticipate.

Let's begin with the influential analysis by Dollar and Kraay (2002), famously entitled, "Growth Is Good for the Poor," in which they concluded that "growth on average does benefit the poor as much as anyone else in society, and so standard growth-enhancing policies should be at the center of any effective poverty reduction strategy" (Dollar and Kraay 2002: 219). The authors also sought to advance a specific agenda about minimal government intervention in the economy when it comes to fostering growth, which is a much more debatable recipe for success at reducing poverty.

But the issue that concerns us is whether inequality may get in the way of reducing poverty or not, given that the poor stand to gain from economic growth, as the cases of China and India amply demonstrate. A recent IMF study concludes that "longer growth spells are robustly associated with more equality in the income distribution" (Berg and Ostry 2011: 3). The underlying mechanism has to do with how inequality (or the lack thereof) changes incentives. While some degree of inequality is inherent to the well-functioning of the market economy, rising inequality reduces the incentives for the poor to invest in education. It can also create the conditions for sociopolitical upheaval, as we shall analyze below. This argument is corroborated by the careful analysis of one of the most influential development economists, William Easterly (2007), who found that structural inequality in the long run reduces per capita income because it undermines the quality of institutions in the country and discourages schooling.

In sum, we can safely conclude that rising inequality within countries is likely to reduce economic growth and economic development, which in turn will make poverty reduction much harder. Thus, there is no paradox between rising inequality and decreasing poverty. Poverty came down at a time when inequality was also coming down. The recent spike in inequality within countries since the turn of the twenty-first century may well thwart further efforts at poverty reduction.

A related aspect of the relationship between inequality and poverty has to do with the impact of globalization. The decline in poverty has occurred precisely at a time of growing economic and financial integration, especially of developing countries. Globalization, however, has not uniformly reduced poverty. According to Harrison and McMillan (2007) there are winners and losers among the poor when it comes to the effects of trade and foreign investment. Only the poor who work in export-oriented or investment-receiving sectors of the economy tend to benefit. Most of the impact of globalization on the poorest developing countries, however, does not have to do with free trade but with the lack thereof. Eliminating subsidies to rich-country farmers and creating a truly free global market for agricultural goods would reduce both poverty and income inequality within countries because the wages of unskilled agricultural laborers would rise more quickly than those for skilled workers in urban areas in the same country and those for unskilled workers in developed countries (Anderson et al. 2011).

A similar process of change is taking place in developed countries. "Employment opportunities and incomes are high, and rising, for the highly educated people at the upper end of the tradable sector of the US economy," argues Nobel Prize-winning economist Michael Spence. "But they are diminishing at the lower end." And he predicts: "As emerging economies continue to move up the value-added chain – and they must in order to keep growing – the tradable sectors of advanced economies will require less labor and the more labor-intensive tasks will shift to emerging economies" (Spence 2011: 32–33).

Gender inequality

Among the most important legacies of the twentieth century are the greater awareness of the importance of gender-based discrimination and inequality, the recognition of women's rights, and the empowerment of women as economic and political actors. The demographic trends discussed in Chapter 4 continue to have a large impact on women, whose role in the society and the economy has changed due to higher educational levels and lower fertility.

Women's rights are still far from equal to those of men. A recent World Bank report covering 128 developed and developing economies found a considerable degree of legal discrimination against women in areas that thwart employment and entrepreneurship. For instance, as of 2009 in 45 countries women did not have the same legal capacity to act or engage in economic transactions as men, in 49 women were prevented from working in certain industries, and in 32 they did not have equal inheritance rights. Equal legal rights were found to result in a greater percentage of businesses owned or managed by women (World Bank 2010a). Women face many different kinds of obstacles when pursuing an entrepreneurial career (see Chapter 9).

More progress has been made in terms of educational attainment, with male–female differentials dropping at all levels and in all parts of the world due to increased demand for educated workers and government policies promoting equality of opportunity. Still, parts of sub-Saharan Africa and the Middle East fall well short of gender educational equality. Labor force participation and employment by women has also increased across the board, but it is still higher in the United States, Canada, and the Scandinavian countries than in Southern Europe or Japan, among rich societies. In many developing countries women work outside of the household as a way to escape poverty, and they often do so in the informal sector. Women's paid labor activity is lowest in North Africa and the Middle East. In most rich societies, the gender pay gap has narrowed, although occupational segregation and lower returns to education continue to exist. Women's economic disadvantages are greater in developing countries than in rich societies (Charles 2011).

It is also the case that the gender division of roles within the household has evolved towards more equality, especially in richer societies, though without closing the gap. Women continue to do most childcare and core household work, even when they are employed. A considerable degree of gender-based segregation occurs in the labor market, mostly due to segregation by field of higher education. The important fact here is that richer societies are home to higher, not lower, degrees of career segregation by gender due to the choice of educational field (Charles 2011). Thus, it is not always the case that higher development leads to greater gender equality.

It is also important to keep in mind that variables other than development may have an impact on women's opportunities and well-being. Among those discussed in Chapter 4, population aging stands out as a potential game-changer. Aging will have very different effects by gender. Women represent a disproportionate number of old people due to both higher life expectancy and the higher exposure of men to violent death. We also know that women tend to have lower income than men within the same age group, and the gap is especially important in the older age intervals because of the diseconomies of living alone (Johnson 2005). Thus, population aging may prevent the socioeconomic status gap between men and women from closing.

One final trend concerning women has to do with their increasing presence in political decision making. Table 6.3 shows the proportion of parliamentary seats occupied by women. In 2014 the world average stood at 22.2 percent, up from 12.5 percent in 1990. Europe and Latin America are above the average, while sub-Saharan Africa, South Asia, East Asia, the Arab World, and the Middle East and North Africa in particular, are below. Rwanda with 63.8 and Sweden with 44.7 percent lead the ranking. South Africa went from 3.0 percent towards the end of the apartheid era to 41.5 percent nowadays. The United States with only 19.3 percent ranks below the averages for Europe, Latin America, and sub-Saharan Africa. Interestingly, countries with more women in government are perceived as less corrupt, net of other factors like economic development, openness to trade, liberal democracy, or a free press (Treisman 2007: 212).

The consequences of shifting patterns of global inequality

In *The Great Transformation*, the social scientist Karl Polanyi (1944) famously argued that on the one hand inequality laid the foundations for the dynamism of the market, but on the other it could undermine the "substance of society." The recent trends in global inequality documented in this chapter perfectly justify the fears of the global leaders gathered at the World Economic Forum in 2011. Changes in inequality patterns could

Table 6.3 Women in parliament (% of total seats)

Region	1990	2014
European Union	16.0	27.7
High income: OECD	12.9	27.6
Latin America & the Caribbean	12.0	27.5
World average	12.5	22.2
Sub-Saharan Africa	. . .	22.1
South Asia	6.3	19.2
East Asia & Pacific	14.9	18.6
Arab World	3.8	17.8
Middle East & North Africa	3.8	16.1
Selected countries:		
Rwanda	17.0	63.8
Sweden	38.0	44.7
South Africa	3.0	41.5
Spain	15.0	39.7
Mexico	12.0	37.4
Germany	. . .	36.5
France	7.0	26.2
China	21.0	23.4
United Kingdom	6.0	22.6
Saudi Arabia	. . .	19.9
United States	7.0	19.3
Indonesia	12.0	16.9
Turkey	1.0	14.4
Russian Federation	. . .	13.6
India	5.0	11.4
Brazil	5.0	9.9
Japan	1.0	8.1

Region	1990	2014
Iran	2.0	3.1
Egypt	4.0	2.0

Note: '. . .' signifies unavailable data.
Source: World Development Indicators.

have a number of consequences in the twenty-first century. Let us discuss the economic, political, business, and geopolitical implications.

Global leaders are right to be alarmed. Rising inequality within countries coupled with a reduction in differences across countries is likely to exacerbate social and political tensions, especially if economic growth in developed countries proceeds at a snail's pace. For decades, we have contained between-country inequality by erecting barriers to the free movement of people and engaging in large-scale development efforts and international aid programs. These efforts were meant to address the larger part of inequality in the world, that between rich and poor countries. Within-country inequality is harder to deal with because boundaries cannot be drawn inside countries – as the Arab Spring and the British riots of 2011 illustrate. Moreover, at the beginning of the twenty-first century, governments are not in a position to redistribute more income and wealth because of their budgetary problems and/or the ideological constraints they face in terms of pressure from the electorate. Some scholars argue that total inequality could also rise in the world, in part driven by the increasing within-country inequality (Hillebrand 2008).

The year 2011 saw dramatic events in both developing and developed countries which cannot be fully understood without taking rising within-country inequality into account. The so-called Arab Spring spread from Tunisia throughout the Middle East and North Africa like wildfire. In most of these countries between 45 and 65 percent of the population is under the age of 25 and faces grim prospects in the labor market; rural–urban inequality and within-urban income inequality are on the rise, and corruption is rampant. Vast disparities in wealth offended not only the populace but also the military elites, which withdrew their support for the long-standing autocratic regimes of Tunisia and Egypt (Goldstone

2011). Protracted fighting and armed conflict broke out in Libya, Yemen, and Syria, amidst international condemnation for the sitting regime's repression of the popular uprising. While distinct and distant from the Arab Spring, the riots that rocked Britain's main cities for four days in August were also driven by a sense of economic and political disenfranchisement by the young, however unjustified the form in which the rioters chose to express their dissatisfaction was. While the root causes were similar, the process and the outcome of the British revolts could not be more different to the Arab Spring. So are the various "occupy" movements in Europe and the United States. As the *Washington Post* (August 9, 2011) editorialized,

this is becoming a year of rebellion by the dispossessed – first in the Arab Middle East, then in Israel and now in one of the world's richest democracies. At a time of economic disruption, no country is immune from such upheaval. But Britain is showing that democracies can respond with responsible policing and robust political debate. It is because they are incapable of such political flexibility or respect for human rights that the Arab autocrats are doomed.

Shifting trends in inequality also have implications for business. Most companies with global aspirations have spent the last decade or so repositioning their assets, employees, and product lineups so as to take advantage of growth in emerging markets. Thus, the decrease in income inequality across countries has triggered a race for the purse of the new, rising middle classes of countries like Brazil, China, India, and other emerging economies. By the same token, increasing inequality within countries should also induce corporations to do their best to cater to the needs of those who are, at least temporarily, left behind as emerging economies grow, especially in the rural areas. The increase in income inequality within developed economies should also trigger the imagination of corporations so that new kinds of jobs and careers can be designed for both the unemployed young and the aging population.

As better-educated women join the labor force and gain access to elected public office, the pressure is on for companies to welcome more of them into the c-suite and the boardroom. According to a McKinsey study of the largest listed firms, the proportion of women on the top executive team or the board of directors was lower than 15 percent in most countries, including the US, France, Germany, Britain, Spain, Russia,

Brazil, China, and India. Only Sweden stood out, though the proportion was still far from perfect equity (*The Economist*, July 21, 2011).

The implications of changing trends in inequality for geopolitics of power are tantalizing. Greater inequality within countries may produce more frequent regime change and instability. Lower inequality across countries will surely affect the geopolitical balance of power on a global scale and within specific regions. Chapter 12 will discuss these and other issues related to the shifting global balance of power during the twenty-first century.

7 The rise of the global middle class and the high-net-worth elite

> **KEY GLOBAL TURNING POINTS**
> By the year 2027, and for the first time in human history, more than half of the world's population will be part of the middle class. Also in 2027, the Indian and Chinese middle-class markets will exceed the European and American markets in purchasing power. Meanwhile, the number of high-net-worth individuals continues to grow, and more than half of them will be women by 2030.

The global economic, social, and political landscape is being transformed by the growth of social categories such as the middle class and the millionaires. In Europe and the United States these two groups took off during the 1920s, and resumed their growth during the 1950s and 1960s, at a time when Japan joined the trend. Nowadays most of the growth, however, comes from the emerging economies, while the tendency towards greater inequality is resulting in a shrinkage of the middle class in the US and an expansion of the class of millionaires and billionaires. These trends are transforming the global economy and society, creating numerous business opportunities, and also posing serious economic, political, social, and environmental challenges.

The growth of the middle class is one of the most important trends of the last 150 years. However, until very recently, the middle class was the largest social stratum only in relatively rich countries. Over the last 30 years, hundreds of millions of people have been lifted out of poverty in many parts of the world, including Brazil, China, India, Indonesia, Mexico, and Thailand, to name but a few countries. As a result of these changes, the size of the global middle class will soon become larger than the number of people living under the poverty line for the first time in history. Given the values, preferences, and yearnings of the middle class, its rise to global prominence will have major implications for society, politics, and the global economy.

The middle class has been defined in various ways. At the time of the French Revolution, the middle class referred to the bourgeoisie, i.e., the new ascending urban traders, artisans, and professionals, vastly outnumbered by the peasantry and seeking to become politically influential at the expense of the landed aristocracy. In the nineteenth century, Karl Marx referred to the middle class as the petit bourgeoisie, namely, a class between the proletariat (i.e., the working class) and the ruling capitalist class. The sociologist Max Weber echoed this distinction in his extensive studies of social stratification. Hard work, security, and frugality are values commonly associated with the middle class.

In a global context, the contemporary middle class, however, refers not only to small business owners and salaried employees, but more broadly to anyone with sufficient discretionary income to purchase goods and services beyond basic necessities such as shelter and sustenance. The middle class thus defined purchases durable goods such as automobiles and household appliances, often on credit, and prefers to consume branded products, for which it is ready to pay a premium price (Murphy *et al.* 1989).

The middle class

The middle class is commonly defined as the social stratum between the working class and the upper class. From a global perspective, the middle class is the stratum between the poor and the rich.

Middle-class people tend to have high levels of educational attainment, moderate political views, aspirational consumption patterns, and yearnings for stability and security.

The middle-class consumer accounts for the bulk of the demand for goods and services in both emerging and developed economies. Middle-class consumers exhibit a taste for branded goods, and they tend to buy homes, automobiles, and household appliances on credit, thus contributing to the development of the financial system.

The size of the global middle class can be defined in different ways. In terms of disposable income, Homi Kharas (2010) defines it as families

(cont.)

with at least $10 to spend per person per day but no more than $100. This would translate into annual incomes of $14,600 and $146,000 for a family of four, always adjusting for local purchasing power. An alternative definition focuses on the ownership of durable goods such as automobiles.

The rise of the global middle class is propelling economic growth and consumption around the world, with important implications for sustainability and for the global balance of economic power. Moreover, the balance of political power within countries also shifts, upsetting the established parties in the case of democratic regimes, and potentially undermining authoritarian regimes.

The growth of the middle class has been historically associated with demands for political representation and democracy (Banerjee and Duflo 2007; Moore 1966), the acquisition of human capital through education (Doepke and Zilibotti 2007), and the accumulation of financial capital through savings. The most distinctive economic behavior of the middle class, however, has to do with consumption of both durable and non-durable goods, and with the use of services such as credit and insurance (Nomura 2009). "The swelling middle class in emerging economies thus has the potential not only to transform the economic balance of power across the globe but also political relations within and between countries" (Dadush and Ali 2012: 3).

Defining and measuring the global middle class

In his landmark study on "The Emerging Middle Class in Developing Countries," Homi Kharas (2010: 7) defined the middle class as people with "the ability to lead a comfortable life." Members of the middle class "usually enjoy stable housing, healthcare and educational opportunities (including college) for their children, reasonable retirement and job security, and discretionary income that can be spent on vacation and leisure pursuits." Instead of using the distribution of income within each country to arrive at a relative definition of who is middle class, Kharas adopted an absolute definition in terms of purchasing power per capita, with the middle class ranging between $10 and $100 per day, and the poor and the rich defined below and above those thresholds, respectively. Using household surveys, he analyzed the distribution of income to determine how many people fall within each of the three intervals in each country. An absolute definition of the middle class is more appropriate than a relative one for the purposes of understanding global shifts and of examining the consequences for the economy, for international trade, and for the environment.

The results of his analysis indicate that there were about 1.8 billion middle-class people in the world as of 2009, or nearly 27 percent of the total population at the time, of which 664 million were in Europe, 525 million in Asia (125 million in Japan), 230 million in the United States, 181 million in Central and South America, and just 32 million in Africa. American middle-class consumers, however, enjoy a disposable income nearly twice as high on average than Europeans or Asians. As of 2009, the United States and Europe combined represented 48 percent of all middle-class individuals, and 59 percent of total middle-class spending (Kharas 2010: 15–16).

Figure 7.1 shows the rapid increase in the proportion of the population classified as middle class and the size of middle-class consumption. The projections made by Kharas (2010) indicate that by the year 2027 more than half of the world's population will be middle-class. By that year, total middle-class consumption will reach nearly 43 trillion dollars. More importantly, the geographical distribution of the global middle class will shift towards Asia. At the turn of the twenty-first century, middle-class consumption in the US and the European Union was 40 times greater than in China and India. By the year 2027, the two Asian giants will surpass the two traditional poles of middle-class consumption. The rest of the Asia-Pacific region, the Middle East and North Africa, and sub-Saharan Africa will also see its share of global middle-class consumption increase, while Latin America will see its share dwindle a bit as a percentage of the total (see Figure 7.2).

The figures involved in middle-class consumption are mind-boggling. The global total was 21 trillion dollars in 2009 and is projected to reach nearly 49 trillion by 2030. The number of middle-class people will swell from 1.8 billion to 4.7 billion. The largest middle-class consumer market will be India at $8.8 trillion, followed by China at nearly $8.3 trillion (see

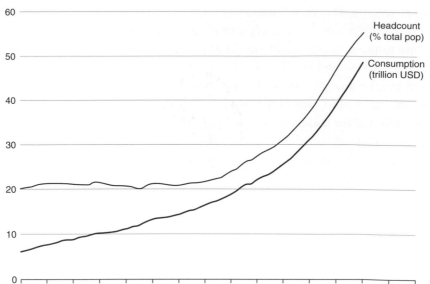

Figure 7.1 The growth of the global middle class, 1965–2009, with projections to 2030
Notes: Using purchasing power parities. USD of 2005.
Source: Brookings Development, Aid, and Governance Indicators. www.brookings
.edu/research/interactives/development-aid-governance-indicators (accessed
March 15, 2015).

Table 7.1). The reasons why India will be a bigger market than China are
diverse. First, India will have a greater population than China by about
2030. Second, the Indian economy relies on domestic consumption to a
much greater extent than China's, 60 versus 34 percent. And third, the
Chinese model of growth generates more inequality over time than India's.

In 2030, the EU will be the third largest middle-class consumer market
at $8.2 trillion, while the United States will only be about half the size. The
reasons are that the growth of the middle class in Eastern Europe will
accelerate, and the overall EU will harbor less income inequality than the
US (see Chapter 6). Still, the United States will be the richest middle-class
market, at $20,971 per capita, followed by Japan at $18,780, and the EU at
$17,838. China and India will be at roughly half those levels.

Excluding India and China, the rest of the Asia-Pacific region will also
witness rapid growth in both the number of middle-class people and

Figure 7.2 Distribution of middle-class consumption by country or region, 1965–2009, with projections to 2030
Notes: Using purchasing power parities. USD of 2005.
Source: Brookings Development, Aid, and Governance Indicators. www.brookings.edu/research/interactives/development-aid-governance-indicators (accessed March 15, 2015).

consumption. Meanwhile, middle-class consumption in Latin America and the Middle East and North Africa will increase to become twice as big by 2030, thus trailing the growth rate of the Asian countries. Finally, sub-Saharan Africa will continue to be the smallest regional middle-class consumer market, although growing rapidly from a very small base.

An alternative way of measuring the middle class is to take ownership of durable goods into consideration. Automobiles and household appliances are markers of middle-class social and economic status. For instance, the "car index" measures the middle class as the number of automobiles in circulation adjusted by household size. According to this metric, there are 550–600 million middle-class people in the G20 emerging economies (Dadush and Ali 2012), a figure about 20 percent lower than the one based on per capita disposable income (Kharas 2010). Figure 7.3 shows the number of passenger and commercial vehicles per 100,000 population. In the US, the EU (with 28 members throughout the entire time period), and Japan the figures are at least twice as high as in Russia or

Table 7.1 The global middle class in 2009 (actual) and 2030 (forecast)

Country or region:	Headcount (millions)		Consumption (2005 billion USD)		Per capita consumption (2005 USD)	
	2009	2030	2009	2030	2009	2030
United States	231.8	208.0	4,401	4,362	18,986	20,971
European Union	464.0	457.9	6,621	8,168	14,269	17,838
India	53.3	1,167.7	341	8,832	6,398	7,564
China	136.9	1,041.1	837	8,281	6,114	7,954
Japan	123.0	108.2	1,710	2,032	13,902	18,780
Rest of Asia Pacific	180.6	541.9	1,859	5,306	10,293	9,791
Latin America	265.1	452.8	2,197	4,629	8,287	10,223
Middle East and North Africa	81.6	173.7	635	1,524	7,782	8,774
Sub-Saharan Africa	29.5	130.9	241	923	8,169	7,051
World total	1,818.7	4,664.7	21,209	48,582	11,662	10,415

Notes: Using purchasing power parities. USD of 2005.
Source: Brookings Development, Aid, and Governance Indicators. www.brookings
.edu/research/interactives/development-aid-governance-indicators (accessed March
15, 2015).

Brazil, and many orders of magnitude greater than in China or India. In
the US and Europe automobile ownership started to grow in the 1920s,
while in Japan it took off during the 1950s. Thus, the potential growth of
the automobile market and the middle class in the emerging world is huge.

Another important indicator of the size of the middle class is enrollments in tertiary education. A university or college degree is not only a
typical aspiration of middle-class individuals, but also a credential that
facilitates access to stable and well-paying white-collar jobs. The top
panel of Figure 7.4 shows enrollments in tertiary education in millions.
The world has today more than twice as many university or college
students as at the turn of the twenty-first century. The largest increases
have taken place in East Asia and the Pacific and in South and West Asia,
followed by Latin America and sub-Saharan Africa, albeit from a very low
base. Tertiary enrollments as a proportion of the population have declined

Figure 7.3 Number of passenger cars and commercial vehicles per 100,000 people, selected countries
Note: The EU-28 includes the 28 members as of 2015 throughout the entire time period.
Source: Cross-National Time-Series Dataset.

in the most developed parts of the world, including the US, Europe, Japan, and, especially, Russia, mostly driven by population aging. Meanwhile, they have quadrupled in China, and approximately doubled in India and Brazil (see lower panel in Figure 7.4). In Nigeria, Africa's largest country by population, the available data until 2005 indicate a level and trajectory similar to India's at the time.

What characterizes the middle-class consumer?

There are several key aspects that characterize global middle-class people as a consumer group with discretionary income to spend. They look for

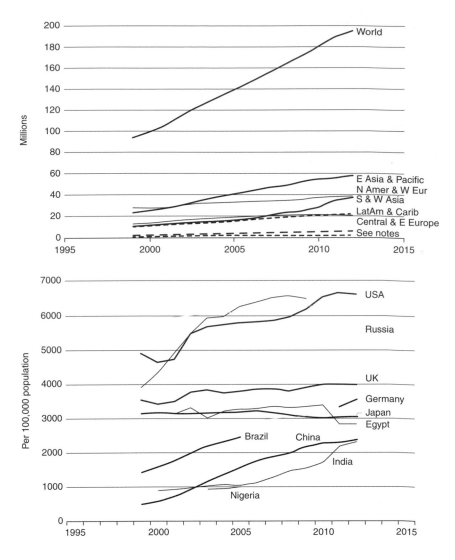

Figure 7.4 Enrollments in tertiary education
Notes: The bottom three lines in the top chart are for Arab states, sub-Saharan Africa, and Central Asia, respectively.
Source: UNESCO.

quality as well as low price. They prefer branded goods, which they see as having better durability. They value education, health, and safety. While they save, they also like to gain access to credit in order to buy durable goods or homes. As consumers, they are motivated not just by survival values but also by self-actualization and by peer influence. They like to consume goods and services that convey their status in the social hierarchy. It is interesting to note that middle-class "consumers in emerging markets in Asia Pacific appear to be much more concerned about maintaining status and appearance relative to their peers than consumers in developed markets or other emerging markets" (Boumphrey and Bevis 2013: 22). Thus, 45 percent of middle-class survey respondents in Thailand and 56 percent in Indonesia say that maintaining or exceeding the standard of living level of their peers is important to them, compared to fewer than 25 percent in Brazil, Colombia, or Mexico. "Similarly, Asian respondents are more likely to agree that their possessions should show others that they are successful, more so than U.S. consumers (30 percent)," who in turn feel this need more acutely than middle-class consumers in Latin American and other developed markets (Boumphrey and Bevis 2013: 22; see also Atsmon et al. 2012).

An example may help illustrate some of the key characteristics of middle-class consumers. The Tata Nano was launched with much fanfare in 2009 by Tata Motors, India's largest automobile company, part of the Tata Group, itself India's oldest and largest. This was the company that stunned the world in 2008 by acquiring Jaguar and Land Rover, the latter a company that not even BMW had been able to manage successfully prior to selling it to Ford. Against all predictions, Tata demonstrated that it could run these companies much better than their previous owners.

The Nano was presented as family transportation for the new middle class of consumers, and priced at the equivalent of $2,000, using exchange rates of the time. That is a very low price tag. For comparison, the Model T Ford was launched in 1908 at the equivalent of 19,800 dollars of 2009, although by 1916 the price had fallen to less than half. The Nano was accurately billed as the world's cheapest car. Equipped with a 634-cc engine, it was not meant to offer many features. In fact, it did not have air conditioning. The company's target was to eventually sell a million units per year.

Well, it did not happen. Tata sold fewer than 75,000 Nanos during each of the first two years after launch, and it has been downhill ever since. "There were huge expectations when the Tata Nano was launched," explains Vipul Vinzuda, an expert on the automobile industry at India's National Institute of Design. "Initially, it was marketed as a family car. That marketing strategy did not seem to have worked, considering there was a lot of dissatisfaction regarding certain features of the car, including the steering, the noise from the engine, etc." (*Indian Express*, April 26, 2012). Quality problems were partly to blame, but most importantly, the Nano was not a car for the middle class.

The story of Shushank Sharma, a 22-year-old computer operator, illustrates the nature of the problem. He was deciding between a Nano and a two-wheeler motorbike, which cost approximately the same, and he ultimately went for the latter. "I don't like the way the Nano looks to people and it's all about the look," Sharma explained. "I take the bike to work. But if I have to go hang out with my friends or go for a marriage, then I prefer a car. But I would prefer to sit at home if I have to go in a Nano" (*Washington Post*, January 3, 2011). In other words, the Nano is not aspirational, and if it is not aspirational, it is not for the middle class. "Those climbing into India's middle class want cheap cars, but they don't want cars that seem cheap," argued the *Wall Street Journal* (October 14, 2013). Or as *The Guardian* put it, the Nano was a "car that was too cheap" (February 3, 2014). Middle-class consumers prefer to buy goods and services commensurate with their status in society.

The Tata Nano is not the first such instance of a powerful company misreading the wants and preferences of the middle-class consumer. The Ford Motor Company launched in 1957 the Ford Edsel, a full-size car named after the son of founder Henry Ford. "Within two months of its highly publicized launch on September 4, 1957 the Edsel became a rolling joke" (Dicke 2010: 486). Edsel sales were abysmal mainly because it was perceived as being too conventional in its styling, had some mechanical failures, was not positioned clearly relative to other Ford or GM models, and the name itself did not catch on. Production of the model ended two years later amidst flagging sales and cumulative losses of $350 million, or $2.8 billion in dollars of 2015. It is also clear from the historical record that future Defense Secretary and World Bank President Robert McNamara, at the time the executive vice president in charge of production at Ford, "had a deep dislike for the Edsel," and "saw it as the epitome of the excesses and deficiencies that characterized American automobiles in the 1950s" (Dicke 2010: 499). In fact, he already had plans to streamline Ford's product lines and pull the plug on the Edsel even before it was launched. Fairly or not, "people and products as diverse as George Romney, New Coke, the C-5A aircraft, the Susan B. Anthony dollar, and the videophone have all been labeled 'Edsels'" (Dicke 2010: 499).

The millionaires

While the global middle class swells, another key trend has gathered momentum. It has to do with the growth in the number of people with more than $1 million in investable assets, excluding their primary residence. These so-called high-net-worth individuals (HNWIs) – a.k.a. millionaires, for short – have become a major category in terms of headcount let alone wealth. Another important category is that of the mass affluent, commonly defined as individuals with at least $100,000 in liquid financial assets but no more than $1 million. This group comprises the upper segment of the middle class in the most developed countries, and is much bigger than that of the millionaires.

According to estimates based on a Lorenz-curve analysis of national household income and wealth surveys, there were 10.1 million millionaires in the world in 2007. The drop in asset prices in the wake of the financial crisis cut that number to 8.6 million by the end of 2008, but it recovered swiftly to reach 11.9 million by the end of 2012. As a group, they owned $40.8 trillion in assets back in 2007, a figure that sunk to $32.8 trillion by the end of 2008 and roared back to $46.2 trillion by the end of 2012. The regions with the largest numbers of millionaires are North America (3.7 million) and Asia-Pacific (3.7), followed by Europe (3.4), Latin America (0.5), the Middle East (0.5), and Africa (0.1). The average millionaire in the world has $3.9 million in investable assets, but in Latin America the mean is around $15.0 million. The countries with the most millionaires are the United States (3.4 million), Japan (1.9), Germany (1.0), China (0.6), and the UK (0.5), and the figures are growing very fast not only in emerging economies like China and India but also in the United States (Capgemini and RBC Wealth Management 2013). The countries with the most billionaires on the Forbes list are the United States (536), China (213), Germany (103), India (90), Russia (88), Hong Kong (55), and Brazil (54), meaning that the distribution of wealth at the very top is more skewed in the BRICs than in the United States, Europe, or Japan.

The growth in the number and wealth of the millionaires around the world bodes well for the luxury industries, including aircraft, automobiles, yachts, hospitality, personal accessories, personal care products, art, and homes. This is a market estimated to move up to $1 trillion annually. It is a segment that continues to be dominated by companies and brands from Western Europe and the United States, and to a lesser extent Japan. Although the luxury business is sensitive to the business cycle, its growth potential is massive, especially given how brand-conscious consumers in emerging markets tend to be.

Gender and wealth

The drivers behind the accumulation of wealth in the contemporary world are complex. To the list of factors and considerations analyzed in Chapter 6, one must add the new role of women as significant owners of financial wealth. Unlike in previous generations, women are not only working in large numbers, but they are much better educated, and many have managed to pursue professional careers in spite of rampant and persistent discrimination in both pay and promotions. As a result, the estimated proportion of all millionaires who are women stood at 24 percent in 2008, growing to 27 percent by 2010. That year, 37 percent of all millionaires in North America were women, the highest proportion in the world, followed by Japan at 31 percent (Capgemini and Merrill Lynch GWMA 2009, 2011). If the trend continues at a similar pace, by the year 2030 there will be more women than men among the world's millionaires. Among the billionaires, the percentage of women is only 10.8 percent, 197 out of 1,826 on the Forbes list for 2015, a slight increase from the 8.8 percent in 2010 (89 out of 1,011).

The proliferation of women with significant financial wealth has been mainly driven by their own ability to accumulate, and also by the fact that they live longer than men. In the developed world, women live on average 6.8 years longer than men, while in the emerging economies the difference is 3.9 and in the poorest countries 2.7. Longer lives may offer the opportunity to continue accumulating wealth through work or investment, and normally increase the probability of inheriting assets from a parent, spouse, or relative. Not surprisingly, more than half of the world's millionaires are above age 55 (Capgemini and Merrill Lynch GWMA 2009, 2011), both because it takes time to accumulate wealth and because the likelihood of inheriting wealth increases with age. To the extent that differences in life expectancy persist and women continue to reach higher levels of education, employment, and income, one should expect the number of female millionaires to grow faster than the number of male millionaires.

Does it matter that the number of women who are millionaires is growing? The broad answer to this question is that it does, although there are many important nuances to take into consideration. Data on affluent men and women, those with at least $250,000 in investable assets, reveal important differences in terms of consumption, saving, and investing. Survey and experimental research also points out many relevant differences.

A first aspect to consider is that affluent men and women differ in terms of their preferences and concerns, which probably translates into different consumption patterns. For instance, 66 percent of affluent US women are concerned about ensuring their retirement assets last throughout their lifetime, compared to 54 percent of men. Naturally, they should be more concerned given that the average US woman lives five years longer than the average man. Similarly, 76 percent of affluent US women are concerned about the future of social security benefits, while only 59 percent of men are. There are other differences that are not driven by life expectancy. For instance, 56 percent of affluent US women are concerned about the rising cost of children's college education, versus 44 percent of men, and 37 percent of affluent US women are concerned about the prospect of what caring for an aging parent could do to their own financial security, compared to 25 percent of men (Merrill Lynch 2012). It is also the case that women are more concerned than men about safety and therefore more interested than men in safer automobiles and in different kinds of property, casualty, and life insurance. Therefore, affluent and wealthy women prefer different kinds of durable goods, including luxury goods, and they are more likely to spend money on healthcare, education, and insurance, not just for themselves but also for their parents, children, and grandchildren.

A second key gender difference has to do with savings, a behavior that is affected by age, marital status, and social roles in exceedingly complex ways. Single women tend to save more than men, especially if they are not expecting to get married soon, while men save more when they are preparing for marriage. At the aggregate level, studies find that "the higher women's income is relative to that of men's, the higher the country's gross domestic savings rate," especially in countries with traditional gender roles. In such countries, the more the woman earns relative to the man, the more she saves and the more the household as a whole saves. By contrast, in countries with more egalitarian gender roles, like Canada, the reverse tends to be true, namely, families save less as women's income catches up with men's. It is also the case that US and Canadian women tend to contribute less to retirement accounts, perhaps because they expect other sources of support in the future (their spouses perhaps), and they are more likely to stop working, and hence saving, while they raise their children (Grossbard and Pereira 2010).

A third dimension involves the ability to manage personal finances. Women tend to score lower than men on standardized financial literacy tests, and this is true of a wide variety of countries around the world, even after taking educational differences into account. The tests assess knowledge concerning the concepts of compound interest, the impact of inflation on investment returns, and risk diversification. "There are likely to be important benefits of greater financial knowledge, including savvier saving and investment decisions, better debt management, more retirement planning, higher participation in the stock market, and greater wealth accumulation" (Lusardi and Mitchell 2014: 30). Survey and experimental research suggests that better financial knowledge leads to better financial planning and better financial decisions.

Finally, gender differences regarding investing behavior have attracted much research, yielding largely consistent results. The conventional wisdom is that women tend to be more cautious and risk-averse than men when it comes to investing. "If instead of Lehman Brothers, we had Lehman Sisters," so the joke goes, "there wouldn't have been a financial crisis." This idea is certainly an exaggeration, but most survey and experimental research shows systematic differences between men and women. In principle, the differences may be related to both nurture and nature, including preferences, emotions, levels of self-confidence, education, financial literacy, or attitudes and expectations about the future, and some studies suggest that gender differences disappear once these variables are taken into account (Croson and Gneezy 2009; Charness and Gneezy 2012). One interesting study using actual investment data on Tunisian men and women finds the same result, but with more financially knowledgeable men being more risk-averse while more financially knowledgeable women are less risk-averse. Education reduced risk aversion for both men and women (Sebai 2014).

The implications of gender differences in investing behavior for financial markets may not materialize for years, but as more women accumulate wealth, it is plausible to expect more of an emphasis on less risky asset classes. This effect, coupled with population aging, could exert considerable downward pressure on stock prices relative to bond prices. There is considerable evidence showing that women's actual investment portfolios are more risk-averse than men's (e.g., Sundén and Surette 1998; Croson and Gneezy 2009), although some studies suggest that, when married, the differences between men and women disappear (Lancaster and Raj 2009). It will also prompt banks and other financial companies to offer products that appeal to risk-averse investors, including indexed funds, funds with downside protection, and bundled investment and insurance products.

The rise of the global middle class of consumers and the accumulation of wealth at the top of the socioeconomic pecking order will certainly create myriad opportunities for businesses. But it also raises daunting challenges concerning the race for natural resources, environmental impacts, climate change, political participation, and the redistribution of global economic and geopolitical power. We will explore these issues in subsequent chapters.

8 The transformative power of technology

> **KEY GLOBAL TURNING POINTS**
> By the year 2014, the number of active mobile broadband subscriptions in the developed countries reached a whopping 84 per 100 inhabitants. In the developing and emerging economies it was only 21 per 100, but growing very rapidly.

Technology has become a core component of the economy, politics, culture, and daily life. It has completely reshaped social relationships, and raised expectations regarding the world's most pressing problems, including energy, poverty, and disease. Technology has fundamentally altered competition in virtually every branch of the economy, disrupting industries, displacing established firms, and creating new business models. Technology, and the knowledge that creates it, has become an instrument of power as well as human advancement. Its many applications to war have raised moral and political issues, especially after Hiroshima, biological warfare, and, more recently, drone attacks.

Technological breakthroughs have occurred at discrete points of time over human history: the control of fire, the agricultural revolution, the wheel, writing, the arch as in architecture, gunpowder, the movable type printing press, the various navigation technologies of the age of discovery, the steam engine, the railroad, the electric motor, refrigeration, artificial fibers, the incandescent lamp, radio communication, and the internal combustion engine, among many others. These inventions all took place before 1900. The rate of technological innovation has arguably accelerated and extended into virtually every field of human activity over the last century, powered by the extension of mass education, a more systematic pursuit of knowledge creation at universities, companies, and the government, and the requirements of war. The list of major breakthroughs could include the powered aircraft, antibiotics, rockets, computers, lasers, biotechnology, magnetic resonance imaging, smart phones, 3D printing, and the collaborative economy, among other developments.

Technology

The word "technology" conveys a number of different images and metaphors. In the strictest economic sense, technology has to do with the characteristics of the production function, namely, the way in which capital, labor, and natural resources are employed to generate valuable products and services.

For most people, the meaning of technology nowadays includes all the gadgetry and systems of gadgets that individuals, companies, and governments use to get things done, including both hard and soft components or elements. Technology has become the most important aspect of the global economy because of its impact on production, distribution, and consumption of all sorts of goods and services, even those with little technological content themselves.

Technological development has become a necessary ingredient in strategies of economic growth. Both governments and private actors have realized that the global economy of the twenty-first century is one driven by knowledge and technology, in which innovations that increase productivity have a disproportionate effect on economic performance.

Analyzing all areas of technology and their implications for the economy and the society is mission impossible. We will focus the attention on information and communications technology, artificial intelligence, and 3D printing as illustrations of the extensive ways in which our lives have already changed and will continue to change in the future. We will also review how governments promote technology, and the ways in which emerging economies are joining the group of countries at the forefront of technological development.

Information and communications technology

Perhaps no area has evolved faster and with more far-reaching implications than information and communications technology (ICT), which has come to epitomize what electronic gadgets and connectivity can do for the economy and how it can affect political and social life. Nowadays, a third of all patents have to do with this area of technology. The story begins in the 1960s with the invention of packet switching and ARPANET, continued during the 1980s with the personal computer and the TCP/IP protocol, and coming to a head in the 1990s with the launching of the World Wide Web, email, and blogs. A few years later e-commerce, e-payments, algorithmic search, and big data became a reality. By the turn of the twenty-first century we are met by broadband and Wikipedia, smart phones and digital social media. The next frontier is perhaps the Internet of Things. Moore's Law and Metcalfe's Law have confirmed the forecasts of significant impacts on various areas of economic and social activity, in terms of organization, and consumer preferences in the transmission of information and the dissemination of ideas, among others. New generations of consumers are now being described in terms of their relationship to technology, as in the "digital natives" (Ontiveros 2015).

ICT has very significantly reduced the cost to create, disseminate, find, and analyze information. Also of spreading it: the decline in the cost of transmission is changing operating models and forms of organization not just in the business world but in politics and private lives as well. The monopoly of formal bureaucracies has been seriously questioned, from governments to large organizations, including business firms. After decades of centralization of resources, ICT enables decentralization. Barriers to entry into industries and fields of activity have been lowered, and entirely new sectors have been created from scratch. Informal networks are now much more powerful than formal organizations.

The efficient use of information technology has become a decisive influence on the composition of economic growth. ICT allows economic agents to become more efficient at making decisions. Back in 1987 Nobel Prize-winner Robert Solow cast doubt on the efficiency gains to be derived from ICT, noting that productivity did not seem to have changed as a result of massive investments in it. It took organizational redesign and an overhaul of business subsystems, from logistics to finance, for the gains to become readily apparent (Brynjolfsson 1993; Brynjolfsson *et al.* 2002; Ontiveros 2000).

It is also important to note that ICT has generated inequality, both across and within countries, as noted in Chapter 6. The IMF estimated in its *World Economic Outlook 2007* that technology was a far greater contributor to income inequality within countries than the globalization of trade and investment, especially in developing and emerging economies. Some people benefit to a greater extent from ICT than others, mostly because of better and cheaper access, and because education matters in that some people can use it more efficiently than others. While according to the International Telecommunication Union the number of active mobile-broadband subscriptions in the developed countries in 2014 was 84 per 100 inhabitants, the average in the developing and emerging economies was just 21 per 100, for a world total of 32 per 100. In the developed world 78 percent of households have Internet access, compared to just 31 percent in the developing and emerging economics. There is no doubt that a "global digital divide" has emerged, one that generates inequality, at least in the short and medium run.

Most importantly, ICT has not rendered geography irrelevant. Labor continues to exhibit very little cross-border mobility. Less than 3 percent of the world's population lives in a country different than the one in which they were born. Meanwhile, capital and information have become almost perfectly and instantaneously mobile at very low cost. As a result, ICT has enabled the organization of industrial value chains across many different locations in which workers with different levels of skill are paid very different wages.

The digital economy

The ubiquity of ICT and its multipurpose character has enabled the creation of a digital economy in which research, development, production, distribution, and consumption take place (OECD 2008). The digital economy facilitates the accumulation and rapid distribution of knowledge, and technological development, two forces that have become key engines of economic growth. Consumers have arguably benefited from falling prices and more choice, while digital entrepreneurs have amassed stupendous fortunes. Lifestyles have been transformed.

Still, the digitization of the economy is not fully universal, although it has exhibited very high rates of growth. The number of users of the network of networks in the economies of the OECD (2013) has risen from less than 60 percent of adults in 2005 to over 80 percent in 2013. In the Nordic countries, the proportion exceeds 95 percent. In 2012, 77 percent of companies in the advanced economies maintained a website and 21 percent sold their products electronically (OECD 2014a). The extension of mobile commerce is growing while advances in the detection and tracking of consumer preferences triggers an unprecedented qualitative leap in marketing strategies, with the help of advances in data analysis that allow a targeted approach to understanding and influencing consumer behavior. According to Gardner, a consultancy, mobile commerce will reach in 2017 half of total digital trade value in the United States. In 2015 there were 7,000 million mobile phone subscriptions globally. The access through mobile devices outnumbered fixed lines, and four fifths of broadband connections were mobile. Ecosystems such as iTunes, the App Store, Google Play, or the Amazon App Store have upended existing industries and created new ones.

The Internet is nowadays considered a critical piece of the infrastructure, similar to electricity, water, or transportation, with an ever larger number of devices connected to it. There is nowadays a greater ability to control simultaneous activities and deploying multiple devices in permanent connection. Value may be added to assets of very diverse nature. New ways of living and interacting have been made possible. Permanent connectivity has become the norm.

As the OECD (2014a) points out, by 2022 the number of connected devices will reach 14,000 million in the advanced economies, compared to 1,400 million in 2012. This emerging Internet of Things has come to be seen as the "Internet of Everything" or an "Industrial Internet" including 50,000 million machines and all kinds of devices that will become interconnected online over the next two decades. Sensors of all kinds will gather information and thus enable driverless transportation, smart cities, behaviorally-based insurance, and many other kinds of new services. The world of manufacturing will also be transformed.

The digital economy will also benefit immensely from the development of artificial intelligence (AI). In 1997 Gary Kasparov was defeated by IBM's Deep Blue. A year later, Tiger Electronics developed a robotic toy with voice-recognition technology. In 2000 Honda launched ASIMO, a humanoid robot serving as a multifunctional personal assistant. In 2011 Apple incorporated Siri into its smart phones, and Google continues to experiment with self-driving car technology. AI facilitates the management of complex systems, such as expert systems. The Internet of Things will also become more useful, especially in terms of analyzing the vast amounts of data collected. It is precisely in this area that learning machines become relevant, especially in areas like health, diagnosis and treatment, agriculture, energy management, transportation, housework, safety, and security.

Realizing the potential gains from the Internet of Things, however, will require significant progress in integrating diverse and complex systems, and in assuring their complete interoperability. Companies will need time to adapt, to learn, and to define new business models. Firms hoping to become fully digital businesses cannot limit themselves to large-scale incorporation of technologies within their own organization. They will need to develop systems to interact with other relevant actors, partners, and of course, their customers. They also need to attract the right talent. The McKinsey Global Institute (2015) anticipates a lag in the realization of the productivity benefits, similar to the delay identified by Robert Solow in the mid 1980s concerning ICT. The end user, i.e., the consumer or a company, will eventually reap the benefits from these new technologies.

The reach of the Internet and mobile broadband will also expand through satellite communications. Several companies are developing projects to provide broadband to remote areas using solar powered terminals, connected to a network of more than 600 micro-satellites. These efforts will help overcome the global digital divide. The McKinsey Global Institute (2015) estimates that the highest potential value of the Internet of Things over the next ten years will be in advanced economies because of higher value per use. However, nearly 40 percent of total value could be generated in the developing economies.

Another tantalizing development is 3D printing, which promises to liberate consumers and businesses from their dependence on supply chains. While the technology still is in its infancy, it is already proving remarkably useful in medicine and some areas of manufacturing (De Jong and de Bruijn 2013). The colonization of the Moon or Mars may become much easier if settlers can print whatever they need at will.

The rise of the collaborative economy

The aftermath of the financial crisis and new technologies have also enabled entrepreneurs to envision new ways of producing and delivering services. Examples include sharing apartments, vehicles, and other types of pricey assets that are not fully utilized by the owner 24/7. It is also quickly extending into financial services, disintermediating banks, and other financial institutions. The connectivity of ICT creates a universe of new possibilities for people to share their assets and engage in collaborative consumption. These innovations effectively circumvent traditional markets, creating direct channels between supply and demand (Khanna and Khanna 2014). Thus, the digital economy is fundamentally about new ways of coordination through ICT, making information available in real time, and enabling economic agents to establish new patterns of exchange.

The effects of collaborative solutions on efficiency are hotly debated. So are the implications for market power, especially by established firms and agents, who see their position eroded by new entrants. Regulatory agencies are also at play because of the need to oversee new forms of economic activity. "Peer-to-peer" capitalism will surely continue to develop because of its efficiency and the transactional transparency that it entails. In general, the collaborative economy reduces transaction costs and provides consumers with more options. It also has the potential of reducing inequality and improving financial inclusion. The severity of the crisis of 2008 has heightened people's desire to share assets they do not fully utilize, and to develop new areas of trust.

The crisis has also fostered the development of alternatives to the banking sector, especially when it comes to funding projects and activities. The credit crunch has been one of the most persistent legacies of the crisis, which has especially affected small and medium-sized enterprises. Crowdfunding in particular has become a very popular trend. It epitomizes the new digital economy driven by technology, common purpose, and a healthy dose of idealism.

The digital economy and employment

According to the OECD (2014a), the weight of ICT-related activity has risen in recent years to represent 6 percent of total added value, 4 percent of total employment, and 12 percent of total fixed investment. The number of companies involved in ICT has continued to grow at a higher pace than in other sectors, with survival rates also higher than those in manufacturing or services. According to the OECD (2014a), between 2009 and 2012, the growth of net entrepreneurial population in the ICT sector was 4.5 percent compared to 1 percent in all economic sectors. Needless to say, the productivity growth recorded in the ICT sector is also significantly higher than in other sectors.

The sector's biggest impact, however, is indirect. Many industries have seen job losses as a result of the introduction of ICT or competition from ICT-centered firms. Still, productivity gains and job creation in ICT have compensated for at least part of the losses. The OECD (2014b) admits that the net effect of these two forces is far from clear and ultimately depends on the specific conditions and policies adopted in each country.

The digital economy continues to create jobs with new content, and many companies in traditional sectors have also created new positions to implement ICT. It also helps create employment in traditional occupations that support the creation of new businesses or the expansion of existing ones. The adverse impact of the growth of ICT occurs when jobs are eliminated or redefined through restructuring, outsourcing, or offshoring.

The crisis, not just new technology, has accelerated the obsolescence of traditional skills and generated new skill requirements. High unemployment is often accompanied by the inability of companies to find enough employees with the skills they need. Technological change creates new demands, and makes retraining programs essential to help displaced workers find new occupations. According to some studies, approximately 47 percent of US employment is at risk as a result of growing computerization, which also acts as a factor depressing wages (Frey and Osborne 2013). The spread of ICT is certainly responsible for at least some of the income inequality in the advanced economies. Without further investments in education and training, the "e-skills" gap will only get wider and deeper. This issue is especially worrisome in the high-unemployment European countries, where youth joblessness exceeds 50 percent.

Information technology and the government

ICT is not just transforming the economy, consumption, and the labor market. It is also reshaping the relationship between citizens and the government. The public space has been redefined by connectivity and mobility. Disintermediation is affecting much more than banking, air transportation, or retail. Eric Schmidt and Jared Cohen, two Google executives, wrote in *The New Digital Age* (2013: 6) that the Internet is "the most comprehensive global space without government." One of its most important aspects is that it tends to "reallocate the concentration of power away from states and institutions and transfer it to individuals." The issue is, however, whether such a shift results in a better-governed world or not, or one that is safer or more dangerous. ICT tends to provide citizens with the tools to challenge authority, and it certainly contributes to transparency, although it also has the potential of increasing the ability of the government to engage in surveillance. Thus, the growth of ICT creates conflicts between freedom and control.

Citizens have used ICT to mobilize politically, as discussed in Chapter 5. Connectivity and the ability to diffuse information almost instantaneously means that ideas, debate, and activism circulate with enormous speed. Moreover, ICT disintermediates traditional political organizations such as parties and unions. It enables citizens to become politically active as individuals or in self-formed groups and networks.

Schmidt and Cohen (2013: 7) go as far as arguing that ICT creates a new "clash of civilizations," one between the physical civilization that evolved over the centuries, and the other the virtual civilization spurred by new technology. "The physical world will impose rules and laws that help contain the anarchy of virtual space and that protect people from terrorist hackers, misinformation and even from the digital records of their own youthful misbehavior." It will be the conflict between the two civilizations that will come to define our world. They end their analysis on an optimistic note, arguing that the world resulting from the ubiquity of ICT will be "more egalitarian, more transparent and more interesting than we can even imagine" (Schmidt and Cohen 2013: 7).

Promoting technology and innovation

Given the widespread impact of technology on the economy, governments the world over are going out of their way to promote technology development and innovation. Policies vary greatly from country to country, almost as much as actual outcomes in terms of technological achievement. There is a very strong correlation between the innovativeness of an economy and its level of economic development, and there is a two-way causal link between the two. Innovation accelerates economic development, and greater economic development facilitates innovation (Fagerberg and Srholec 2008).

Countries differ, however, in how they are organized to develop technology and to generate innovations. One model is based on patient capital and seeks to foster basic science and innovation in mature fields and industries such as chemicals, metals, or automobiles. Germany has historically excelled in them. Another model is more entrepreneurial, and is focused on disruption, creative destruction, and the launching of new industries. The United States is the global leader in this area. Finally, another model is orchestrated by the state, and it concentrates in large-scale projects in sectors such as energy and transportation. France is generally proposed as an example (Furman *et al.* 2002; Liu and White 2001; Gittelman 2006).

Different countries devote to R&D very different amounts of resources. According to the World Bank, in 2011 very few countries spent more than the world's average of 2.1 percent of GDP: South Korea (4.0), Israel (4.0), Finland (3.8), Japan (3.4), Sweden (3.4), Denmark (3.0), Germany (2.9), Austria (2.8), the US (2.8), Iceland (2.6), Slovenia (2.5), Estonia (2.4), France (2.2), Singapore (2.2), and Belgium (2.2). R&D budgets in the European Union have been declining since the crisis, and they stood at 2.0 percent. Both China (1.8) and India (0.8) continue to lag behind. It is important to note that the countries that spend the most as a proportion of their GDP do so not because the government spends more but because the business sector does. Thus, in Israel, Sweden, South Korea, Japan, Switzerland, the US, and Germany, more than two-thirds of total spending on R&D is accounted for by companies.

The BRICs are stepping up their investments in R&D, though starting from a very low base (Thomson Reuters 2013). They are being smart about focusing their efforts on scientific and technical fields in which they have some kind of comparative advantage: agriculture, plant and animal science, and pharmacology in Brazil; physics, space science, and geosciences in Russia; chemistry, pharmacology, and agriculture in India; and materials science, pharmacology, and physics in China.

Most of the results of R&D efforts accrue to the richest countries. One useful indicator is patents. More than 99 percent of the world's patents are accounted for by inventors based in the top 25 countries, led by the US, Japan, Germany, South Korea, France, the UK, Canada, Italy, Sweden, Switzerland, and the Netherlands. Brazil, Russia, and China are making impressive headway, however, especially in fields such as materials, machinery, engines, transportation, and electronics. India has become a star in areas such as pharmaceuticals, fine organic chemistry, and bio-technology (Thomson Reuters 2013).

It is also worth noting that there are just eight countries in the world with a significant surplus in their balance of payments in royalties and fees, namely, a surplus greater than 1 billion dollars: the US, Japan, France, Sweden, the UK, Germany, Finland, and the Netherlands. There are five small countries with a modest surplus. The rest of the world has a deficit.

Another important aspect has to do with institutions. Some countries have strong institutions in place geared towards the development of new technology, including the educational system, research centers, venture capital, and intellectual property laws. Most countries lack all of those institutions, and their performance is accordingly poor. The countries at the top of the technological and innovation league have developed very solid institutions over long periods of time. Thus, their present advantages are unlikely to erode any time soon.

Countries, however, are not the only relevant units of analysis when it comes to innovation and technology. Cities are increasingly important as nodes in the global economy. A few of the most influential of them play a disproportionate role in financial services, education, and technology. According to a recent study (Matthiessen *et al.* 2006), the ten most important research metropolitan areas in the world are, in decreasing order: Tokyo–Yokohama, London, San Francisco Bay Area, Osaka-Kobe, Paris, New York, Boston, Los Angeles, Amsterdam–The Hague–Rotterdam–Utrecht, and Beijing. In the specific area of ITC, the ranking is somewhat different: Tokyo–Yokohama, San Francisco Bay Area, Seoul, Hong Kong, Beijing, London, Singapore, Paris, Los Angeles, and Amsterdam–The Hague–Rotterdam–Utrecht. And in the field of biotechnology, the most important are: Tokyo–Yokohama, Osaka–Kobe, London, San Francisco Bay Area, Boston, New York, San Diego, Paris, Philadelphia, and Los Angeles.

Whether we use countries or cities as the locus of technology and innovation, we find that the geographical patterns are very skewed in favor of the most advanced countries, with some of the emerging economies partially succeeding at joining the major leagues. In the next chapter we further explore the attempts by governments to create institutions and to formulate policies that favor entrepreneurship.

9 Development, institutions, and entrepreneurship

> **KEY GLOBAL TURNING POINTS**
> After decades of emphasizing investments in infrastructure and large-scale industry, recent years have seen a growing emphasis on institutions as a determinant of economic development, including culture, laws, regulation, taken-for-granted assumptions, and other artifacts that enable economic actors to play a role in the economy, shape their preferences, and provide them with tools for pursuing their goals.

Economic development was once seen as a process mainly driven by the alignment of a country's natural and labor endowments with the map of relative comparative advantage prevalent in the global economy. Thus, developing countries were routinely advised that the road to development entailed taking advantage of natural resources and cheap labor, making investments in infrastructure, and looking for ways to differentiate themselves in the global marketplace. Governments wanted to stage a large-scale transformation of the economy and the society, including the abandonment of traditional values in favor of modern ones, the development of cities, and investments in new types of industrial activities, typically capital-intensive ones. Different countries, however, took different paths to accelerate economic growth, including inward-looking industrialization based on import substitution and export-led growth with a protected domestic market to enable firms to become more sophisticated over time (Amsden 1989; Gilpin 1987; Guillén 2001; Haggard 1990).

During the 1980s and 1990s – in the wake of the oil crises and the sovereign debt defaults in the developing world – a new policy toolkit emerged at the IMF and the World Bank focused on the idea of free markets. It was dubbed the "Washington Consensus." The list of policy prescriptions became longer and more focused on the business sector and on a retreat of the state from the economy. Fiscal discipline, financial liberalization, openness to trade and investment, privatization, deregulation, and protection of property rights were presented as necessary to create the foundations for sustained economic growth (Rodrik 2006). Many countries, out of their own volition or as an imposition of the IMF, adopted privatization policies (Henisz *et al.* 2005).

Economic development and institutions

Economic development is a complex process that entails a wholesale transformation of not only the economy but also social and political relationships. Traditionally, economic development was seen as a matter of eliminating obstacles such as traditional values, lack of infrastructure, insufficient skills, and scarcity of capital.

More recently, the emphasis of development efforts has focused on institutions, which are formal and informal arrangements that provide the foundations for actors such as managers, investors, workers, consumers, and policymakers to make sense of the options available to them, figure out their preferences, and implement their preferred course of action.

At the national level, institutions have become a key way of understanding what factors facilitate and impede development, and what are some of the policies that can be put in place to accelerate development. Those institutions include the legal system, regulation, culture, and taken-for-granted assumptions.

The lackluster results of these policies in Latin America and Africa led development theorists and policymakers to enlarge the agenda to include an even more sweeping list of necessary reforms, including corporate governance, labor market flexibility, independent central banks, and anti-corruption measures, among others. This "augmented" Washington Consensus, while theoretically on target, placed too much emphasis on eliminating inefficiencies and on the virtues of free financial flows without seriously considering dynamic innovation as the engine of growth (Rodrik 2006). Moreover, the success of this model of economic growth required wholesale institutional reform on several fronts simultaneously, something that is likely to be opposed politically, and may not always be conducive to superior economic outcomes (Guillén 2001; Rodrik 2006). Institutions became the cornerstone of economic growth, and institutional reform the elixir for success. Once again, many countries adopted institutional reforms voluntarily or were coerced into adopting them (Polillo and Guillén 2005; Weber *et al.* 2009).

The underlying assumption was that "economic activity requires good rules," an idea that was first proposed by sociologist Max Weber (1978: 328–329). The "old institutional" school in economics provided some of the foundations for this line of thinking, one that Hernando de Soto, an influential Peruvian economist, helped popularize in policy circles during the 1990s with his emphasis on the protection of property rights as a way to empower poor people, especially subsistence farmers, and help them access credit. A major boost to the revival of institutional economics came in 1993 when the Nobel Prize was awarded to economic historians Robert Fogel and Douglass North, who had independently demonstrated the role of institutions in the historical development of the market economy. Further validation came in 2009 when it went to Elinor Ostrom, a political scientist who analyzed the implications of the "tragedy of the commons," and Oliver Williamson, who theorized why firms undertake many production activities that could be performed by the market, a topic that had already been recognized in 1991 when the prize went to Ronald Coase for his research on transaction costs and property rights.

The importance of institutions was further demonstrated in a series of landmark economic analyses by Andrei Shleifer and Daron Acemoglu, two economists interested in very different topics. Shleifer is the leading proponent of the view that legal institutions underpin modern finance, and that different kinds of legal traditions shape financial practices by companies and governments, and ultimately affect the development of financial markets (see Shleifer *et al.* 2008 for a review). Acemoglu has championed the theoretical and historical understanding of what types of institutions foster innovation and growth versus which generate extraction, corruption, and backwardness (Acemoglu *et al.* 2001; Acemoglu and Robinson 2012).

It is important to note that the concept of institutions in economics often bills them as mechanisms to overcome situations in which the market fails due to the costliness of measurement and enforcement (North 1990, 1997). Institutions, however, do much more than fill in the gaps of the market. They constitute and enable actors – entrepreneurs, investors, managers, consumers, and so on – to engage in socially meaningful action. Institutions also shape actors' preferences. Thus, a sociological concept of institutions includes other aspects in addition to those related to the establishment and well-functioning of markets (Biggart and Guillén 1999; Guillén 2001).

Enter entrepreneurship

The forgotten actor in many economic analyses and policies of development is the entrepreneur. For decades, entrepreneurship – the complex array of activities involved in imagining, launching, and managing a venture, whether for profit or not – did not receive enough attention from economic theorists, advisors, and policymakers, who preferred to think about development in terms of macroeconomic policymaking, cultural obstacles, and the lack of physical infrastructure. The increasing attention paid to institutions as "soft infrastructure" also served to reignite interest in new firm formation, small firms, and their contribution to economic and employment growth (OECD 2004; Naudé 2010). In particular, micro and small enterprises (MSEs), those with fewer than 50 employees, were found to represent a greater share of employment in developing countries than in developed ones (Nichter and Goldmark 2009), thus presenting more opportunities to accelerate economic development.

In his landmark 1911 book, *The Theory of Economic Development*, Joseph Schumpeter presented the entrepreneur as the hero of the market economy. Decades later, in his famous book, *Capitalism, Socialism, and Democracy* ([1942] 1975: 82), he argued that

Capitalism [. . .] is by nature a form or method of economic change and not only never is but never can be stationary. The fundamental impulse that sets and keeps the capitalist engine in motion comes from the new consumers' goods, the new methods of production or transportation, the new markets, the new forms of industrial organization that capitalist enterprise creates. [. . .] The opening up of new markets, foreign or domestic, and the organizational development from the craft shop and factory to such concerns as U.S. Steel illustrate the same process of industrial mutation [. . .] that incessantly revolutionizes the economic structure *from within*, incessantly destroying the old one, incessantly creating a new one. This process of Creative Destruction is the essential fact about capitalism.

As a result of the new emphasis on institutions and entrepreneurship, the concept and metaphor of "creative destruction" became perhaps as famous and influential as Adam Smith's "invisible hand." Schumpeter also reminded us of another important feature of entrepreneurs. The entrepreneur is not necessarily an investor who puts his or her own capital at risk, but rather someone who combines resources (including capital) to launch a venture.

Measuring and tracking institutions

There is a bewildering number of agencies, think tanks, and other organizations that generate annual indicators of institutional conditions in different countries around the world, including the World Bank, the OECD, the World Economic Forum, Transparency International, the Heritage Foundation, the Fraser Institute, and many others. The World Bank has published since 2003 a very comprehensive database on "Doing Business" in different countries, and some specific regions or cities within the largest economies. Over the years, comparative data on more than 190 economies and 20 regions and cities have been compiled using teams of local experts. The World Bank's focus is on the formal sector of the economy, under the assumption that informality tends to limit firm growth and the potential contribution to economic development (Nichter and Goldmark 2009). The World Bank presently tracks more than 50 quantitative indicators, including the ease of starting a business, dealing with construction permits, getting electricity, registering property, getting credit, protecting minority investors, paying taxes, trading across borders, enforcing contracts, and resolving insolvency.

The general ranking of the "ease of doing business" is quite predictable. It includes 189 countries and territories. Economies such as Singapore, New Zealand, Hong Kong, Denmark, South Korea, Norway, Finland, and Australia tend to be among the top ten along with the United States and the United Kingdom, namely, countries with a common-law legal tradition and those in Scandinavia. Most Western European countries score in the 10–40 places, while Eastern European countries are further down the list. The top-ranked Latin American country in the 2014 ranking was Mexico (#39), followed by Chile (#41), with Haiti (#180) and Venezuela (#182) ranking lowest. The BRICs do not fare particularly well: Russia (#62), China (#90), Brazil (#120), and India (#142). The United Arab Emirates (#22) is the highest-ranked Middle Eastern country, and South Africa (#43) is the highest-ranked in sub-Saharan Africa (World Bank 2014).

Since the World Bank began to measure and track the conditions for doing business in 2003, many countries have gone out of their way to improve their rankings. Between 2003 and 2014, 42 of the indicators show a decline in the standard deviation across countries, only three indictors show an increase (credit registry coverage, cost to export, cost to import), and two remained roughly stable over time (minimum paid-in capital and recovery rate during insolvency). There are two consequences to this trend. The first is that creating the best conditions for doing business is no longer as effective a differentiator as a decade ago because laggards have caught up with the leaders, as indicated by the decline in the standard deviations (Berry *et al.* 2014). The second consequence is that countries have become more alike one another, reducing the amount of institutional diversity, and perhaps making it harder for the global system as a whole to recover from episodes of crisis (Guillén 2015).

The indicators included in the "Doing Business" database are highly correlated with other indices of the overall business environment and competitiveness, such as those compiled by the OECD, the World Economic Forum, or IMD. The body of empirical research that uses these indicators seems to confirm that better institutional conditions reduce informality, facilitate new firm formation, encourage entrepreneurship, and increase employment (World Bank 2010a; Klapper *et al.* 2010). These findings make a great deal of sense given that the institutional indicators measure such egregious obstacles to doing business as the number and cost of bureaucratic procedures to start a firm, do construction, register property, resolve a commercial dispute, pay taxes, or engage in international trade, although other indicators are more controversial, including those having to do with labor market rigidities and investor protections.

Another useful set of indicators on institutional conditions for doing business is the Global Entrepreneurship Monitor, which publishes data on entrepreneurial activity and attitudes towards entrepreneurship since 2001 based on representative surveys of the adult population in as many as 104 countries and territories (GEM 2015). One interesting indicator is the proportion of the adult working population (ages 18–64) that is engaged in early-stage entrepreneurship with a venture less than 42 months old. Figure 9.1 shows the data plotted against GDP per capita for 67 economies. There is a curvilinear relationship indicating that at low levels of economic development the proportion of the adult population engaged in early-stage entrepreneurship can be as high as 35 percent, while at intermediate levels it is much lower, in some cases less than 5 percent. In the countries with the highest GDP per capita the proportion is slightly higher. Another useful indicator is the proportion of the adult population that is the owner-manager of an established business more than 42 months old. A similar curvilinear pattern with GDP per capita obtains (see Figure 9.2).

The main reason for the intriguing U-shaped relationship, especially in the case of early-stage ventures, is that there are two kinds of entrepreneurship. Some entrepreneurs launch a venture out of necessity, that is, because they lack other viable options to make a living, while others launch it in response to an opportunity. In developed countries, for each entrepreneur driven by necessity, there are many more driven by opportunity: Norway (19.5), Denmark (11.1), Sweden (7.1), Singapore (6.2), Luxembourg (5.1), Taiwan (5.0), the US (5.0), France (4.3), or the UK (4.1). Two less developed countries with high ratios are Suriname (7.3) and Trinidad and Tobago (5.4). At the other end of the spectrum, in Greece (0.9), Georgia (0.6), Croatia (0.6), and Bosnia & Herzegovina (0.5), there are more entrepreneurs driven by necessity than those driven by opportunity (GEM 2015).

It is also revealing to see how early entrepreneurship and business ownership correlate with attitudes. Using a sample of 104 countries between 2001 and 2014, we find that early-stage entrepreneurship is very highly correlated with the proportion of the population that intends to start a business within three years (+0.78), knows someone who started a business within the past two years (+0.52), considers starting a business as a desirable career choice (+0.48), or sees entrepreneurs as receiving high status in their country (+0.29). It is negatively correlated with the fear of failure (−0.26). The correlations are significant though lower in the case of

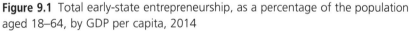

Figure 9.1 Total early-state entrepreneurship, as a percentage of the population aged 18–64, by GDP per capita, 2014

Note: The country codes stand for AGO Angola, ARG Argentina, AUS Australia, AUT Austria, BRB Barbados, BEL Belgium, BLZ Belize, BOL Bolivia, BIH Bosnia and Herzegovina, BWA Botswana, BRA Brazil, BFA Burkina Faso, CMR Cameroon, CAN Canada, CHL Chile, CHN China, COL Colombia, CRI Costa Rica, HRV Croatia, DNK Denmark, ECU Ecuador, SLV El Salvador, EST Estonia, FIN Finland, FRA France, GEO Georgia, DEU Germany, GRC Greece, GTM Guatemala, HUN Hungary, IND India, IDN Indonesia, IRN Iran, Islamic Rep., IRL Ireland, ITA Italy, JAM Jamaica, JPN Japan, KAZ Kazakhstan, LTU Lithuania, LUX Luxembourg, MYS Malaysia, MEX Mexico, NLD Netherlands, NZL New Zealand, PAN Panama, PER Peru, PHL Philippines, POL Poland, PRT Portugal, PRI Puerto Rico, ROM Romania, RUS Russian Federation, SGP Singapore, SVK Slovak Republic, SVN Slovenia, ZAF South Africa, ESP Spain, SUR Suriname, SWE Sweden, CHE Switzerland, THA Thailand, TTO Trinidad and Tobago, UGA Uganda, GBR United Kingdom, USA United States, URY Uruguay, and VNM Vietnam.

Source: Global Entrepreneurship Monitor and World Bank, for 2014 and 2013, respectively.

Figure 9.2 Owner-managers of an established business, as a percentage of the population aged 18–64, by GDP per capita, 2013
Note: See Figure 9.1 for country code list.
Source: Global Entrepreneurship Monitor and World Bank, for 2014 and 2013, respectively.

the proportion of the population that is an owner-manager of an established business, except for status of entrepreneurs in society, which is slightly higher (GEM 2015).

Gender, development, and entrepreneurship

The world of development and entrepreneurship is also affected by gender as an institutional factor. Development scholars and policymakers did not pay systematic attention to women until a Danish economist working for the United Nations, Ester Boserup, published her influential book, *Woman's Role in Economic Development* (1970). Boserup's analysis was so powerful because she showed the enormous extent to which women contribute to economic development. She forcefully argued that women play a key role in development, inside and outside the household. Her work inspired the United Nations Decade for Women (1975–1985) and laid the foundations for the wave of studies and programs arguing that promoting women's role in the economy could become a major contributor to development (OECD 2004; World Bank 2001; Browne 2001; see Jaquette and Staudt 2006 for a review). The concern by development scholars interested in gender was not only to advance gender equality as a goal in its own right, but also to explore ways in which women's economic activities could contribute to economic growth and to economic development, in the sense of a transformation of the economy through innovation.

These and other subsequent studies documented that development created a segregated labor market along gender lines, with women clustering in more labor-intensive activities in light manufacturing (e.g. textiles, food-processing) that paid lower wages, or being self-employed in the service sector (Boserup 1970; Browne 2001). Attempts were also made conceptually and statistically to distinguish among the prevalence and contributions to development of unpaid household labor, unpaid work at the family farm or business, self-employment, and entrepreneurship by women (UNIFEM 2005; ILO 2009). A related argument about women's role in economic growth and development was formulated by Gøsta Esping-Andersen (1999), a Danish sociologist, who argued that in advanced postindustrial societies the incorporation of women into the labor force triggered the growth of all manner of market-oriented service activities that women used to perform in the household without pay.

By the beginning of the 1990s entrepreneurship by women was fully recognized as a dynamic contributor to economic development. The main argument in this new line of inquiry and policymaking became that countries that did not make it possible for women to participate fully as economic agents would be underutilizing half of the talent pool (OECD 2004; World Bank 2001). As Helen Clark, the Administrator of the United Nations Development Program has recently put it, "by unlocking the tremendous potential of women entrepreneurs and addressing the obstacles they face, such as access to credit and finance, and their inability to inherit or hold land titles or benefit from government budgetary allocations, we can reduce inequality and stimulate economic growth" (UNI-FEM 2010: 3).

Women and men pursue entrepreneurship for different reasons. In 42 out of 68 countries, women's ratio of opportunity-driven versus necessity-driven entrepreneurship is significantly lower than men's. The exceptions are Italy, Japan, Romania, the Netherlands, Belgium, Taiwan, Singapore, Lithuania, Tunisia, Switzerland, Poland, and Sweden. In Iran, Russia, Portugal, Ireland, Algeria, Germany, Estonia, Slovakia, the US, Uganda, Slovenia, Bosnia-Herzegovina, and Egypt the differences by gender are very small (GEM 2013).

Obstacles to entrepreneurship by women

Entrepreneurship, however, has never been an easy path for women. Researchers reported that entrepreneurs, whether men or women, tended to initiate activities related to their previous job experience. Given the preexisting gender segregation by type of sector, industry, or activity, the effect of previous experience on entrepreneurial activity generated a segregated pattern of entrepreneurship by gender, with women overwhelmingly launching new ventures in the service sector in general, and in retail and personal services in particular, where capital requirements tend to be lower and their household and self-employment experience more relevant (Carter *et al.* 2001; Carter and Shaw 2006). It is important to note that this sector of the economy produces for the most part nontradable services, thus reducing the potential for international growth. As we shall see in the next section, the self-selection of women entrepreneurs into specific industries and activities helps explain many of the observed gender differences. In addition, in many developing countries researchers found that more than half (and in some cases more than three quarters) of the smallest firms, accounting for a large share of total employment, were owned by women, and that they were generally characterized by slower growth rates and informal practices (Nichter and Goldmark 2009). Lastly, there is virtually no research on whether better educated women from advantaged social backgrounds are more likely to benefit from entrepreneurial opportunities, new aid or government programs, and the like, thus perpetuating other sources of inequality.

As is true of other related fields of inquiry, research on women and entrepreneurship is split between two seemingly irreconcilable models (Guillén 2013). First, there are researchers who propose that there is one unique and universal model of entrepreneurship, which is gender-free. From this perspective, when studying entrepreneurship by women, the most important task for the researcher is to understand, explain, and provide solutions to the difficulties they may encounter, such as securing the necessary resources to launch a new venture. This type of analysis may be useful for educational and policymaking purposes, but it suffers from a serious theoretical and methodological shortcoming. Understanding differences in entrepreneurship between men and women by reference to a universal model of entrepreneurship can easily succumb to the temptation of an essentialist conception of how gender affects entrepreneurial processes and outcomes. Essentialism consists of characterizing a group of people or other entities by a small set of fixed properties, while ignoring the conditions under which such identities emerged, discounting any possibility of change or variation within the group (for a review of these arguments and the empirical evidence, see Mirchandani 1999; Lewis 2006).

A second group of researchers argues that there are many types of entrepreneurship, and that gender is not just one more variable that may help explain certain processes or outcomes. Rather, women entrepreneurs may have distinct preferences for choosing, organizing, and managing a venture, and may define success in terms of goal achievement, a better work/family balance, or community benefits as opposed to growth, profits, and fame. Ahl (2006) reported that the foundational texts in the field of entrepreneurship (including Schumpeter 1934) used words such as self-efficacious, strong-willed, resolute, skilled at organizing, visionary, daring, courageous, detached, achievement oriented, and astute to describe the entrepreneur, terms that correlate very highly with index scales of what psychologists refer to as "masculinity." Ahl also found that the opposites of those traits correlated with index scales of "femininity." Other researchers observed that entrepreneurship is often defined by reference to masculine traits such as ambition, independence, individualism, competitiveness, self-reliance, and risk-taking. According to these scholars, entrepreneurship by women, however, draws on different resources and opportunities, resulting in a qualitatively different kind of economic activity based on women's distinctive characteristics (for reviews, see Ahl 2006; Bird and Brush 2002; Guillén 2013; Brush 1992; Brush *et al.* 2006b, 2010; Fielden and Davidson 2010a, 2010b; Mirchandani 1999; Lewis 2006).

These opposing ways of looking at entrepreneurship by women resonate with the two classic strands in feminist thought. Liberal feminist theory holds that men and women are similar and that any differences in opportunity or achievement are the result of discrimination or structural barriers. By contrast, social or radical feminist theory maintains that men and women are different, and that the latter's traits constitute resources that can be mobilized to pursue meaningful social or economic action in ways that are distinct from those observed in men.

Perhaps the most useful way to reconcile these two perspectives is to view gender not as a given, but as a socially constructed category, as we have seen in the previous chapters. Women are socially constructed individually and as a group in different ways depending on time and space. Thus, all gender research, including research on entrepreneurship by women, should start by unveiling the assumptions underlying such constructions in the specific context and time in which it is taking place (Ahl 2006). This preliminary step is very important in the case of studies of women entrepreneurs across time and/or space, when political, cultural, religious, and other social variables are not constant.

The empirical evidence comparing men and women entrepreneurs does not offer a clear picture as to the presumed differences in terms of the motivations, processes, and outcomes of entrepreneurship. The existing reviews of the massive literature on this topic conclude that overall there is little support for differences between men and women engaged in entrepreneurship, with only two exceptions: (1) men and women self-select into different kinds of entrepreneurial activities, sectors, and industries, mostly based on their prior work experience; and (2) ventures founded, owned, and/or managed by women tend to grow less over time, mostly as a result of structural constraints of various sorts. The existing literature does not find systematic differences in terms of the motivations to become an entrepreneur, attitudes towards entrepreneurship, the social or psychological characteristics of entrepreneurs, the process of starting the business, the management or leadership style, or even ongoing access to finance, except as noted below (for reviews of the literature, see: Guillén 2013; Brush 1992; Brush *et al.* 2006a, 2010; Carter and Shaw 2006; Carter *et al.* 2001; Ahl 2006; Nichter and Goldmark 2009).

Perhaps the most intensively studied aspect of entrepreneurship by women is access to finance. The emerging consensus in the literature, based on more representative samples, is that access to startup capital is more limited for women than for men. Aspiring women entrepreneurs tend to be asked to provide guarantees that lie beyond their existing assets, relationships, or track record. The evidence on discrimination when it comes to accessing capital on an ongoing basis, i.e., after the business is up and running, yields more ambiguous and inconsistent results, although most research indicates that the relationship between women entrepreneurs and bankers is mired by gender stereotyping. Still, much of the gap between men's and women's access to finance can be explained by previous business experience, self-selection into specific activities, sectors, and industries, or track record (Carter *et al.* 2001; Carter and Shaw 2006; Guillén 2013).

Another heavily researched area is networking. Women entrepreneurs tend to rely on extensive personal and professional networks in order to launch and grow their ventures, just as men do. The existing literature documents that women entrepreneurs often complain that they do not have access to the necessary resources for launching and growing their venture because their network connections are not the most appropriate for success. Those resources include not only material ones but also advice, mentorship, and role models. The existing body of research shows that women entrepreneurs, when compared to men, have fewer network ties in general, and weak (i.e., intermediary or brokerage) ties in particular. Both men and women entrepreneurs tend to have same-gendered ties, which makes it more difficult for women to find mentors and role models in fields in which there are few of them. These differences are largely attributable to prior employment history and job experience. In fact, regardless of gender, salaried men and women tend to have more network contacts than the self-employed (Carter *et al.* 2001; World Bank 2011: 233). Although evidence for entrepreneurs is lacking, research on salaried men and women managers in the United States shows that women reap fewer benefits from weak ties and encounter more difficulties obtaining mentorship and advice. They also face different, and often more demanding, role expectations when they are "tokens," i.e. in the numerical minority in their fields of activity (for a review, see Rothbard and Brett 2000).

Yet another area of controversy concerns work/family balance. Women's role in the family is seen in the literature as both constraining and enabling entrepreneurship. On the one hand, research has shown that the family obligations shouldered by women can detract energy and time from other activities and make it harder for them to build the experience, reputation, and networks necessary for success. On the other, research also indicates that entrepreneurship can help women make more flexible arrangements to balance work and family than the typical 9-to-5 job. These arrangements, however, may imply that the venture is located in the household, which tends to be a major constraint on growth, at least in developing countries (Nichter and Goldmark 2009).

It is important to note that the most important explanations for the differences found between men and women entrepreneurs when it comes to accessing resources, including networking – lack of experience, limited track record, or self-selection into specific activities – in no way imply the absence of discrimination or the futility of public programs and policies geared at providing women with more opportunities. Analyzing the impact of experience and self-selection are precisely key to determining the best solutions to the obstacles that women experience when becoming entrepreneurs, which the literature has identified as having to do with a long list of interrelated factors: insufficient education or experience, barriers of access to various material resources (especially capital), lack of mentors and role models, competing demands on time, and so on (Carter *et al.* 2001; Carter and Shaw 2006; OECD 2004; Ahl 2006).

The evidence indicates that enabling women entrepreneurs to participate in all manner of activities, sectors, and industries – not just in those in which they have prior experience – and to maximize the growth opportunities of their ventures will surely help them make an even greater contribution to economic development (Brush *et al.* 2006a, 2010; Carter *et al.* 2010a, 2010b). This is perhaps the most solid conclusion that can be reached from our efforts to understand the drivers of women entrepreneurship, one that justifies the efforts at creating programs aimed at improving women's access to professional education and social activities.

While self-selection is a powerful force shaping the activities of women entrepreneurs, there is no denying that discrimination places limits on women's entrepreneurial opportunities. Perhaps the most blatant aspect of discrimination has to do with laws and regulations that place women at a disadvantage. A recent report by the World Bank covered 128 developed and developing economies. As of 2009, in 45 countries women did not have the same legal capacity to act or engage in economic transactions, in 49 women were prevented from working in certain industries, and in 32 they did not have equal inheritance rights. Legal discrimination has an impact on entrepreneurship. Equal legal rights were found to result in a greater percentage of businesses owned or managed by women, and higher gender legal equality correlated with per capita income, although it was not clear what the direction of causality is (World Bank 2010b; see also WEF 2011).

The set of institutions relevant to economic development are not just those enshrined in laws, regulations, and other formal arrangements. Culture, taken-for-granted assumptions, and categories such as gender also matter. We shall see in the next chapter that institutions are also fundamental to understanding a key concern of our time, namely, the relationship between human populations and the physical environment.

10 The quest for sustainability

At a time when the most pressing priority has to do with accelerating economic growth so that unemployment recedes, one runs the risk of relegating the long term to the background. The ways in which we generate economic growth and well-being in the short term, however, are intimately linked to our ability to keep the momentum going over the long run. It is not always easy to make temporal perspectives compatible and complementary. Indeed, it is very hard to establish priorities and to distinguish between what is important and what is urgent. It is at the intersection of these treacherous cross-currents that the concept of sustainability lies.

From an economic point of view, sustainability has to do with ensuring that satisfying present needs does not come at the expense of doing so in the future. This idea concocts social and political dimensions as well because sustainability involves delicate inter-generational trade-offs. Thus, the concept of sustainability – the sustainable development of human societies – goes well beyond the concerns about energy, natural resources, and the environment supporting life on the planet to include all aspects of social, economic, and political life insofar as present actions may place limitations on future actions. Thus, pension schemes, educational programs, the banking system, and political regimes have varying degrees of sustainability built into them. Having covered some of these broader concerns in Chapters 2, 5, and 6, in this chapter we will focus on the challenges of global warming, energy, food, and water, and on the opportunities they represent for business (Matthew 2012; Waughray 2011; WWF 2010).

The rise of environmental awareness

By the beginning of the twenty-first century, there was around the world a widespread perception that natural resources on Earth are finite. This is by no means a new concern. The controversial premonitions made by British political economist Thomas R. Malthus more than two hundred years ago generated a first wave of awareness. Interest in sustainability has ebbed and flowed over the last few decades, with the Club of Rome's famous 1972 report on *The Limits to Growth*, the oil crisis of 1973, the 1979 US National Academy of Sciences report linking greenhouse gases to global warming, and the Chernobyl nuclear accident of 1986 as major milestones igniting heated debates among experts, policymakers, and the general public. The twenty-first century was ushered in with the signing of the Kyoto Protocol in 2001, a set of limits on greenhouse gas emissions that came into force in 2005. While its effectiveness is in doubt, it further signals growing awareness of environmental problems. And so did the famous 700-page report by British economist Nicholas Stern, *The Economics of Climate Change: Stern Review* (2007), which estimated that without coordinated intervention by governments around the world, climate change would reduce global GDP by more than 1 percent annually, and possibly up to 3 percent, by 2050, while the measures needed to mitigate the risks would cost no more than 1 percent. These estimates are averages, with the dispersion around them being quite large. Developing countries are widely predicted to suffer the most from global warming.

The case of global warming helps gain an understanding of the drivers of environmental degradation and the prospects for achieving sustainability. While environmental disasters tend to be local in scope, global warming has significantly raised the stakes by creating the potential for worldwide disasters due to changes in sea levels, atmospheric instability, the geographic distribution of species, and agricultural yields, among others. "The Earth's climate is nearing, but has not passed, a tipping point beyond which it will be impossible to avoid climate change with far-ranging undesirable consequences," asserts NASA's Jim Hansen (2006), widely recognized as the world's leading climate change expert.

As in the cases of demography and inequality, the Industrial Revolution represents a watershed for the environment. Emissions of carbon dioxide have increased about 40 percent since the beginning of industrialization, and may double or treble before the twenty-first century comes to a close. During the twentieth century the consumption of fossil fuels grew by a factor of 14. As urban life becomes the norm for a majority of the world's population (see Chapter 4), the demand for transportation and food will also increase. Cities are responsible for 80 percent of greenhouse gas emissions, and each week the number of urban residents grows by 1.5 million. As the twenty-first century goes on, global needs for clean water, energy, and food seem harder and harder to meet. As more and more people in different parts of the world demand a better standard of living (see Chapter 6), and middle-class consumption swells (Chapter 7), the race for natural resources intensifies.

Technology represents in the minds of many the hope for a solution to the seemingly intractable problems related to sustainability in general and global warming in particular. It is true that over the last three decades automobile engines, electricity generation from fossil fuels, household appliances, and heating and cooling systems have become three to four times more efficient. In the field of renewable energy – especially solar and wind – the present pace of improvement can make these sources of energy competitive with coal, which still provides the cheapest way of generating massive amounts of electricity.

An often forgotten aspect of sustainability is human behavior. Better awareness about pollution and sustainability has had a major impact on energy savings, especially in the areas of heating and cooling, transportation, and food and diet. People forget that methane from belching cattle and other sources related to livestock generate up to 18 percent of total carbon emissions (FAO 2006). Consumption of beef has increased rapidly in emerging economies with rising incomes. Thus, dietary changes contribute to global warming but can also be the source of reduction on emissions. Another example is tourism, which is responsible for about 5 percent of total greenhouse gases (Neiva de Figueiredo and Guillén 2011).

Another aspect present in virtually every debate about sustainability is the role that regulation and taxation should play in encouraging more efficient and greener production and consumption in general, and of energy in particular. In the case of global warming, governments have deployed a battery of incentives to reduce emissions, including gasoline taxes, carbon emission taxes, tax credits and guaranteed feed-in tariffs for renewable energy sources, and other forms of positive or negative taxation. Much of the debate in this area is about the real or perceived trade-off between economic growth in the present and sustainability in the future. Also important is the discussion as to whether government intervention should promote innovation as opposed to production, under the assumption that sustainable production needs to be sustainable itself, that is, competitive in cost (Victor and Yanosek 2011). The global financial imbalances discussed in Chapter 2 could be reduced if energy-importing countries were able to develop indigenous sources of energy. Finally, there are a host of national security issues related to energy independence that will surely shape geopolitics in the twenty-first century (see Chapter 12).

Thus, the debate about sustainability in general and global warming in particular lies at the intersection of economic, technological, political, geopolitical, and behavioral forces. As Paul Roberts has recently argued in one of the most important books on the subject, *The End of Oil* (2004: 309), "the energy challenge of the twenty-first century will be to satisfy a dramatically larger demand for energy while producing dramatically less carbon. Yet the availability of carbon-free energy on a mass scale will not happen without significant technological developments." Roberts puts his faith in economic incentives by arguing that progress on climate change will not occur "until the market regards carbon as a cost to be avoided – not just in 'progressive' economies like Germany or England, but in the big economies of Russia, China, and above all the United States."

Food and water

Energy is not, however, the only pressing environmental problem humanity will face in the twenty-first century. Back in 1987 the United Nations' Brundtland Commission report, *Our Common Future*, called for international cooperation to address the issues raised by not only fossil fuel consumption and nuclear energy but also deforestation and famines. In its report *Towards Green Growth*, the OECD (2011a) estimated that threats to

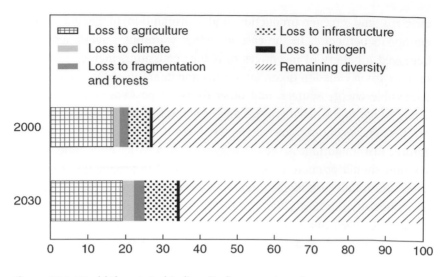

Figure 10.1 World threats to biodiversity (in percentages)
Source: OECD (2011a: 19).

biodiversity, a useful summary indicator of our combined effect on the sustainability of life, are increasing fast, especially those related to climate change, but that the most significant problem had to do with agriculture (see Figure 10.1).

Droughts and famines have besieged subsistence societies for centuries. It is alarming to note, however, the extent to which agricultural crises and rising food prices can increase poverty in urban areas. For instance, the food crisis that started in 2007, triggered by droughts and aggravated by incentives for corn-based ethanol in the US, increased the number of hungry people in the world by more than 25 percent, according to the FAO. The "green revolution" in agriculture during the last third of the twentieth century made food plentiful in the developed world, while the developing countries continued to face problems feeding their expanding populations. Biofuels production could compete with food production. The calories in a sport utility vehicle's (SUV) full tank are enough to feed one person for an entire year.

Global warming is also starting to have its effects on harvests. A recent study focused on European wheat production found that "heat stress" could reduce yields by as much as 7 percent by 2050 (Semenov and Shewry 2011), which could have a big impact on the price of this staple food for hundreds of millions of people and livestock. Oxfam, the international relief group, predicts that food prices could double by 2030 from their 2011 levels (Willenbockel 2011). Most of the effects of such steep increases would be felt in the developing world because families spend on food more than three quarters of their income. Half of the predicted hike in prices is attributed to global warming.

The availability of water, although a renewable resource, will also become a top topic on the global agenda during the twenty-first century. The changing geographical distribution of population growth, the process of urbanization, and the growth of the middle class will fundamentally reshape the economics and politics of water (see Chapters 4 and 7). In the *Towards Green Growth* report, the OECD estimated that almost 4 billion people – nearly half of the world's predicted population – will live in areas with serious water shortages by the year 2030 (OECD 2011a; see Figure 10.2; see also WWF 2010). Roughly 70 percent of worldwide human water consumption is for agricultural purposes, while industrial usage accounts for 20 percent, and households for the remaining 10 percent. Sustainability in agriculture thus poses the greatest challenge, and it involves not just the efficient use of water but also the judicious use of

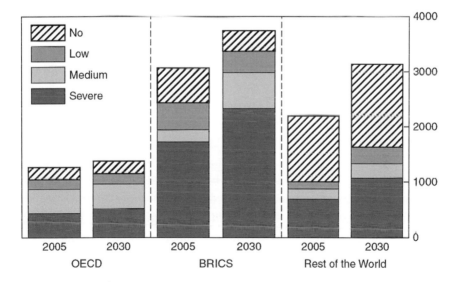

Figure 10.2 People living under severe water stress (millions)
Source: OECD (2011a: 19).

soil, fertilizers, and other inputs (Sydorovych and Wossink 2008). It is important to note that only 11 percent of Earth's surface is apt for agricultural use, and the indiscriminate use of fertilizers, erosion, and global warming might further reduce it. Another major challenge will be to remove subsidized water prices for agricultural use, which discourage conservation. Overall, much progress has been made in terms of preserving water resources. Since the 1960s conservation efforts and new technologies have reduced consumption from 0.3–0.4 cubic meters per dollar of GDP to less than 0.1 in most developed countries. Developing and emerging economies have also reduced water use to comparable levels (UNESCO 2009: 88, 99, 108, 109, 111). Still, for a major water crisis to be avoided in the next two decades, large-scale technological, policy, and behavioral changes will be needed.

Energy

Most people associate sustainability with solutions to the energy problem. Although there are many other aspects of sustainability that deserve a place on the global agenda for the twenty-first century, it is true that energy production and consumption patterns are not only related to global warming but to political instability, *coups d'état*, and even wars. The most important debates about energy revolve around the so-called energy mix, that is, the combination of energy sources a country uses and its evolution over time. Thus, for example, coal accounts for half of the increase in energy use over the past decade worldwide, according to the International Energy Agency. Renewable sources such as hydro, wind, solar, tidal, geothermal, and biomass have grown quickly over the last two decades. These technologies, however, are not yet competitive in cost. The very large subsidies to renewable energy ($66 billion in 2010, according to the International Energy Agency) will continue to grow in the coming decades, to quadruple by 2035. In addition, hydro, wind, and solar are relatively unpredictable sources. Another important dimension has to do with global warming. Nuclear power has won many supporters because of its lower contributions to global warming – although the Fukushima accident in Japan in 2011 has undermined the public's confidence in this form of energy. Over the next quarter century, energy trends will vary

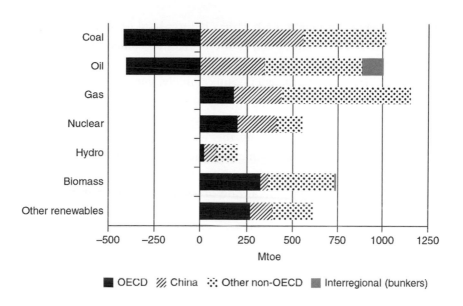

Figure 10.3 Incremental primary energy demand by fuel and region, 2008–2035
Note: All data are projections.
Source: International Energy Agency, *World Energy Outlook* (2010, figure 2.6, p. 86). © OECD/International Energy Agency.

from country to country. In the developed countries renewable energy will become more important at the expense of fossil fuels (oil and coal). In emerging and developing countries, by contrast, all energy sources are predicted to increase (see Figure 10.3).

Renewable energy has the potential to supply a substantially larger part of the world's anticipated energy needs. Barriers to sustainable energy production and consumption include technical limitations, lack of awareness and information, economic constraints, regulatory barriers, market failures, and consumer behavior (Lior 2008; Reddy and Painuly 2004). First of all, the cost of renewable green energy must come down. At the present time, sustainable sources like solar and wind are competitive thanks to direct or indirect subsidies, unless one includes all of the externalities of dirty sources such as coal, gas, and nuclear (Sovacool 2008). One of the key debates is whether subsidies should encourage production or innovation. To the extent that subsidies foster innovation, the outlook for energy sustainability looks brighter (Victor and Yanosek 2011). Consumers – both corporate and residential – can make a large impact in terms of energy consumption efficiency, but it is hard for them to alter the energy mix if renewable green sources are not competitive in price. Therefore, technological innovation is perhaps the most important force shaping the evolution of the energy mix. Finally, geopolitics will play an important role in future energy policy decisions given that the most important oil reserves are located in politically unstable areas.

The clock continues to tick as the world consumes non-renewable energy sources and global warming proceeds. According to the International Energy Agency, between 2008 and 2035 the demand for energy will grow at a cumulative annual rate of 1.2 percent, down from the 2.0 percent increase in the period 1980–2007 (IEA 2010). This is only in part good news because at the reduced growth rate, energy demand will be 36 percent higher in 2035 when compared to 2008. Moreover, greenhouse gas emissions will soar (see Figure 10.4). In spite of widespread efforts,

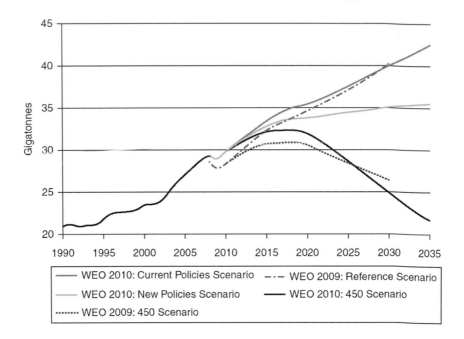

Figure 10.4 Global CO_2 emissions (gigatonnes)
Note: The 450 Scenario aims at limiting the long-term concentration of greenhouse gases in the atmosphere to 450 parts per million of carbon-dioxide equivalent.
Source: International Energy Agency, *World Energy Outlook* (2010, figure 13.2, p. 384). © OECD/International Energy Agency.

renewable sources (hydro, wind, solar, geo-thermal, biomass, tidal), which do not contribute to global warming, represented just 7 percent of total primary energy demand in 2008, and they are not likely to be more than 14 percent in 2035 (IEA 2010). In spite of subsidies, wind energy does not contribute much more than 5 percent to total electricity generation, although in some countries like Spain it reaches 14 percent on average and as much as 50 percent during peak periods (EWEA 2011). Still, the criticism is that a large installed base of wind power generation using current technology needs to be subsidized on an ongoing basis. Therefore, technological innovation is key to the economic sustainability of wind power (Victor and Yanosek 2011). And it is also true that production and consumption of fossil fuels is subsidized in many parts of the world directly through exploration credits or indirectly through expenditures on infrastructure such as highways.

China's central role in global sustainability

As the world's soon-to-be largest economy, China will hold the key to global sustainability. Its rapid industrialization and urbanization has turned the country into the largest consumer of energy. Although on a per capita basis China is still far behind developed countries, its impact on global energy markets is massive. The International Energy Agency estimates that one third of global energy demand growth to 2035 will be accounted for by China.

It is quite clear that the world's prospects for arresting climate change will depend to a very large extent on China's actions. In spite of efforts to foster renewable and clean energy sources, the country is likely to consume ever bigger quantities of coal and oil in the foreseeable future.

China could slow down its impact on global warming and also improve local air and water pollution by promoting public transportation, mid-sized cities, and energy efficiency through both technological innovation and behavioral change. Public awareness of environmental problems will also serve as a catalyst for corrective action. The transition to a service-based economy will also have a large beneficial impact.

Emerging economies and sustainability

The growing problems with supplying energy, water, or food apparently have much to do with the rise of the emerging economies. It is true that in general they are very inefficient users of energy, and that changes in dietary preferences driven by rising incomes are also having major environmental consequences. It is estimated that 93 percent of the increase in primary energy demand until 2035 will come from emerging and developing countries (IEA 2010). China's development to 2035 is projected to account for 90 percent of the increase in coal demand, and over 50 percent of the growth in oil demand and in greenhouse gas emissions (Figure 10.5 and the Box).

While the raw figures indicate that rapidly growing emerging economies have become major polluters, it is true that their economies are necessarily more inefficient and dependent on industry as opposed to services. As these countries grow richer, social and political pressure, combined with the sheer necessity to avoid environmental disaster, will most likely lead to more sustainable policies and practices. Still, it is sobering to remember the scenario described by Chandran Nair, founder and chief executive of the Global Institute for Tomorrow (GIFT): "Imagine 5 billion Asians living like Americans" (OECD 2011b). Indeed, the United

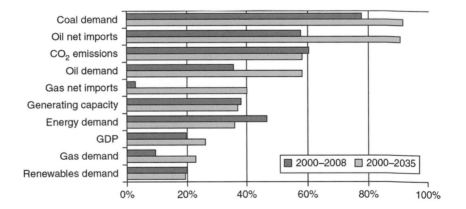

Figure 10.5 China's share of projected net global increase for selected energy indicators
Source: International Energy Agency, *World Energy Outlook* (2010, figure 2.16, p. 99). © OECD/International Energy Agency.

States is responsible for three times as much per capita greenhouse emissions as China, and more than twice as Europe.

It also fair to note that emerging economies are making a big effort at promoting renewable energy. China and India are among the most active investors and innovators in wind energy (Kristinsson and Rao 2008; Lema and Ruby 2007), China is also promoting solar (Chien and Lior 2011), and the Gulf Cooperation Council countries are aggressively pursuing renewable energy even though they have no shortage of fossil fuels (Alnaser and Alnaser 2011). Perhaps the most impressive case is Brazil, widely recognized as a global technology leader in renewable energy production for automobiles. Its ethanol policy targeted sugarcane as the key source, which offers many advantages over corn. After three decades of government intervention, some studies indicate that Brazil's sugarcane ethanol industry is competitive without subsidies (Goldemberg *et al.* 2008; Lèbre La Rovere *et al.* 2011). In addition, government entities and companies invested heavily in a host of related technologies, including the flex automobile engine and bioplastics, among others.

Sustainability, competitiveness, and business opportunities

One of the most heated debates concerning sustainability has to do with whether it undermines competitiveness, with negative consequences for job creation and economic well-being in those countries that adopt sustainable policies. The belief in a trade-off between economic growth and sustainability is giving way to more sophisticated analyses in which government intervention to reduce "dirty production" of energy and other goods and encourage sustainable growth is warranted (Acemoglu *et al.* 2010; Nordhaus and Kokkelenberg 1999). It has become clear by now that fossil sources are "competitive" because we do not take into consideration all costs, especially those that are not borne directly by the producer or the consumer, like pollution, geopolitical tensions, or global warming (Sovacool 2008). The market for energy is clearly failing to price different energy sources accurately. National economies will not easily gravitate towards sustainable production and consumption practices (Bhagwati 2004). But the balance of public opinion and policymaking has taken a turn towards a reconfiguration of the relationship between humanity and nature, a process in which government intervention designed to compensate for market failures needs to play an important role in spite of the fact that environmental regulation is very much under debate.

While the discussion about sustainability and competitiveness is important, there is another angle from which to examine the opportunities for value creation that a sustainable approach to growth might offer. In a recent article written for business executives, management guru C. K. Prahalad and his co-authors argued that companies with a greater ability to adapt and to innovate will benefit immensely from the trend towards sustainability (Nidumolu *et al.* 2009).

Sustainable or green business has become the subject of much analysis and debate (Neiva de Figueiredo and Guillén 2011). A recent McKinsey survey conducted in developed and emerging economies showed that nearly 90 percent of consumers worry about the environmental and social impact of the goods and services they buy, although no more than one in three is specifically willing to buy green products, defined as those that are environmentally friendly and sustainable. The most popular green products among consumers are efficient lighting and organic foods. By contrast, few consumers buy green automobiles or green detergents (Bonini and Oppenheim 2008). The main challenge facing green business practices is to incorporate green principles throughout the entire product life cycle, from design and production to distribution and sale, and to consumption and recycling (Albino *et al.* 2009; Glavic and Lukman 2007).

The evidence indicates that improvements made to goods and services so as to reduce negative environmental impacts may result, on the one hand, in higher development and production costs, and, on the other, in higher product differentiation, increased margins, and larger market shares for those firms which successfully move to commercialize green products (Reinhardt 2008). It is also important to note that packaging is another area susceptible to greening, including design, consumption, and disposal practices. Let's hope that business-based ingenuity and innovation will one day play a much greater role in delivering sustainable solutions to the problems of energy, food, and water. In the meantime, regulation and policy coordination across countries are necessary to prevent the twenty-first century from witnessing large-scale environmental catastrophes, which could lead in some parts of the world to further state failure, violent conflict, massive migration, repeated refugee crises, and a reversal of the trend towards poverty reduction (Matthew 2012).

11 The trials and tribulations of the financial system

> **KEY GLOBAL TURNING POINTS**
>
> In 2011 the proportion of the adult population with a bank account surpassed 50 percent for the first time, though still leaving half of the world's population financially excluded. In the developed countries, the proportion was 85 percent. Meanwhile, the younger generation of millennials exhibited the highest rates of mobile technology usage, including mobile payments and other digital financial services.

The financial system globally and within various countries has undergone massive change during the last three decades. Deregulation, liberalization, and privatization created during the 1980s and 1990s a radically new scenario. The London Big Bang of 1986 positioned the City once again as one of the world's leading financial centers. Tokyo, Shanghai, Hong Kong, Paris, Frankfurt, and Madrid also became important hubs for financial services. The financial sector's share of the economy became much larger than in the past (Philippon and Reshef 2013), something that has not tended to accelerate growth, as Raghuram Rajan, as of 2015 the Governor of the Reserve Bank of India, presciently argued before the crisis (Rajan 2005).

Then the crisis hit in 2008, and the landscape shifted in dramatic ways. The exceptional became normal. The virulence of the crisis itself – which spread globally like wildfire from a relatively small corner of US financial markets – was responsible for the greatest shakeup in financial services since the Great Depression of the 1930s. The permissive monetary policies deployed by the major central banks further contributed to creating a situation rather unprecedented, one in which liquidity is abundant, and yet many financial institutions continue to operate on the brink, requiring massive amounts of government support, especially in Europe.

At the same time, long-standing trends concerning population aging, the rise of the "digital natives," and the proliferation of technology have taken the financial sector by storm, enabling new types of competitors to gain market share and thus exacerbating the problems of the traditional financial institutions, especially deposit-taking banks (Berges *et al.* 2014). The financial sector of the economy is engaged in a tedious process of deleveraging while the global economy continues to grow slowly, deflation sets in, and new technologies and companies threaten its very existence.

The financial system

The financial system is an indispensable set of institutions. At the national level it includes banks, financial companies, shadow financial institutions such as hedge funds and private equity firms, all manner of intermediaries, regulatory agencies, sovereign wealth funds, and the central bank. At the international level, the International Monetary Fund, the Bank for International Settlements, and the World Bank, among others, provide the foundations for a well-functioning global financial architecture.

Banks and other financial institutions have come under intense scrutiny and criticism in the wake of the 2008 financial crisis. Their reputation has suffered immensely. At the same time, population aging, the rise of the millennial generation, new technology, and increased regulations, among other important trends, are putting enormous pressure on their traditional business model, which involves some combination of deposit taking, borrowing, lending, and investment and advisory services.

No market economy can function properly without a financial system. Yet, countries differ massively in terms of the characteristics of their financial system, especially in terms of the role and importance of deposit-taking banks, non-bank financial institutions, equity markets, debt markets, currency markets, and foreign capital flows. The diversity of national financial systems, for instance, represents a major obstacle preventing Economic and Monetary Union in Europe from functioning smoothly.

The crisis and its impact

The financial sector has changed beyond recognition. The crisis has had one major effect, which is the greater scrutiny which every financial company will be subject to in the future. Trust in the sector has deteriorated very rapidly. The financial sector itself has become a source of uncertainty and instability for the overall global economy. The "Great Moderation" from 1985 to 2007, in a context of widespread liberalization and deregulation of financial activity, led not to a more solid financial system but to myriad problems which manifested themselves at the levels of individual financial businesses, financial conglomerates, national financial systems, and the entire global financial architecture. Risk management and risk rating were at the epicenter of the crisis, with speculative bubbles exploding sooner or later. Public authorities at the national treasuries and at the central banks were forced to intervene buying bad assets, acquiring equity stakes in banks and other institutions, purchasing government bonds, and expanding the supply of money more generally.

The way in which academics study financial activity has also changed as a result of the crisis, granting much more importance to behavioral aspects and less so to market mechanisms per se (Akerlof and Shiller 2009; see also Cassidy 2010). As highlighted by Jakab and Kumhof (2015), macroeconomic theory was initially unprepared to provide much guidance when it came to studying the complex interactions between the banking sector and the economy. The reason was simple. Banks were not a part of most macroeconomic models, perhaps because for decades banks were not considered to be sources of vulnerability and volatility. Almost all of the attention devoted to banks was of a microeconomic nature.

This inattention to banks concealed their role as pro-cyclical providers of financing. The crisis and its aftermath have made it impossible to ignore the leverage ratios of households and non-financial companies. In addition to banks, the rise of "shadow banking" requires a different kind of financial supervision. Recent experiences and failures amplify the importance of considering psychological and sociological aspects when analyzing the financial sector and its impact on the broader economy.

Traumas and disappointments

The crisis has been a trauma with various manifestations within the financial sector. Lack of confidence is the most explicit. The technical requirements for risk management and best practices of financial operators have been seriously called into question. Although the bubble that burst was in the real estate market, its broadest and adverse consequences manifested themselves within financial services companies, especially banks. The reconsideration of the role of banks as enablers of productivity gains and economic growth may have far-reaching implications for the future of the global economy.

Banks deserve this attention and the regulation that it may ultimately bring with it given their behavior during the years prior to the crisis. Banks found many ingenious ways to circumvent regulations, especially to make their leverage ratios appear deceptively low (Acharya and Richardson 2009). Agency problems – a breakdown of the incentives to make decisions following reasonable risk-management criteria – proliferated, leading many banks to forget about the interests of those providing them with funds, i.e., shareholders, bondholders, and depositors. Mutual funds and insurance companies also engaged in behaviors that benefited portfolio managers at the expense of their investors and customers (Lang *et al.* 2013).

Seven years after the crisis, one can still point to numerous anomalies in the behavior of many financial companies, some with important legal implications. Examples include subprime mortgages, fixing the interbank interest rates (Libor), the manipulations in the foreign exchange markets, and the enabling and facilitation of tax evasion or money laundering. A recent report by Keefe, Bruyette & Woods, a New York investment firm, has tracked 264 ongoing investigations involving 46 banks around the world.

Other institutions considered fundamental to the functioning of financial markets have been seriously questioned. The most egregious case is that of the rating agencies, which investors rely on in order to assess and compare risks of various financial instruments. The three agencies with greater global significance have seen their reputation eroded. Their favorable ratings of financial instruments that proved to be toxic have been the focus of much disappointment and some litigation. In addition, conflicts of interest and other anomalies have been investigated. It seems inevitable that more regulation will be needed to prevent similar occurrences in the future, given that self-regulation has worked so poorly. The oligopolistic nature of the sector also requires further examination.

Banks have rightly been the target of much criticism. To add insult to injury, the damage sustained by shareholders, customers, and taxpayers was compounded by a reluctance to rein in executive pay and perks (Suárez 2014). In fact, executive pay is commonly identified as a major source of rising income inequality. Both the technical reputation and the ethical standards of bankers have been compromised. Even the "social utility" of banking – a term coined by Lord Turner, then a chairman of the Financial Services Authority (FSA) – has come under attack. Insurance companies were less complicit than banks, with notable exceptions such as AIG. Still, guilt by association has undermined the reputation of all financial intermediaries.

Financial services companies, especially banks, have needed important support of governments in many advanced countries. The most important was public resources to restore their solvency and liquidity, with monetary measures by central banks ranking as a close second. In fact, those decisions of exceptional liquidity expansion and reduction to zero, or even negative, levels of real interest rates, have defined a new habitat for the activity of all financial actors, from banks to insurance companies, and from hedge funds to mutual funds. Those extremely low interest rates coexist with growing levels of public debt, at a time when governments have seen their tax revenue capacity eroded.

That situation is beginning to have an impact on the income statements of all financial companies. For instance, the requirement of matching delivery obligations to holders of life insurance contracts with historically low interest in risk-free assets places some companies in a difficult position. The guarantee of returns does not always correspond to the possibilities of low-risk investment (especially government bonds) that the companies have in order to guarantee them. In addition to this conundrum, insurance companies must also deal with new regulatory pressures.

Banks will not be what they used to be

Besides the shame of having had to rely on taxpayer money to make it through the crisis, banks have seen their entire business model called into question. Traditional banking intermediation is under stress due to changing demographics and new technology. And low interest rates with relatively high levels of risk aversion make it very hard to rely on traditional intermediation as a major source of income. Banks need to cut costs and develop new sources of income in order to continue persuading their shareholders and bondholders to fund them. Retail banks have no choice but to generate economies of scale, especially in economies with saturated banking markets, as in the Eurozone. The search for economies of scale, however, is not always compatible with customer satisfaction.

Another consequence of the environment of very low interest rates is the tendency towards excessive risk-taking, not only by financial firms, but in general by all types of investors, with its corresponding deleterious effects on financial stability. Banks have become less prone to offer credit, making many small and medium-sized firms suffer a severe shortage of capital, especially in the bank-based financial systems of Continental Europe.

Regulation

Banks cannot escape the new scenario of tighter regulation and supervision, new technology, and financial disintermediation (Berges *et al.* 2014). Increased regulation and stricter supervision are the logical reaction to the specific responsibilities that financial companies, especially banks, have concerning the emergence of the crisis, and the massive support they have received from taxpayers in some countries. There is indeed a sense that current regulations did nothing to curb the excesses of banks. Insufficient capital and excessive leverage were two factors that, in the best of cases, exacerbated the consequences of the instability and hindered the ability of regulatory authorities to bring it under control. In 2008, Lehman Brothers, for instance, held equity representing only 3.3 percent of its balance-sheet. It is not surprising, therefore, that in the future banks will be required to have a larger base of capital, and more controls over their amount and type of debt.

Governments may also question the continuity or at least the magnitude of tax incentives for debt financing, especially in the case of banks, and perhaps also households. The tax advantages, and possibilities of maintaining control, make borrowing cheaper against the equity financing, especially if the market takes a presumption that in case of bankruptcy the government will bail out the bank. But the preferences of regulators, especially after the crisis, tend to go in the direction of a strengthening of equity. In any case, they are receptive to the development of new hybrid instruments that combine the advantages of debt with the greatest responsibility in the event of solvency problems of financing through equity.

In the case of the Eurozone, such monitoring was adopted in late 2014 as part of the emerging Banking Union. In fact, the beginning of the Single Supervisory Mechanism, one of the main pillars of banking integration, is a ray of hope in an otherwise complex post-crisis environment. Greater capital requirements will limit credit to smaller firms, with negative consequences for job creation.

The top managers at some of the biggest financial companies made public in May 2015 a document in which they adopt a more positive attitude towards regulation intended to avoid future financial crises (WEF 2015). They support macro prudential policies, including the use of tools to limit the adoption of systemic risk positions in order to ensure an appropriate balance between financial stability and economic growth. However, it is much easier to define the purpose of these policies than to anticipate the effects of their implementation.

It should be ultimately accepted that financial stability is a public good, and that producing it requires a close scrutiny of the various kinds of inefficiencies that emerge in the financial system. Regarding the supply of credit, it is important to examine not only the amount but also how it is allocated. The experience in the US with off-balance-sheet transactions and the lack of transparency in securitization loom large as problems to be avoided.

In sum, regulations will reshape the banking sector, especially those regarding new capital requirements, risk management, separation of commercial deposit-taking and investment banking so as to avoid explicit or implicit guarantees of non-core activities by core activities, incentives at the organizational level and for certain types of employees, and enhanced consumer protections. Pressure is also building to levy new taxes on financial activity. These new regulations will make it harder for banks to lend money, with smaller firms being the most affected.

Technology

Mobile telecommunications technology has already disrupted many parts of the economy. Banking and financial services more broadly will not be an exception. In addition, technology can also revolutionize back-office operations, reducing entry costs, and enabling nimbler competitors to enter the market. The banking business model predicated on a ubiquitous geographical presence through branches may well be approaching its end. The future does not necessarily hold branchless banks, but certainly a much leaner distribution network and a so-called "omni-channel" experience for the customer. New intermediaries, new forms of financing and brokerage are constantly emerging. "Crowdfunding" and other forms of collaborative finance do not yet represent a serious threat to traditional banking, but could well become one. The traditional relationship of loyalty between the bank and the client is breaking down.

As a result, non-bank and non-financial companies are entering the financial sector by developing and leveraging technology. Non-traditional operators can provide payment services, mobile transfers, trading, insurance, financial advisory, and other types of financial services. Firms with deep pockets like Amazon, Apple, Facebook, or Google will soon become relevant competitors for traditional banks, fragmenting their value chains, and disintermediating them. The risk for banks is that these new digital competitors will confine them to a limited role as utilities that provide only basic banking services to customers.

These trends are unfolding in an environment in which cash transactions are losing ground to the point that in some countries, such as Denmark, money as currency is literally disappearing. Regulatory initiatives, as proposed by the Danish Chamber of Commerce, may enable small businesses to reject payments in cash, something that would help in the fight against the underground economy and tax fraud. Accountability and security are additional reasons for the extension of cards and mobile payments. Big data also opens new horizons for the expansion and development of financial services, albeit subject to considerations of privacy and security. "Cash is expensive, dirty, difficult to transport, unreliable, and does not generate tax revenues. Governments would increase revenue by promoting digital payments," argues Mehmet Sezgin, who is responsible for global payments at BBVA, the large Spanish bank (*El País*, May 5, 2015).

Disintermediation

Regulation and technology will eventually reduce the scope for bank intermediation both in terms of sources of funding and sales of financial products. This effect will be more pronounced in economies in which banks have historically been more important than capital markets, as in Continental Europe and some Latin American and Asian countries. The banking industry will be transformed by the emergence of alternative forms of financial intermediation, from shadow banking to peer-to-peer lending. New forms of finance are maturing at the same time that the structure and activities of traditional banks are under scrutiny. Some of those new finance alternatives, like shadow banking, mainly emerge as a way to circumvent regulations or limitations to traditional banking. Others, like peer-to-peer lending or crowdfunding, are preventing banks from performing their traditional lending function to specific borrowers.

As noted above, the case of the Eurozone is especially important. Dependence on bank financing is very high: about 70 percent of the external funding of European companies comes from banks, compared with only 30 percent in the United States. This "bank-dependency" has made managing the effects of the crisis even more complicated. Using data from the European Commission for 2013, roughly 35 percent of small and medium-size companies in the Eurozone failed to obtain from their banks the amount of financing they requested. The costs of bank financing for these companies are significantly higher than for larger companies. Thus, in addition to a Banking Union, the Eurozone also needs a Capital Market Union (CMU) in order to compensate for the lack of enough bank financing (Véron and Guntram 2015). The CMU is scheduled to be in operation by 2019.

The key form of disintermediation refers to "shadow banking," or lending by institutions that are not banks. Those funds may represent today as much as a quarter of the global financial system, with assets that have tripled in value during the decade preceding the crisis. The growth rates of these assets in the shadow have led to reasonable concerns about their destabilizing potential. Due to regulatory pressure, banks will perhaps try to avoid higher risk weights and equity requirements through securitization, or to evade limitations on leverage by investing in non-bank financial institutions. According to the 2014 report of the Bank for International Settlements, asset management companies have already become a major source of credit. Their larger role, together with the high degree of concentration in the industry, may influence market dynamics, and hence cost and availability of funding for firms and households. The concern of supervisors about the migration of activities due to regulatory arbitrage is reasonable.

Shifting demographics

Banks' exposure to regulation, technology, and disintermediation comes at a time when their customer base is shifting by age and gender, developed markets are mature, under-banked markets are witnessing high growth by non-bank institutions, and middle-class consumers in emerging economies are increasingly aspirational, brand oriented, and status seeking. To this one must add the new millennial generation of "born digital" individuals, who are highly connected and skeptical about traditional banks and banking practices, if not hostile to them. They want to be entertained while they shop for goods and services of all kinds, including financial services. They display very little brand and vendor loyalty.

This confluence of demographic, economic, social, financial, and technological trends poses distinct challenges for banks (Berges *et al.* 2014). Their business model and strategies have been rendered partially obsolete. The financial system of the future may not be as bank-centric as it is today.

The new normal is financial instability

New financial competitors and business models, however, do not guarantee a risk-free and tension-free future. Quite on the contrary, every transition phase brings with it instability and uncertainty. The financial sector will need to answer the key question as to whether it has the ability to benefit society (Zingales 2015). Financial development makes an unequivocally positive contribution during the early stages of growth of any country, but its excessive growth beyond a certain point does not always contribute to the development of the real economy, and can become a major factor of instability.

If the 2008 crisis has made something clear, it is that financial markets do not generally operate efficiently or deliver efficient outcomes, as much of the academic literature promised since the 1970s. To the inherent tensions of modern financial systems one must add those generated by the performance of monetary policy and other policies such as interventions in the foreign exchange markets. Over the last few years, several central banks have engaged in "currency wars" with the purpose of manipulating the real exchange rate and thus affecting export competitiveness, trade balances, and capital movements. It should be remembered that an ever-increasing proportion of the profits of large companies listed on the stock market comes from foreign sales. In the case of companies in the S&P 500 index, for instance, that proportion is around 40 percent.

One last source of uncertainty refers to emerging economies, whose financial markets and banking systems have grown very rapidly over the last two decades. This development has not been accompanied by an increase in the capacity of regulators and supervisors to rein in unwanted behaviors, prevent financial meltdowns, and minimize the chances of contagion. The head of the Financial Stability Board and Bank of England Governor, Mark Carney, issued a stark warning about the growth of various forms of shadow banking in emerging markets as the main threat to financial stability in the future. Therefore, coordination of regulation and overall supervision will remain a central aspect of global governance. It is important to remember, for instance, the enhanced role of the G20 during the months immediately following the collapse of Lehman Brothers. Completely neutralizing the possibilities for regulatory arbitrage is not an easy task, but the world needs to at least afford some degree of cross-national oversight.

12 The global powers of the twenty-first century

> **KEY GLOBAL TURNING POINTS**
> During most of the twenty-first century India will be the biggest country in terms of population, China the largest in output, and the United States the richest among the major economies on a per capita income basis.

Perhaps the most tantalizing question about the twenty-first century has to do with the identity of the dominant global power, or whether there will be one at all. If the United Kingdom reigned supreme during much of the nineteenth century and the United States dominated the second half of the twentieth, are we to assume that a different global power will emerge during the twenty-first? For some, the answer is obvious and it points to China (e.g., Jacques 2009; Subramanian 2011). For others, the United States will hold its sway, albeit with a severely diminished capacity to act unilaterally (Nye 1990, 2010). For a third group of observers and commentators, including cold-warriors like Henry Kissinger, the twenty-first century will be characterized by an uneasy balance among several global powers (Bremmer 2010a; CSM 1989; Kissinger 2011). It is clear that "we are now at the start of what may become the most dramatic change in the international order in several centuries, the biggest shift since European nations were first shuffled into a sovereign order by the Peace of Westphalia in 1648" (Ramo 2009: 7–8).

A millennial perspective on the comparative size of populations and economies might be a good place to start analyzing this debate. Table 12.1 presents the data for selected economies. Back in the year AD 1000 China was not even the largest country in terms of population or GDP – India was and had been for at least the previous one thousand years. Five hundred years later the two countries were still running head to head,

Table 12.1 Population, GDP, and GDP per capita, selected economies, 1–2008

	Year								
	1	1000	1500	1820	1850	1870	1913	1950	2008
Population (millions)									
Western Europe	25.1	25.6	57.3	133.0	166.2	187.5	261.0	305.6	401.4
Of which: UK	0.8	2.0	3.9	21.2	27.2	31.4	45.6	50.1	60.9
USA	0.7	1.3	2.0	10.0	23.6	40.2	97.6	152.3	304.2
Latin America	5.6	11.4	17.5	21.6	31.8	40.4	80.8	165.5	580.2
China	59.6	59.0	103.0	*381.0*	*412.0*	*358.0*	*437.1*	*546.8*	*1324.8*
India	*75.0*	*75.0*	*110.0*	209.0	235.8	253.0	303.7	359.0	1148.0
Japan	3.0	7.5	15.4	31.0	32.0	34.4	51.7	83.8	127.3
Africa	17.0	32.3	46.6	74.2	...	90.5	124.7	227.9	974.5
World total	225.8	267.3	438.4	1041.7	...	1275.7	1792.9	2528.0	6694.8
GDP (billion)									
Western Europe	14.4	10.9	44.2	158.9	*260.3*	*366.2*	*902.1*	1396.3	8698.0
Of which: UK	0.3	0.8	2.8	36.2	63.3	110.2	224.6	347.8	1447.0
USA	0.3	0.5	0.8	12.5	42.6	98.4	517.4	*1455.9*	*9485.1*
Latin America	2.2	4.6	7.3	14.9	...	27.3	120.8	415.3	4045.9
China	26.8	27.5	*61.8*	*228.6*	247.2	189.7	241.4	245.0	8908.9
India	*33.8*	*33.8*	60.5	111.4	125.7	134.9	204.2	222.2	3415.2

Table 12.1 (cont.)

	Year								
	1	1000	1500	1820	1850	1870	1913	1950	2008
Japan	1.2	3.2	7.7	20.7	21.7	25.4	71.7	161.0	2904.1
Africa	8.0	13.7	19.3	31.2	…	45.2	79.5	202.6	1734.9
World total	105.4	121.2	248.3	693.5	…	1109.7	2733.2	5335.9	50,973.9
GDP per capita									
Western Europe	*576*	427	*771*	1194	1567	1953	3457	4569	21,672
Of which: UK	400	400	714	*1706*	*2330*	*3190*	*4921*	6939	23,742
USA	400	400	400	1257	1806	2445	*5301*	*9561*	*31,178*
Latin America	400	400	416	691	…	676	1494	2510	6973
China	450	*466*	600	600	600	530	552	448	6725
India	450	450	550	533	533	533	673	619	2975
Japan	400	425	500	669	679	737	1387	1921	22,816
Africa	472	425	414	420	…	500	637	889	1780
World total	467	453	566	666	…	870	1524	2111	7614

Notes: GDP and GDP per capita calculated using constant 1990 Geary–Khamis international dollars. Largest figure for each year noted in bold type.

Source: Angus Maddison, *Historical Statistics of the World Economy: 1–2008 AD*. www.ggdc.net/maddison (accessed Angust 20, 2011).

each still larger than all of Western Europe combined in terms of population or GDP. It was not until the power of steam worked its magic in Western Europe that Asia started to fall behind, and not until after World War II that the United States took the lead. At the turn of the twenty-first century, China and India commanded a large lead in terms of population, with the former's economy poised to become number one in size. Still, as of 2008 China was about a fourth as rich on a per capita basis as the most advanced countries in the world. The United States has been the world's richest large economy for nearly two centuries. Contrary to the conventional wisdom, the UK never was the world's largest economy, given that China passed on the baton directly to the US.

It is sobering to remember that India was the world's largest economy for at least fifteen centuries (since at least the year AD 1 until around 1500). China held the number one spot for three and a half centuries (from 1500 to about 1840). According to Kissinger (2011: 32), China's decline had to do with the way it "entered the modern age," namely as

a state claiming universal relevance for its culture and institutions but making few efforts to proselytize; the wealthiest country in the world but one that was indifferent to foreign trade and technological innovation; a culture of cosmopolitanism overseen by a political elite oblivious to the onset of the Western age of exploration; and a political unit of unparalleled geographic extent that was unaware of the technological and historical currents that would soon threaten its existence.

Western Europe's period as the world's largest economy was a historical "anomaly" by world-time standards, lasting just a century, from about 1840 to 1943. Britain was never the largest economy because China was larger until the early twentieth century, and by that time the United States had overtaken Britain. The United States has thus far been the largest economy for a bit more than six decades (since 1943), if you consider Western Europe as one bloc, or for the 120 years since approximately 1890 if you do not – that was the year the American economy surpassed the Chinese economy in size. In April 2011 the International Monetary Fund predicted that China would become the world's largest economy by 2016. Thus, it is quite likely that during most of the twenty-first century India will be the biggest country in terms of population, China the largest in output, and the United States the richest among the major economies on a per capita income basis.

Global powers

A global power is a state with the ability to shape events and conditions worldwide. Global powers typically exert their influence through economic, political, diplomatic, military, ideological, religious, and/or cultural means. The political theorist Joseph Nye distinguished between hard and soft power, predicting that in the twenty-first century global powers would turn to less coercive and tangible means of exerting their influence.

The modern concept of global power has its origins in the Peace of Westphalia of 1648, which introduced the concept of the sovereign state and set the stage for the diplomatic interaction among states. Historians consider the Congress of Vienna of 1814–1815 as the first explicit recognition of the status of the various European powers, although one could also point to the Treaty of Tordesillas of 1494, which defined global spheres of influence for Portugal and Spain.

During the second half of the twentieth century the term superpower was used almost interchangeably with global power, and was meant to represent a notch above the status of a mere great power. Superpower status came to be associated with the possession of nuclear weapons and with the ability to project force around the world. For instance, after World War II, France and Britain, though nuclear armed, were not deemed superpowers because they could no longer independently project force everywhere on the planet.

As of 2011, nine countries possessed aircraft carriers, six possessed nuclear-powered submarines, and seven possessed nuclear weapons (the US, Russia, the UK, France, China, India, and Pakistan). Israel had neither confirmed nor denied that it possessed them. The South African apartheid regime developed nuclear weapons in the 1970s, but destroyed them prior to the coming of majority rule in 1994. The United States, with 11 aircraft carriers and dozens of submarines, was the only state with the ability to project military force worldwide.

Patterns of rise and decline

Let us state the obvious. Civilizations, empires, and specific countries rise and fall, with some recovering from decay while others descend into chaos and even extinction. Examples of decline and collapse abound: the ancient civilizations, Athens, Rome, Byzantium, and more recently Ming China in the seventeenth century, the Spanish empire during the early nineteenth century, the Ottoman and Hapsburg empires during the early twentieth century, the British Empire during the mid twentieth century, and the Soviet Union during the late twentieth century (see the Box). What is in dispute is whether the pattern of rise and decline can be explained, and whether there is something one can do to arrest or reverse decline once it starts occurring.

Twentieth-century historiography devoted much energy to the task of discerning patterns in the rise and decline of civilizations, empires, and individual countries. Much of it was directly or indirectly influenced by the Hegelian idea that there is a dialectic pattern to history, one in which opposed concepts and ideologies become the engine of change.

Two historians, one German and one British, dominated the early debates about the rise and decline of civilizations, empires, and nations. Writing during and immediately after World War I, Oswald Spengler proposed in *The Decline of the West* (1932 [1918–1923]) to study the topic from a biological perspective, suggesting that civilizations are living organisms following entirely predictable patterns of birth, growth, maturation, and decline. Eighteenth-century British political philosophers like Henry St. John, First Viscount Bolingbroke had already advanced this thesis, maintaining that "the best instituted governments carry in them the seeds of their destruction: and, though they grow and improve for a time, they will soon tend visibly to their dissolution. Every hour they live is an hour the less that they have to live" (quoted in Ferguson 2010). Although based on impressive scholarship, this simplistic and facile view of history came under heavy attack by many historians.

The second contemporary systematic attempt at world history was undertaken shortly thereafter by an amazingly learned British historian, Arnold Toynbee, whose monumental *A Study of History*, written over the span of almost three decades beginning in the early 1930s, was published as 12 separate volumes. He identified 23 "full-blown" civilizations

(Toynbee 1961, vol. XII: 546–561), tracing their origins, development, and evolution. He proposed that civilizations and empires go through cycles of challenge, response, and suicide driven by moral and political decay.

The current debate about global powers properly begins with the publication in 1987 of a book mostly about the last two centuries by the British, though American-based, historian Paul Kennedy. He famously advanced and documented the theory that global powers decline when their global interests and military commitments exceed their economic might and ability by a wide margin, in a way reminiscent of Keohane's (1984: 32) definition of hegemony as "the preponderance of material resources." Kennedy's "imperial overstretch" thesis helps explain the downfall of Napoleon, the British Empire, Nazi Germany, and perhaps American dominance in the twenty-first century, given that in 2012 the US economy represented about 18.2 percent of the global economy, down from 30.5 in 2000, but the country accounted for about 39.2 percent of global military expenditures, slightly down from 41.8 in 2000 (World Bank 2011a).

The financial historian Niall Ferguson (2010) has advanced a different view of the pattern of rise and decline observing that "most great empires have a nominal central authority – either a hereditary emperor or an elected president – but in practice the power of any individual ruler is a function of the network of economic, social, and political relations over which he or she presides." In this sense, "great powers and empires are … complex systems, made up of a very large number of interacting components that are asymmetrically organized," adding that "such systems can appear to operate quite stably for some time; they seem to be in equilibrium but are, in fact, constantly adapting. But there comes a moment when complex systems 'go critical.' A very small trigger can set off a 'phase transition' from a benign equilibrium to a crisis." For instance, the Spanish empire faced such a critical moment in the wake of the Napoleonic invasions, the Hapsburg, Ottoman, and Romanov empires during World War I, the British Empire after World War II, and the Soviet Union following Afghanistan and Chernobyl. "When things go wrong in a complex system, the scale of disruption is nearly impossible to anticipate … a relatively minor shock can cause a disproportionate – and sometimes fatal – disruption." This pattern of change is what biologists call "punctuated equilibrium."

Other historians and social scientists have focused the debate over the rise and decline of various parts of the world – especially the West – on the influence of a bewildering array of factors: demography, disease, and happenstance (e.g., Landes 1998); the "unbound prometheus" of technology (Landes 2003); the incorporation of the Americas and Africa into a modern "world-system" of economic exchange dominated by the European powers (Wallerstein 1974); the free exchange of ideas and the development of experimental, mathematics-based science that fostered "close social relations among entrepreneurs, scientists, engineers, and craftspeople" (Goldstone 2009: 169); "a combination of inventiveness, markets, coercion, and fortunate global conjunctures" (Pomeranz 2000: 23); the benefits of stable economic, social, and legal institutions (Acemoglu *et al.* 2001; Clark 2007; North 1991); the interaction among several "complexes of institutions," namely political and economic competition, science, property rights, medicine, the consumer society, and the work ethic (Ferguson 2011: 12); or geography and disease, coupled with Europe's fragmentation, which led to the "advance of technology, science, and capitalism by fostering competition among states and providing innovators with alternative sources of support and havens from persecution" (Diamond 2005a: 454).

Another historian, Ian Morris, has attempted to synthesize these and other perspectives into a long term theory of the rise and decline of human societies from 14,000 BCE to the present time. He argues that "biology, sociology, and geography jointly explain the history of social development, with biology driving development up, sociology shaping how development rises (or doesn't), and geography deciding where development rises (or falls) fastest" (Morris 2010: 592). He equates social development – "societal development" might be a better term – with the extent to which a society increases its human energy capture, social organization, war-making capacity, and information technology capabilities over time, on the assumption that societies emerge to take care of "lazy, greedy, frightened people ... looking for easier, more profitable, and safer ways to do things" (Morris 2010: 559). As to the decline of civilizations, he adopts a quasi-Marxian perspective, noting that "rising social development generates the very forces that undermine further social development" as over the course of history "societies fail to solve the problems that confront them, [and] a terrible package of ills – famine, epidemic, uncontrolled migration, and state failure – begins to afflict them," with stagnation eventually turning into decline or collapse: "the same pattern … played out again and again" (Morris 2010: 28, 35). He recognizes that societies benefit from their interaction with others, but that over time internal and external pressures create challenges that most are not able to cope with.

Sociologists and political scientists have also made contributions to this burgeoning area of research by focusing on the breakdown of states, especially as a result of social revolutions, as in France in the late eighteenth century, Russia in the early twentieth century, or China during the mid twentieth century. These analyses essentially found that a combination of fiscal strain, elite conflict, international pressure, and popular revolt tends to cause state breakdown. These theories have implications for the analysis of the demise of global powers. For instance, the collapse of the Soviet Union can be readily explained in terms of its commitment to the arms race, its territorial overextension, ethnic hostility to centralized government, a fiscal crisis, and intra-elite conflict between reformers and hardliners (Collins 1999). Economists also jumped into the fray, arguing that institutional rigidities and political sclerosis built over long periods of uninterrupted social and political development could produce a decline relative to other societies that constantly reinvent themselves or are forced to do so in the wake of military defeat (Olson 1982).

From *Pax Americana* to *Pax Sinica*?

Theories aside, the key debate about the rise and decline of nations in the twenty-first century centers on the dynamic between the United States and China. Martin Jacques, a British scholar, columnist, and former editor of the journal *Marxism Today*, has perhaps been most sweeping and extravagant in his prediction that China will become the dominant global power well before the twenty-first century comes to a close, relegating the United States to a distant second place in global affairs. In his book, *When China Rules the World: The Rise of the Middle Kingdom and the End of the Western World* (2009), he displayed a solid knowledge of Chinese history and global stature. However, he made projections into the future which are unwarranted and likely to be proven wrong. "China, with continuing economic growth (albeit at a reduced rate), is destined to become one of the two major global powers and ultimately *the* major global power," he asserted, while hedging a bit in arguing that "what would demolish it is if, for some reason, China implodes in a twenty-first-century version of the intermittent bouts of introspection and instability that have punctuated Chinese history" (Jacques 2009: 363).

Although Jacques dutifully noted China's mounting challenges concerning the sustainability of economic growth, yawning income disparities, population aging, political fossilization, environmental threats, and ethnic fractionalization (affecting two fifths of its territory), he wholeheartedly embraced the notion that not only will China be the dominant political-economic power of the twenty-first century, but also that the renminbi will be adopted as the preferred reserve currency, Chinese universities will become the world's best, Chinese culture will spread around the world, East Asia will become a China-centric tributary-state system, and Beijing will become the new global capital (Jacques 2009: 363–409). In his view, the whole world is about to be swept by a Chinese tsunami of unprecedented proportions. Moreover, "it is clear that Chinese modernity will be very different from Western modernity, and that China will transform the world far more fundamentally than any other new global power in the last two centuries" (2009: 429). As Chris Patten, the British Governor of Hong Kong who negotiated the handover to China, once put it, "this is a people with a sense of their past greatness, recent humiliation, present achievement and future supremacy" (quoted in Carr 2010: 9).

When China Rules the World ends with a dire prediction: "There are two powerful forces that will serve to promote the steady reconfiguration of the world on China's terms." The first is that "China's mass will oblige the rest of the world largely to acquiesce in China's way of doing things," and the second that China "is possessed of a 5,000-year history and an extremely long memory, and unsurprisingly conceives of the future in terms of protracted timescales. As a result, it is blessed with the virtue of patience, confident in the belief that history is on its side" (Jacques 2009: 431–432).

More careful and analytical in the assessment of China's rise is Arvind Subramanian, an economist with experience at the IMF and the GATT, who focuses on GDP, trade, and external financial strength as the key determinants of world domination. In his book, *Eclipse: Living in the Shadow of China's Economic Dominance*, he presents a series of scenarios to 2030 in which China becomes the dominant global economic and financial power even if its growth rate drops to about 5 percent and the United States successfully addresses its growth, fiscal, and distributional problems. For him, the only question is whether in 2030 China will be 50 or 100 percent more dominant than the United States taking into account output, trade, and currency strength. Most importantly, he notes that "China's future dominance is more China's to gain than America's to lose," arguing that China's position as the world's leading trading and financial power is almost beyond reasonable doubt, while the dynamics of economic convergence make it very likely that China's economy will become bigger and bigger over time relative to those of other countries. "The United States cannot escape the inherent logic of demography and convergence," he asserts without mustering any empirical evidence, but admits that "the baseline scenario of a dominant China can be altered materially by a resurgent America (of course, aided by a faltering China)." And he continues to assert that in order for the inevitable dominance of China to be derailed, "not just will the United States have to grow substantially faster than the long-run trend but it must be seen as strong fiscally and, above all, able to reverse the pall of economic and social stagnation that has enveloped its middle class" (Subramanian 2011: 190–195).

While Subramanian is quick to point out the economic, financial, political, and social weaknesses of the United States, which are not to be taken lightly, he can only see strengths in China, utterly ignoring the country's growing economic, financial, social, political, and environmental problems. To arrive at his conclusions, Subramanian (2011: 194) makes rather untenable assumptions, including that "the location of technological progress thus begins to matter less," as if the profits stemming from scientific and technical discovery were enjoyed by others than those who own the technology. He never contemplates a growth rate in China of less than 4.9 percent, while assuming no more than 3.5 percent in the case of the United States. And in truly hyperbolic fashion, he even argues that "one should not rule out the future possibility of a G-1, with that one not being the United States of America. China in solitary dominance is a possible, sobering, and not-too distant reality" (Subramanian 2011: 114).

As Joseph Nye has shrewdly noted, "China's current reputation for power benefits from projections about the future . . . China does have impressive power resources, but we should be skeptical about projections based on current growth rates and political rhetoric" (Nye 2011: 178–179).

While more balanced observers acknowledge the significance of China's rise, they also alert to the obvious flaws in the argument about the inevitable emergence of Chinese global dominance. For instance, the author of a recent special report on China's new role in the world published in *The Economist* cogently argued that the surge in Chinese self-confidence, assertiveness, and nationalism is certainly of consequence, but perhaps will not change the global balance of power in any funda mental way. However, China, at least for now, purely represents itself, does not have an ideology to export, and benefits massively from globalization and the present state of the global economy to engage in aggressive expansion through coercion or war (Carr 2010).

China is the only large economy in the world under threat due to environmental reasons. In *Collapse: How Societies Choose to Fail or Succeed*, Jared Diamond (2005b: 358) argued that "China's environmental problems are among the most severe of any major country, and are getting worse," adding that "the list ranges from air pollution, biodiversity losses, cropland losses, desertification, disappearing wetlands, grassland degradation, and increasing scale and frequency of human-induced natural disasters, to invasive species, overgrazing, river flow cessation, salinization, soil erosion, trash accumulation, and water pollution and shortages." In fact, Diamond observed that China's size is not an advantage, but a serious drawback: "China's large population and large growing economy, and its current and historic centralization, mean that China's lurches involve more momentum than those of any other country" (Diamond 2005b: 377).

It is also worth noting that China has a public-relations problem when it comes to becoming a leader in regional, let alone global, affairs, although other aspiring powers such as Brazil or India suffer from a similar limitation (Castañeda 2010). It is a country with a poor record in terms of bettering the world through diplomacy and policymaking. It has frequently sought dangerous showdowns with its neighbors, including the tensions over the Paracel Islands with Vietnam in 1974, the Spratly Islands with both Vietnam in 1988 and the Philippines in 1994, the Okinotori

Islands with Japan in 2004, the Socotra Rock with South Korea in 2006, and the Senkaku/Diaoyu Islands with Japan in 2010 (Carr 2010: 11). It has active border disputes with the other emerging Asian influential, India. It is increasingly perceived as a neo-colonialist power in Africa, where it has made headway by nurturing ties to corrupt and genocidal governments. It has failed to curb North Korea's nuclear ambitions. And for all its financial and economic muscle, vast parts of China are still poor and the country's ability to project force is anemic given that it is militarily outspent by its immediate neighbors taken as a group, and more than sixfold by the United States (Carr 2010). One wonders as to exactly what kind of tectonic shift might be in the making that would render China the most powerful country in the world within the relatively short span of a generation or two. In *The Next 100 Years: A Forecast for the 21st Century*, George Friedman (2009: 88) put it succinctly: "I don't share the view that China is going to be a major world power. I don't even believe it will hold together as a unified country. But I do agree that we can't discuss the future without first discussing China."

As for China's potential cultural leadership in the world, it is readily apparent that the country is home to one of the great civilizations of all time, which has manifested itself in great contributions to philosophy, science, literature, and the arts. However, cultural creativity is by no means to be equated with cultural influence. The United States continues to be the dominant cultural force in the world, especially in terms of helping spread a liberal international order (Gilpin 1981; Ikenberry 2006; Nye 2004). This can be easily verified by quantifying the impact of popular mass culture and innovation in cultural artifacts, including new products such as the iPhone or new services such as Facebook. Box office revenues in the world, for instance, are overwhelmingly accounted for by US movies.

In *Soft Power* (2004), Joseph Nye offered a sound analysis of China's limitations as a global power. Back in 1990 he coined the term "soft power," noting that "power is becoming less fungible, less coercive, and less tangible . . . Co-optive behavioral power – getting others to want what you want – and soft power resources – cultural attraction, ideology, and international institutions – are not new . . . Yet various trends are making co-optive behavior and soft power resources more important," including the fragmentation of world politics, the great powers' use of force only as a last resort, the rise of multinational corporations, and emergence of mass cultural consumption markets (Nye 1990: 188). "Soft power rests on the ability to shape the preferences of others," he argued, noting that "a country may obtain the outcomes it wants in world politics because other countries – admiring its values, emulating its example, aspiring to its level of prosperity and openness – want to follow it" (Nye 2004: 5). And regarding the rise of Asian powers, he observed: "Further in the future, China and India loom as the giants of Asia, and there are already signs of the expansion of their soft-power resources," citing Chinese novels, movies, and basketball players as examples.

But the real promise for China and India still lies in the future ... While culture provides some soft power, domestic policies and values set limits, particularly in China, where the Communist Party fears allowing too much intellectual freedom and resists outside influences ... In foreign policy as well, both countries' reputations are burdened with problems of longstanding conflicts, over Taiwan and Kashmir, respectively. (Nye 2004: 88–89; see also Castañeda 2010)

China's reaction to the decision to award the 2010 Nobel Peace Prize to a jailed Chinese dissident further contributed to undermining China's claim to global power status. At the turn of the twenty-first century, not only the United States, but also Europe and Japan, possessed much more soft power than China.

Joseph Nye has also contributed to the debate about global powers in the twenty-first century the concept of "smart power," or "the combination of the hard power of coercion and payment with the soft power of persuasion and attraction" (Nye 2011: xiii). Table 12.2 summarizes the indicators of hard – i.e., military and economic – and soft power for the various global contenders. It is clear that as of 2012 China did not possess the combination of power resources to be a major global player; Japan, Germany, Brazil, Russia, and India even less so. Only the European Union – if it were truly a united and cohesive bloc of countries – musters formidable economic and soft resources, in many ways exceeding those of the United States, which remains the only country in the world with a military capable of intervening anywhere on the planet.

The prospects of a *Pax Sinica* during the twenty-first century thus appear to be rather slim when one considers not just the relative weight of the United States and China, but the overall balance among the most

Table 12.2 Nye's indicators of power resources, 2012

Indicator	World	USA	China	Japan	EU	Germany	Brazil	Russia	India
Basic:									
Territory, thousand sq km	148,940	9827	9597	378	4325	357	8515	17,098	3287
Population, mn	7046.4	313.9	1,350.7	127.6	509.0	81.9	198.7	143.5	1236.7
Literacy, % adult population	84.1	99.0	95.9	99.0	99.5	99.0	90.0	99.5	61.0
Military:									
Deployed nuclear warheads	4400	2,150	0[b]	0	450	0	0	1800	0[b]
Expenditure, $bn	1742.2	682.5	166.2	59.3	274.9	45.8	33.2	90.1	44.8
Expenditure, % of world	100.0	39.2	9.5	3.4	15.8	2.6	1.9	5.2	2.6
Economic									
GDP, $bn PPPs	86,057	15,685	12,471	4487	17,067	3349	2366	3373	4793
GDP, current $bn	71,918	15,685	8358	5960	16,634	3400	2253	2015	1842
Per capita GDP, current $PPPs	12,213	49,965	9233	35,178	33,527	40,901	11,909	23,501	3876
Internet users per 100 people	35.6	81.0	42.3	79.1	75.3	84.0	49.8	53.3	12.6
Stock of outward foreign direct investment, $bn[a]	23,593	5191	509[c]	1055	9837[h]	1547	233	413	118

Soft:

Universities ranked in top 100	100	30	3[d]	6	32	3	0	0	0
Films produced	6573	819	584[e]	441	1512[f]	212	99	140	1255
Foreign students, thousands	3573	685	72[g]	142	1215[h]	201	15	130	22

Notes: [a] Not included in Nye (2011: 159).

[b] China has 250 non-deployed warheads and India 110.

[c] Excluding Hong Kong ($bn 1310).

[d] Excluding Hong Kong (3 universities).

[e] Excluding Hong Kong (70 films) and Macao (4).

[f] Includes Denmark, Finland, France, Germany, Ireland, Netherlands, Spain, Sweden, and the UK.

[g] Excluding Hong Kong (10,300 students) and Macao (13,500).

[h] Includes foreign investments and foreign students within the EU, i.e., from one member country into another.

Sources: World Development Indicators, except for territory (CIA World Factbook), literacy (United Nations Development Program, and World Development Indicators), nuclear warheads (SIPRI Yearbook 2013), stock of outward foreign direct investment (World Investment Report 2013), universities (Top University Rankings, www.topuniversities.com), films produced (UNESCO Institute for Statistics), and foreign students (UNESCO Institute of Statistics, Global Education Digest 2012, and Institute of International Education).

important economies and economic regions. While China's economic performance since the mid 1980s is impressive, it is nowhere near becoming the dominant force that Britain was during much of the nineteenth century and the United States during the twentieth. For starters, the US is not the only large economy in the world. Western Europe and Japan are large and unlikely to decline in absolute terms, although they certainly

Figure 12.1 Major economies, 1870–2008 (GDP in million dollars)
Note: GDP calculated using constant 1990 Geary–Khamis international dollars.
Source: Angus Maddison, *Historical Statistics of the World Economy: 1–2008 AD.*
www.ggdc.net/maddison (accessed August 20, 2011).

will relative to others (see Figure 12.1). Moreover, India, Indonesia, and Brazil are also likely to become much larger economies, partially diluting China's relative economic weight. The World Bank estimates that China will be the most important growth pole in the global economy over the next two decades, but by no means the only one (World Bank 2011b: 46). Moreover, from a demographic point of view, China will be second to India in terms of population size by 2030 (1.6 billion versus 1.4 billion), and NATO countries will almost reach 1 billion (Sciubba 2012: 67). Therefore, China's new status must be examined in a global context, not just relative to the United States. And it is also important to note that while the US and China may soon become economies of comparable size, the former will continue to be about four times as rich on a per capita basis as the latter, with enormous implications for technological development and geopolitical power.

From an economic point of view, China already is the second largest economy in the world, but it is unlikely to ever represent half or even one third of the global economy simply because the other large economies probably will not decline much, and there are several other emerging economies – such as Brazil and India – that are also likely to grow vigorously. Most importantly, China will continue to be haunted by sharp income inequalities and a relatively low level of per capita income (Figure 12.2). Demographically, China is on the decline, as discussed in Chapter 4, and may soon be outnumbered by India (Howe and Jackson 2012). It is relevant to note that there is no instance in history of a society with a shrinking population becoming a regional or global leader. The launching of the Spanish and British empires, for example, were preceded by rapid population growth. China's economic transformation has no parallel in human history for a society as large, especially because of the pace and intensity of the change, although young India may well surprise the world with an equally breathtaking makeover.

Similarly, and in spite of China's new role as a major creditor nation (see Chapters 2 and 3), the renminbi is unlikely to displace the dollar and a European currency (the Deutsche Mark or the euro) as the world's most important stores of value. For starters, the Chinese currency is not convertible. One would need to first see a successful transition to convertibility staged over many years. Moreover, a reserve currency requires free capital flows, something that the relatively backward Chinese banking system cannot presently cope with (Walter and Howie 2011). In addition,

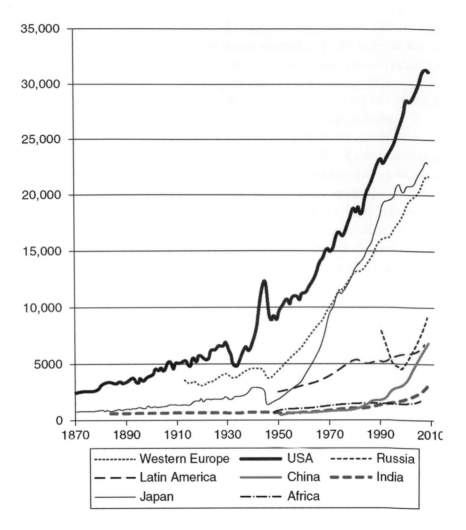

Figure 12.2 GDP per capita for major economies, 1870–2008 (in dollars)
Note: GDP per capita calculated using constant 1990 Geary–Khamis international dollars.
Source: Angus Maddison, *Historical Statistics of the World Economy: 1–2008 AD*. www.ggdc.net/maddison (accessed August 20, 2011).

political stability and a democratic form of government subject to checks and balances are also important foundations underpinning global reserve currencies. As far as the eye can see, then, the twenty-first century does not include a globally dominant Chinese currency. In sum, based on current levels and trends, it is difficult to envision a world in which China could be the dominant global military, economic, financial, or soft power.

Chinese views on China's global ascendancy

To further put in perspective China's potential rise as a global power, it is instructive to examine the views of Chinese academics and policymakers. Contemporary Chinese foreign policy hesitates between keeping a low profile and asserting Chinese interests abroad, with political stability (i.e., continued Communist Party rule) as a big factor looming large in the background. Among his many contributions to Chinese statecraft, Deng Xiaoping's proposal to "hide brightness, cherish obscurity," is still influential within Chinese foreign policy circles, but by no means the dominant approach anymore (Economy 2010).

There is considerable disagreement among scholars, policymakers, and even party officials over the sustainability of China's economic growth given competition from lower-wage countries, overreliance on exports, asset-price inflation (especially in real estate), rampant pollution, population aging, urban congestion, rising income inequality, and domestic political instability (for reviews, see Cheng 2011 and Kokubun and Wang 2004). For instance, according to Hu Angang, an influential professor at Tsinghua University, China faces many challenges, but will continue to grow economically and eventually become "a new type of superpower," focused on science, technology, culture, and human well-being. After painstakingly cataloguing the economic, social, and environmental constraints on China's continued development, he concludes that "China's rise, or whether or not China is able to emerge as a superpower by 2020, is a scenario rife with uncertainty" (Hu 2011: 157). Equally keen on noting China's limitations is Justin Yifu Lin, Senior Vice President and Chief Economist of the World Bank, the first Chinese national to hold the position. (He was born in Taiwan, but defected to the People's Republic of China in 1979.) In his book, *Demystifying the Chinese Economy*, originally written in Chinese, he concludes that "China has great potential to continue the current dynamic growth for another two decades or more . . . To achieve that, China needs to overcome many intrinsic problems," including income disparities, the rural–urban gap, inefficient use of resources, environmental imbalances, external imbalances, currency appreciation, corruption, and education focused on quantity rather than quality (Lin 2012: 17–19).

In a rare article co-authored by leading experts from both the US and China, Joseph Nye and Wang Jisi, Dean of School of International Studies at Peking University, document that, while China is increasingly adopting policies to promote its influence, the country "is far from the United States' or Europe's equal in soft power at this point, but it would be foolish to ignore the important gains it is making" (Nye and Wang 2009: 22).

Given these constraints on Chinese global influence, many Chinese experts propose a focused and somewhat limited foreign policy agenda that is more congruent with a country seeking to protect its interests on the global stage than with one vying for superpower status let alone global supremacy. According to Wang Jisi, "for both policy analysts in China and China watchers abroad, China's grand strategy is a field still to be plowed." He emphasizes that the Chinese foreign policy community contains many different views about the role of China in the world. Based on a realist assessment of China's power and the pronouncements of its leaders, Wang notes that China's foreign policy agenda will be limited to safeguarding "the interests of sovereignty, security, and development," to quote President Hu Jintao. Thus, Chinese foreign policy is likely to be geared towards maintaining the Communist Party in power and securing the resources for continued economic growth as opposed to global domination. While some Chinese policy experts see the US as the enemy to be confronted on the global stage, Premier Wen Jiabao has pragmatically stated that "our common interests far outweigh our differences" (Wang 2011). In a similar vein, Hu Angang, the economics professor at Tsinghua University, favors a foreign policy shift in order to sustain its development and to ensure that "China and the world can respond to [the] challenges together" (Hu 2011: 157, 161).

These views are echoed by Zhu Feng, a professor at Peking University, who argues that "China's rise will be peaceful" because it has everything to gain from being a participant in a US-dominated world – at least for now. "Only the United States possesses the full range of traditional great power attributes: size of territory and population, military capability and readiness, economic and technological superiority, political stability, and 'soft power' attributes, such as cultural and ideological appeal" (Zhu 2008:

40–41). He believes that China is at best an "adolescent" power facing significant domestic political challenges. "Given Beijing's economic and domestic political objectives, it is in China's interest to cooperate with the American strategic order ... In the present unipolar system, China is a satisfied, cooperative and peaceful country" (Zhu 2008: 54). There are, however, more assertive voices within the Chinese foreign policy community. For example, Shen Dingli, Executive Vice Dean of the Institute of International Affairs at Fudan University, is among the more nationalist scholars. He has provided a rationale for the establishment of Chinese military bases abroad (Economy 2010; see also Shen 2009).

Is global influence a zero-sum game?

It is often forgotten that the rise of Europe, Japan, and even China could be a boost to the position of the United States as a global leader. Each of the other three big political–economic actors has an intimate relationship with the United States, albeit of a different kind. They are different in scope and nature, to be sure, but the United States continues to play the central role in brokering deals among the other relevant powers in the world, and in providing leadership for new initiatives and policies or in hindering them. The historian William McNeill (1963) highlighted the importance throughout the centuries of contact between civilizations for mutual growth and prosperity. He coined the term "ecumene" to refer to such synergistic relationships. These exchanges, shaped by geography, biology, and technology, explain patterns of development of societies and global powers (Morris 2010). It is simply wrong to assume that civilizations, empires, and global powers are always in conflict with one another, that one's rise comes at the expense of another's decline, or that established powers cannot possibly benefit from the rise to prominence of others.

In a similar vein, the economist Paul Krugman (1994) has duly noted that countries in general, and global powers in particular, can and often do have complementary economies, with each of them specializing in different types of products and services, or designing and branding them differently, and mutually benefiting from trade and investment. "While competitive problems could arise in principle, as a practical, empirical matter the major nations of the world are not to any significant degree in economic competition with each other," he argued, adding that "of course, there is always a rivalry for status and power, countries that grow faster will see their political rank rise." Noting that mercantilist policies rarely succeed in the long run, he famously observed that "countries do not compete with each other the way corporations do."

A similar argument holds on the issue of global political, diplomatic, and military influence and competition. Aaron Friedberg, a professor at Princeton and former deputy assistant for national security affairs in the Office of the Vice President under Dick Cheney, embraces the view that global power is not zero-sum. "China's rise presents an intellectual challenge," he argues in his book, *A Contest for Supremacy*, because it does not conform to conventional categories. China is "neither a friend nor, at this point, an avowed enemy" (Friedberg 2011: 264). He advocates policies of engagement and openness that help the US benefit from the rise of China as an economic and technological superpower.

Another prominent debate is how China's rise might affect the global economic order. Ian Bremmer's book, *The End of the Free Market* (2010a), offered an analysis of the contrast between the free-market ideology championed by the US and the state capitalism of China and other emerging economies as a key characteristic of the twenty-first century. Bremmer argued that free markets and state capitalism are not only dependent on each other, but also complementary in other ways. For instance, during the crisis that started in 2007, continued growth in China and other emerging economies helped cushion the impact of financial catastrophe on the global economy. While Bremmer is an advocate of a free-market system supported by effective political institutions, he argues that there is room for mutual learning and adaptation. A related argument to Bremmer's has been proposed by John Ikenberry (2011: 57), who observed that "China and the other emerging great powers do not want to contest the basic rules and principles of the liberal economic order; they wish to gain more authority and leadership within it."

Joseph Nye has grasped the landscape of global power in the twenty-first century best when he reminded us that the decline of one power need not necessarily result in the rise of another, as illustrated by the case of Rome, or vice versa, that is, when the rise of one power brings about the relative decline of another. "The problem of American power in the twenty-first century, then, is not one of decline but what to do in light of the realization that even the largest country cannot achieve outcomes it wants without the help of others" (Nye 2010: 12; see also Kissinger 2011: 526; Nathan 2011; Swaine 2011). The argument equally holds if one substitutes "Chinese" for "American," and "resurgence" for "decline." It seems safe to assume that, unlike the nineteenth and twentieth centuries, the twenty-first will probably lack a dominant, let alone hegemonic, global power. We are headed towards a polycentric or multipolar world. "We are now living in a G-Zero world," Ian Bremmer and Nouriel Roubini argued, "one in which no single country or bloc of countries has the political and economic leverage – or the will – to drive a truly international agenda" (2011: 2). We still do not know how a multipolar world will operate, and whether international cooperation or conflict will be the norm.

13 Coping with uncertainty and complexity

We have documented in previous chapters the key economic, socio-demographic, political, and geopolitical global turning points. Taken as a whole, these points of inflexion define the ways in which the twenty-first century is so tantalizingly mercurial, uncertain, and complex when compared to the twentieth. Table 13.1 summarizes the turning points as well as the key drivers and consequences.

As far as the economy and business are concerned, the key turning points into the twenty-first century have to do with the rise of the emerging economies. By the end of the second decade of the new century, more than half of global output will be accounted for by emerging and developing countries. These economies are also positioning themselves as big exporters of commodities, manufactured goods, and services. This turning point is driven by differentials in growth rates for both GDP and population. A second, related turning point has to do with the fact that emerging and developing countries have come to own more than half of total foreign exchange reserves in the world, a shift fueled by their large current account surpluses. They are also blessed by historically low levels of external debt, which implies that they enjoy an unprecedented capacity to invest abroad. Emerging and developing countries have actually become a key source for the funding needs of developed economies.

These two turning points hold important consequences, including a redistribution of geo-economic power, shifts in the location and characteristics of consumer markets, a rising potential for systemic global financial disruptions as far as current account imbalances persist, and, on a more optimistic note, a reduction in poverty, assuming that the emerging economies allocate their increasingly abundant financial resources in a fruitful way.

The rise of the emerging economies has come hand in hand with the appearance of large and capable emerging-market multinationals in a variety of industries. A third of the largest firms in the world, 29 percent

Table 13.1 Major turning points, drivers, and consequences in the twenty-first century

Turning point	Key drivers of sustained shift	Main consequences
Economy & Business:		
Emerging & developing economies account for nearly half of total output (Ch. 2).	Differentials in growth rates for both GDP and population.	• Redistribution of geo-economic power. • Shifts in consumer markets.
Emerging & developing economies own 75 percent of foreign exchange reserves (Ch. 2).	Large surpluses in the current account of the balance of payments.	• Potential for systemic global financial disruptions. • Reduction in poverty.
Nearly 30 percent of the total number of multinational firms are emerging-market multinationals, and they accounted for 41 percent of new foreign direct investment flows in 2006–2010 (Ch. 3).	Search for markets, inputs, and strategic assets; large current account surpluses.	• Enhanced competition in global industries. • New hubs of decision making.
By the year 2027 more than half of the world's population will be part of the middle class, and the Indian and Chinese middle-class markets will exceed the European and American markets in purchasing power (Ch. 7).	Growth of emerging economies. Rising income and wealth inequality in Europe and the United States, which squeezes the middle class.	• Shift in global consumer markets towards Asia. • China and India will participate in writing the rules of competition and product standards for a wide variety of industries.
The number of high-net-worth individuals continues to grow, and more than half of them will be women by 2030 (Ch. 7).	Increasing income and wealth inequality. Women get more education, and they live longer than men.	• Social and political tensions. • More prominent role for women in business, finance, and society.

Table 13.1 (cont.)

Turning point	Key drivers of sustained shift	Main consequences
By the year 2014, the number of active mobile broadband subscriptions in the developed countries reached a whopping 84 per 100 inhabitants. In the developing and emerging economies it was only 21 per 100 (Ch. 8).	Investments in the infrastructure for information and communications. Declining cost of new technology.	• Reconfiguration of production, distribution, and consumption on a global scale. • Increasing inequality, at least initially (the global digital divide). • Redefinition of how citizens relate to the government.
Growing emphasis on institutions as a determinant of economic development, including culture, laws, regulation, taken-for-granted assumptions (Ch. 9).	Failure of development efforts based on infrastructure and large-scale industry.	• Rethinking of development policies. • Danger of institutions becoming a new panacea.
In 2011 the proportion of the adult population with a bank account surpassed 50 percent for the first time, though still leaving half of the world's population financially excluded. In the developed countries, the proportion was 85 percent (Ch. 11).	Failure of the traditional business model of banking, especially in developing countries.	• Financial exclusion. • Opportunities for use of new technology to reach a majority of the population.
Society & Demography: Population aging: Inverted age pyramids (Ch. 4).	Decline in fertility due to new role of women in society; increased life expectancy.	• Changes in consumer, social, and political behavior. • Increasing income inequality. • Increasing government debt.

More people live in cities than the countryside (Ch. 4).	Relative prices and changes in productivity by sector.	• Growing urban challenges. • Declining fertility. • Sedentary lifestyle.
Africa and South Asia will be fastest-growing regions in terms of population (Ch. 4).	High, though declining, fertility rates, which are higher than in other parts of the world.	• Global redistribution of consumption and geo-economic power.
More people suffer from obesity than from hunger (Ch. 4).	Rising incomes; abundance of (bad) food; sedentary lifestyles.	• Changes in consumption and social behavior. • Improved life opportunities.
Income inequality within countries on the rise (Ch. 6).	Skills gap; rural–urban duality; lower taxes and transfers.	• Growing social problems and political protests.
Poverty on the decline (Ch. 6).	Economic growth in emerging and developing countries.	• Improved life opportunities.
Politics:		
Budget deficits and sovereign debt a bigger problem in rich than in emerging and developing economies (Ch. 2).	Declining competitiveness; population aging; political paralysis.	• Further budget cuts. • Decline in state capacity. • Financial tensions.
Declining legitimacy and capacity of the state (Ch. 5).	Social unrest; political revolts; state retrenchment; inequality.	• Reduced ability to deal with problems, local and global. • Failed states.
Geopolitics:		
Income inequality across countries on the decline (Ch. 6).	Higher growth rates in emerging and developing countries.	• Redistribution of geo-economic power.

Table 13.1 (cont.)

Turning point	Key drivers of sustained shift	Main consequences
Proliferation of failed states, which outnumber dictatorships (Ch. 5).	Income inequality; civil wars; resource curse.	• Supply and shipping risks. • Illicit trade. • Terrorism.
Top scientists predict that, without corrective action, climate change will become irreversible at some tipping point during the twenty-first century (Ch. 10).	Greenhouse emissions.	• Food shortages. • More frequent and severe environmental disasters. • Flooding of coastal areas.
By 2030 food prices could be twice as high as in 2011, and half of the world's population could be affected by serious water shortages (Ch. 10).	Climate change; pollution; changes in dietary preferences; urbanization.	• Social unrest and political protests. • Geopolitical instability.
India will be the biggest country in terms of population, China the largest in output, and the United States the richest of the large economies (Ch. 12).	Global demographic shifts; higher growth in emerging economies; technological innovation.	• Global redistribution of power. • Multipolarity. • Geopolitical instability. • G-zero world.

of the total number of multinational firms, and 29 percent of new foreign direct investment flows originate from emerging and developing economies. These firms are expanding throughout the world in search of markets, inputs, and strategic assets, especially technology and brands. Emerging-market multinationals have provoked a fundamental reshaping of competition in global industries and the formation of new hubs of decision making in the leading cities of the emerging world, from São Paulo to Dubai, Mumbai, and Shanghai. Due to the rise of the middle class in emerging economies, the center of gravity of global consumption will shift towards Asia. China and India will participate in setting the rules of competition and product standards for automobiles, consumer electronics, and financial services, among other industries.

Rising income and wealth inequality will expand the markets for luxury goods and services, and the rapid increase in the number of women who are millionaires will bring important changes to savings, consumption, and investing. Global patterns of inequality have also been shaped by technological change, which has generated a global digital divide, at least in the short run. Another important shift will be the emphasis on soft institutions as opposed to infrastructure and heavy industry when it comes to designing policies to help developing countries improve the lot of their populations. Finally, the breakdown of the traditional business model of banking was made readily apparent by the financial crisis of 2008, but had been in the making for decades given the slow adoption of new technology in financial services and the persistence of financial exclusion in the developing world.

In social and demographic terms, the twenty-first century will be characterized by rapid population aging primarily due to the decline in fertility, itself the result of women's new role in society, and to increased life expectancy. Japan and many Western and Eastern European countries already have more people above age 60 than below age 20. China, Russia, the United States, and 30 other countries are following suit. The consequences of aging are complex and still unfolding, and they include changes in consumer, political and social behavior, increasing income inequality, and rising government indebtedness. A second key sociodemographic turning point is that more people live in cities than in the countryside for the first time in human history, a process driven by differences in relative prices and changes in productivity between rural and urban areas in addition to shifting cultural preferences and social aspirations. As a consequence, the world will face mounting urban challenges, including pollution and infrastructure deficiencies, among others. Fertility will most likely decline as a result of urbanization, thus accelerating population aging. The sedentary urban lifestyle will also bring with it social and behavioral changes. Africa and South Asia will be the fastest-growing regions in terms of population, leading to a global redistribution of consumption and geo-economic power. Urbanization and rising incomes are also fueling a fourth socio-demographic turning point, namely, the rise in obesity, which has now become a greater problem than hunger.

Inequality within countries continues to rise due to the skills gap, differences in opportunities in rural versus urban areas, and a drastic decline in the state's role as a redistributor of income and wealth. Inequality's most momentous consequence will be a greater potential for political frictions and upheavals. Paradoxically, poverty is on the decline thanks to growth in emerging and developing countries.

From a political perspective, the twenty-first century is synonymous with high levels of government debt in the richest countries, driven by declining competitiveness relative to the emerging economies, population aging, and political paralysis. Further budget cuts, a decline in the state's capacity to address and solve social and economic problems, and global financial tensions are the main consequence of the sovereign debt burden inherited from the last quarter of the twentieth century and the aftermath of the global financial crisis. The declining legitimacy and capacity of the state has been exacerbated by social unrest, political revolts, budget cuts, and rising inequality within countries. States are steadily losing their monopolies over information, communication, and violence. The Internet and mobile telecommunications were invented in the twentieth century, but their effects on the state's legitimacy and capacity to act have only become readily apparent since 2001. Phenomena such as WikiLeaks, the Arab Spring, and the sharp increase in terrorist attacks remind us that we live in a brave new world.

The shrinking legitimacy and capacity of the state in the United States and Europe is worrisome. In Europe, the row over the future of the common currency has induced an identity crisis and raised many doubts about the effectiveness of European institutions. Young people are suffering from the consequences of a bad economy more than any other group. Europe faces fundamental decisions if it is to overcome the challenges of the twenty-first century. For instance, it seems impossible to promise pension and healthcare benefits to a retiree over his or her life expectancy of 20 years after age 65 given that the cost is roughly equivalent to the lifetime taxes paid by two young working people. The United States has also gone down a path that seems unsustainable and utterly paradoxical. For example, it leads the world in incarceration rates and urban social dislocation, with a year in prison now costing taxpayers more than two semesters at an Ivy League university.

The world also looks very different through a geopolitical lens. Income inequality across countries is on the decline due to the rise of the emerging economies, leading to a redistribution of geo-economic power. In some countries the state has failed or nearly failed in the sense that central authority has broken down, with fatal consequences in terms of illicit trade, terrorism, and disruption to global supply networks and shipping lines.

A third major turning point has to do with the environment. Scientists predict that climate change could become irreversible beyond a tipping point if corrective action is not taken, with grave consequences for food production, the frequency of environmental disasters, and the flooding of coastal areas. Food and water are in fact likely to become scarce and pricey, heightening social unrest, political protests, and geopolitical instability.

As to the overall balance of power in the world, during most of the twenty-first century India will be the biggest country in terms of population, China the largest economy in output, and the United States the richest among the largest economies. Multipolarity is likely to be the norm.

The four institutional gearboxes shaping global dynamics

The set of trends, changes, and events just described feed into each other in highly complex ways. We have only analyzed them in this book if they represent a major turning point in the global context. Globalization has in fact produced a worldwide system in which economic, socio-demographic, political, and geopolitical variables interact with each other to potentially create outcomes that are complex in their consequences and uncertain in the sense that we cannot even begin to calculate the probability of their occurring within a certain time frame. They are difficult to anticipate in the raw sense that we have little basis for adapting our present behavior in response to their potential unfolding in the future.

Let us use the concept of the *gearbox* to capture the uncertain and complex interactions among the turning points and variables in the four domains of the economy, the society, politics, and geopolitics. A gearbox is an essential part of the transmission mechanism in vehicles because it regulates the speed of the wheels independent of the rotational speed of the engine. Thus, a gearbox can be seen as a device that allows the vehicle to operate under fluid circumstances, such as starting, stopping, cruising, or going uphill. Societies, economies, and the entire global system also need "institutional gearboxes" that transform one dynamic into another in different situations. Change is a quintessential aspect of economic, social, political, and geopolitical life; its causes and consequences are regulated by a series of institutional gearboxes.

The four most important institutional gearboxes shaping global dynamics in the twenty-first country are the labor market, the political representation system, the state apparatus, and the international system of states. If they work properly, they help economies, societies, and the entire global system grow and prosper. But if they don't function well, they transform tensions in one domain into tensions in another, thus increasing the potential for systemic disruptions. Figure 13.1 captures the complex interactions among the key economic, socio-demographic, political, and geopolitical variables within and across the four domains.

As an institutional gearbox, the labor market operates at the boundary between the economic and socio-demographic domains. It has become readily apparent that labor markets are no longer working for citizens – for all of them, that is. Duality in work opportunities and outcomes has become a rampant feature in developed, emerging, and developing economies alike. The gulf between rural and urban areas, younger and older age groups, skilled and unskilled workers, tradable and non-tradable sectors, permanent and temporary, full-time and part-time, and formal and informal has widened considerably over the last two or three decades. One important consequence is rising income inequality within countries;

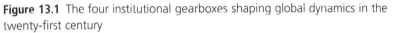

Figure 13.1 The four institutional gearboxes shaping global dynamics in the twenty-first century
Notes: Solid arrow indicates increase while dotted arrow indicates decrease. For the role of the financial system, see the text.

another is persistently high unemployment among the young in developed, emerging, and developing countries.

The political representation system works at the intersection between the socio-demographic and the political domains. While democracy has never been so widespread around the world, nearly a quarter of humanity continues to live under authoritarian or totalitarian regimes. In addition, there are a record number of failed states. If that weren't enough, serious doubts could be cast on the quality of democratic life in many parts of Latin America, Eastern Europe, Africa, and South and Central Asia. Ecuador, Venezuela, the Ukraine, Russia, Thailand, Nigeria, and Angola are just a few examples. Analysts are divided as to whether the Arab Spring of 2011 will prove to be a harbinger of democracy or not. Even in the mature democracies of Western Europe and North America one observes an alarming degree of disenfranchisement and a loss of legitimacy of the basic democratic institutions. Protest and "occupy" movements are proliferating.

The state apparatus, the third key gearbox, is situated at the border between the political and geopolitical domains. As a machine of administration, the state is presently broken or nearly broken in many parts of the world. In the developed countries, government indebtedness has skyrocketed due to changes in international competition, loss in competitiveness, and population aging. In many developing countries, and even some emerging economies, state-building is incomplete, with persistent problems of legal predictability and personal security. The retrenchment of the state has both economic and ideological roots, and it has reduced state capacity, i.e., the ability to anticipate and cope with problems. The increasing weakness of the state apparatus has made it far more difficult to deal with economic inequality, political disenfranchisement, environmental degradation, and terrorism, to name but a few challenges of our time.

Finally, the international system of states operates at the edge separating the economic and geopolitical domains. The twenty-first-century system of states is increasingly becoming a G-zero world as a result of the coincidence of two interrelated trends, namely, the rise of the emerging economies and the lack of clear global leadership over persistent problems such as financial instability, failed states, terrorism, environmental degradation, and climate change. It has become readily apparent that there is considerable strain and confusion in the international system of states as the balance of geo-economic power shifts.

The pervasiveness of financial markets

We have not yet dealt with the role that financial markets play across the space described in Figure 13.1. They actually permeate each of the four domains. Financial markets are both local and global in their reach, and they can reduce or exacerbate system disruptions, as the crisis that started in 2007 illustrates. A dynamic and solid financial system is absolutely necessary to ensure economic development and social cohesion. The financial system allocates resources and rewards within and across the economic, socio-demographic, political, and geopolitical realms. We have seen in the first decade of the twenty-first century a situation in which the financial system can tailspin into an episode of severe instability generating immense economic and social dislocation and hardship.

The global economic and financial crisis has been the most complex, though not yet the deepest, in history, precisely because it has taken place in a context of intense globalization. Its rapid spread around the developed world calls into question some basic aspects of modern finance. The ill effects of sophisticated financial products have exposed the potentially destructive effects of big financial institutions and operators. Policy-makers and central bankers have wrestled, and continue to struggle, with the consequences. Most developed economies simultaneously went into recession for the first time in more than half a century. Unemployment rose to levels not seen since the Great Depression.

The lack of proper financial regulation and the absence of sufficient and effective supervision lie at the origins of the crisis and its propagation throughout the world. These problems have afflicted both "market-based" financial systems such as those of the US and the UK, and "bank-based" systems like those of Continental Europe. Financial globalization can only work if regulation and supervision aim at limiting the frequency and intensity of the seemingly inevitable episodes of financial distress that are likely to occur. Regulation needs to pay attention to different kinds of financial activities (from deposit-taking and loans, to trading and invest-ment banking), and different kinds of financial operators by size and complexity. Financial innovation in a context of free capital flows needs to be structured in such a way that economic growth is sustained and sustainable.

The crisis has also exposed the inadequacy of international institutions. The G20 has become the most important club when it comes to global economic and financial matters. It is not yet clear if its size and membership is ideal for effective policy coordination and decision making. The insuffi-cient presence of emerging economies in international agencies, especially the IMF, continues to pose problems of global governance given that some of the most important players do not have enough representation.

What is to be done?

Complexity and uncertainty make for an explosive combination in any system, be it a candy manufacturing plant, a nuclear power station, an economy, or the global community of states. The landscape depicted in

Figure 13.1 is rather daunting until one begins to realize that the tensions leading to systemic disruptions could be ameliorated by improving the functioning of the four key institutional gearboxes. Labor markets can be reformed and reinvigorated through concerted action by governments and key stakeholders in the private sector, always in the direction of greater flexibility and attention to the needs of both employees and firms. The engagement and involvement of employees is generally conducive to higher productivity and satisfaction.

Systems of political representation will need to address the growing dissatisfaction of citizens with government. People are increasingly disappointed and resorting to unconventional ways to manifest their displeasure, as in the cases of the various "occupy" and "indignant" movements. It seems as if in contemporary democracies, taking the temperature through periodic elections is not enough to ensure that citizens' needs and wants are taken into account. Corruption has also contributed to the high levels of political indifference among the public. The disaffection of the young is particularly worrying because they are the mainstream electorate of the future.

The view that a smaller government is always better must also be debated and reassessed. The revolution initiated by Thatcher and Reagan in the 1980s framed the discussion in the wrong way. What matters is efficiency and effectiveness, not size. We need to ensure that states have the capacity to act locally and globally. The financial crisis has made it readily apparent that we need a state with the ability to gather information, constrain perilous behavior, and anticipate problems. Unfortunately, this debate is now overshadowed by the sovereign debt crisis affecting most of the developed world. The state's capacity to act, however, is our first line of defense against present and future economic, financial, political, environmental, and security dangers. Moreover, the ideology of minimal government has artificially cast the business community and the state as being at odds with each other, as if they were sworn enemies. We must abandon this idea and look for ways to make the private and public sectors collaborate to tackle the challenges of the twenty-first century.

The international system of states needs new institutions for representation and decision making. We must strike a balance between inclusiveness and effectiveness without side-tracking smaller states and communities. The world of the twenty-first century is dancing to a new

musical score played by a new set of musicians. We need to institutional-
ize who plays each instrument and to what tune. We cannot afford
simplistic solutions in a multipolar world in which several major global
and regional powers will be the norm.

Turning points are not destiny. They are not tipping points, necessarily.
Some may be reversible while the impact and meaning of others may be
malleable and subject to the countervailing forces of human and societal
agency. The economic, socio-demographic, political, and geopolitical
global turning points analyzed in this book are certainly game-changers.
They are fundamentally reshaping life on the planet. The sooner we
understand their implications, the better prepared we will be to cope with
them and potentially turn them to our advantage. And in order to do so,
we need to repair the four key institutional gearboxes: the labor market,
the representation system, the state apparatus, and the international
system of states.

References

Abdelal, Rawi. 2007. *Capital Rules: The Construction of Global Finance.* Cambridge, MA: Harvard University Press

Acemoglu, Daron and James A. Robinson. 2012. *Why Nations Fail: The Origins of Power, Prosperity, and Poverty.* New York: Crown Business.

Acemoglu, Daron, Philippe Aghion, Leonardo Bursztyn, and David Hemous. 2010. "The Environment and Directed Technical Change." www.econom ics.harvard.edu/faculty/aghion/files/Environment%20and%20Directed.pdf (accessed September 2, 2011).

Acemoglu, Daron, Simon Johnson, and James A. Robinson. 2001. "The Colonial Origins of Comparative Development: An Empirical Investigation." *American Economic Review* 91(5): 1369–1401.

Acharya, Viral V. and Matthew P. Richardson. 2009. "Causes of the Financial Crisis." *Critical Review* 21(2–3): 195–210.

Ahl, Helene. 2006. "Why Research on Women Entrepreneurs Needs New Directions." *Entrepreneurship Theory and Practice* 30(5): 595–621.

Aker, Jenny C. and Isaac M. Mbiti. 2010. "Mobile Phones and Economic Development in Africa." *Journal of Economic Perspectives* 24(3): 207–232.

Akerlof, George A. and Robert J. Shiller. 2009. *Animal Spirits: How Human Psychology Drives the Economy, and Why it Matters for Global Capitalism.* Princeton University Press.

Albino, Vito, Azzurra Balice, and Rosa Maria Dangelico. 2009. "Environmental Strategies and Green Product Development: An Overview on Sustainability-Driven Companies." *Business Strategy and the Environment* 18(2): 83–96.

Alnaser, W. E. and N. W. Alnaser. 2011. "The Status of Renewable Energy in the GCC Countries." *Renewable and Sustainable Energy* 15(6): 3074–3098.

Amsden, Alice H. 1989. *Asia's Next Giant: South Korea and Late Industrialization.* Oxford University Press.

Amsden, Alice H. and Takashi Hikino. 1994. "Project Execution Capability, Organizational Know-How and Conglomerate Corporate Growth in Late Industrialization." *Industrial and Corporate Change* 3(1): 111–147.

Anand, Sudhir and Paul Segal. 2008. "What Do We Know about Global Income Inequality?" *Journal of Economic Literature* 46(1): 57–94.

Anderson, Kym, John Cockburn, and Will Martin. 2011. "Would Freeing Up World Trade Reduce Poverty and Inequality? The Vexed Role of Agricultural Distortions." *The World Economy* 34: 487–515.

Atsmon, Yuval, Peter Child, Richard Dobbs, and Laxman Narasimhan. 2012. "Winning The $30 Trillion Decathlon: Going for Gold in Emerging Markets." *McKinsey Quarterly* (August). www.mckinsey.com/insights/strategy/winning_the_30_trillion_decathlon_going_for_gold_in_emerging_markets (accessed March 25, 2015).

Banerjee, Abhijit and Esther Duflo. 2007. "What is Middle Class about the Middle Classes around the World?" MIT Department of Economics Working Paper 07-29.

BCG. 2009. *The 2009 BCG 100 New Global Challengers*. The Boston Consulting Group.

Beetsma, Roel and Massimo Giuliodori. 2010. "The Macroeconomic Costs and Benefits of EMU and Other Monetary Unions." *Journal of Economic Literature* 48(3): 603–641.

Berg, Andrew G. and Jonathan D. Ostry. 2011. "Inequality and Unsustainable Growth: Two Sides of the Same Coin?" IMF Staff Discussion Note SDN/11/08.

Berges, Angel, Mauro F. Guillén, Juan Pedro Moreno, and Emilio Ontiveros. 2014. *A New Era in Banking: The Landscape after the Battle*. Brookline, MA: Bibliomotion.

Berry, Heather, Mauro F. Guillén, and Arun S. Hendi. 2014. "Is there Convergence across Countries? A Spatial Approach." *Journal of International Business Studies* 45: 387–404.

Bhagwati, Jagdish. 2004. *In Defense of Globalization*. Oxford University Press.

Biggart, Nicole Woolsey and Mauro F. Guillén. 1999. "Developing Difference: Social Organization and the Rise of the Auto Industries of South Korea, Taiwan, Spain, and Argentina." *American Sociological Review* 64(5): 722–747.

Bird, Barbara and Candida Brush. 2002. "A Gendered Perspective on Organizational Creation." *Entrepreneurship: Theory and Practice* 26: 41–65.

BIS. 2014. *84th Annual Report*. Basel: Bank for International Settlements.

Blundell-Wignall, Adrian and Patrick Slovik. 2010. "The EU Stress Test and Sovereign Debt Exposures." OECD Working Papers on Finance, Insurance and Private Pensions, No. 4. Paris: OECD.

Boix, Carles. 2011. "Democracy, Development, and the International System." *American Political Science Review* 105(4): 809–828.

Bonini, Sheila M. and Jeremy M. Oppenheim. 2008. "Helping 'Green' Products Grow." *The McKinsey Quarterly* (October): 1–8.

Boserup, Ester. 1970. *Women's Role in Economic Development.* London: Earthscan.

Bosworth, Barry and Susan M. Collins. 2008. "Accounting for Growth: Comparing China and India." *Journal of Economic Perspectives* 22(1): 45–66.

Boumphrey, Sarah and Eileen Bevis. 2013. *Reaching the Emerging Middle Classes beyond BRIC.* New York: Euromonitor International.

Bremmer, Ian. 2010a. *The End of the Free Market.* New York: Portfolio.

  2010b. "Democracy in Cyberspace." *Foreign Affairs* 89(6): 86–93.

Bremmer, Ian and Nouriel Roubini. 2011. "A G-Zero World." *Foreign Affairs* 90(2): 2–7.

Breznitz, Dan and Michael Murphree. 2011. *Run of the Red Queen: Government, Innovation, Globalization, and Economic Growth in China.* New Haven, CT: Yale University Press.

Browne, Katherine E. 2001. "Female Entrepreneurship in the Caribbean: A Multisite, Pilot Investigation of Gender and Work." *Human Organization* 60(4): 326–342.

Bruni, Attila. 2005. *Gender and Entrepreneurship: An Ethnographic Approach.* New York: Routledge.

Brush, Candida G. 1992. "Research on Women Business Owners: Past Trends, a New Perspective and Future Directions." *Entrepreneurship: Theory and Practice* 16: 5–26.

Brush, Candida G., Anne de Bruin, Elizabeth J. Gatewood, and Collette Henry, eds. 2010. *Women Entrepreneurs and the Global Environment for Growth: A Research Perspective.* Cheltenham: Edward Elgar.

Brush, Candida G., Nancy M. Carter, Elizabeth J. Gatewood, Patricia G. Greene, and Myra M. Hart, eds. 2006a. *Growth-Oriented Women Entrepreneurs and their Businesses: A Global Research Perspective.* Cheltenham: Edward Elgar.

  2006b. *Women and Entrepreneurship: Contemporary Classics.* Cheltenham: Edward Elgar.

Brynjolfsson, Erik. 1993. "The Productivity Paradox of Information Technology: Review and Assessment." *Communications of the ACM* 36: 66–67.

Brynjolfsson, Erik, Lorin Hitt, and Shinkyu Yang. 2002. "Intangible Assets: Computers and Organizational Capital." *Brookings Papers on Economic Activity: Macroeconomics* 1: 137–199.

Cain, J. Salcedo, Rana Hasan, Rhoda Magsombol, and Ajay Tandon. 2008. *Accounting for Inequality in India: Evidence from Household Expenditures.* Manila: Asian Development Bank.

Cairncross, Frances. 1997. *The Death of Distance: How the Communications Revolution Will Change our Lives*. Boston, MA: Harvard Business School Press.

Capgemini and Merrill Lynch GWMA (Global Wealth Management Advisor). 2009. *World Wealth Report 2009*. www.capgemini.com/resource-file-access/resource/pdf/World_Wealth_Report_2009.pdf (accessed April 3, 2015).

2011. *World Wealth Report 2011*. www.capgemini.com/resource-file-access/resource/pdf/World_Wealth_Report_2011.pdf (accessed April 3, 2015).

Capgemini and RBC Wealth Management. 2013. *World Wealth Report 2013*. www.capgemini.com/resource-file-access/resource/pdf/wwr_2013_1.pdf (accessed April 3, 2015).

Carr, Edward. 2010. "Friend or Foe? A Special Report on China's Place in the World." *The Economist* (December 4).

Carter, N. M., C. Henry, B. Ó Cinnéide, and K. Johnston, eds. 2007. *Female Entrepreneurship: Implications for Education, Training and Policy*. London: Taylor and Francis.

Carter, Sara, Susan Anderson, and Eleanor Shaw. 2001. *Women's Business Ownership: A Review of the Academic, Popular and Internet Literature*. Glasgow: Department of Marketing, University of Strathclyde.

Carter, Sara and Eleanor Shaw. 2006. *Women's Business Ownership: Recent Research and Policy Developments*. Report to the Small Business Centre. Stirling: University of Stirling.

Cassidy, John. 2010. "After the Blowup: Laissez-Faire Economists Do Some Soul-Searching – and Finger-Pointing." *The New Yorker* (January 11): 28–33.

Castañeda, Jorge. 2010. "Not Ready for Prime Time." *Foreign Affairs* 89(5): 109–123.

Castells, Manuel. 1996. *The Rise of the Network Society*. Cambridge, MA: Blackwell.

Charles, Maria. 2011. "A World of Difference: International Trends in Women's Economic Status." *Annual Review of Sociology* 37: 355–371.

Charness, Gary and Uri Gneezy. 2012. "Strong Evidence for Gender Differences in Risk Taking," *Journal of Economic Behavior and Organization* 83(1): 50–58.

Chen, Chuan and Ryan J. Orr. 2009. "Chinese Contractors in Africa." *Journal of Construction Engineering and Management* 135: 1201–1210.

Chen, Jiandong, Dai Dai, Ming Pu, Wenxuan Hou, and Qiaobin Feng. 2010. "The Trend of the Gini Coefficient of China." Manchester: Brooks World Poverty Industry Working Paper 109.

Cheng, Li. 2011. "Introduction: A Champion for Chinese Optimism and Exceptionalism." In Hu Angang, *China in 2020: A New Type of Superpower*. Washington, DC: Brookings Institution Press, pp. xv–xl.

Chien, John Chung-Ling and Noam Lior. 2011. "Concentrating Solar Thermal Power as a Viable Alternative in China's Electricity Supply." *Energy Policy* 39(12): 7622–7636.

Clark, Gregory. 2007. *A Farewell to Alms: A Brief Economic History of the World*. Princeton University Press.

Collins, Randall. 1999. *Macrohistory: Essays in the Sociology of the Long Run*. Stanford University Press.

Cottarelli, Carlo and Andrea Schaechter. 2010. "Long-Term Trends in Public Finances in the G-7 Economies." IMF Staff Position Note SPN/10/13. Washington, DC: International Monetary Fund.

Croson, Rachel and Uri Gneezy. 2009. "Gender Differences in Preferences." *Journal of Economic Literature* 47(2): 448–474.

Crow, Ben, Nichole Zlatunich, and Brian Fulfrost. 2009. "Mapping Global Inequalities: Beyond Income Inequality to Multi-Dimensional Inequalities." *Journal of International Development* 21(8): 1051–1065.

CSM. 1989. "Kissinger's World View." *Christian Science Monitor* (January 6): 19.

Dadush, Uri and Shimelse Ali. 2012. *In Search of the Global Middle Class: A New Index*. New York: Carnegie Endowment for International Peace.

Davies, James B., Susanna Sandstrom, Anthony Shorrocks, and Edward Wolff. 2009. "The Global Pattern of Household Wealth." *Journal of International Development* 21(8): 1111–1124.

De Jong, Jeroen P. J. and Erik de Bruijn. 2013. "Innovation Lessons from 3D Printing." *Sloan Management Review* (Winter), reprint 54212.

Diamond, Jared M. 2005a [1997]. *Guns, Germs, and Steel: The Fates of Human Societies*. New York: W. W. Norton.

2005b. *Collapse: How Societies Choose to Fail or Succeed*. New York: Viking.

Dicke, Tom. 2010. "The Edsel: Forty Years as a Symbol of Failure." *Journal of Popular Culture* 43(3): 486–502.

Doebke, Matthias and Fabrizio Zilibotti. 2007. "Occupational Choice and the Spirit of Capitalism." NBER Working Paper 12917. Cambridge, MA: National Bureau of Economic Research.

Dollar, David and Aaart Kraay. 2002. "Growth Is Good for the Poor." *Journal of Economic Growth* 7(3): 195–225.

Easterly, William. 2007. "Inequality Does Cause Underdevelopment: Insights from a New Instrument." *Journal of Development Economics* 84(2): 755–776.

Economy, Elizabeth C. 2010. "The Game Changer: Coping with China's Foreign Policy Revolution." *Foreign Affairs* 89(6): 142–153.

Eichengreen, Barry. 2009. "The Dollar Dilemma." *Foreign Affairs* 88(5): 53–69.

Eisenhardt, Kathleen M. 1989. "Building Theories from Case Study Research." *Academy of Management Review* 14(4): 532–550.

Epstein, Ethan B. and Nathan Converse. 2008. *The Fate of Young Democracies.* Cambridge University Press.

Esping-Andersen, Gøsta. 1999. *Social Foundations of Postindustrial Economies.* Oxford University Press.

Euromonitor. 2010. *Global Clothing & Footwear: Unlocking Opportunity in a Challenging Operating Climate.* London: Euromonitor International.

Evans, Peter. 1997. "The Eclipse of the State? Reflections on Stateness in an Era of Globalization." *World Politics* 50(1): 62–87.

EWEA. 2011. *Annual Report 2010: Powering the Energy Debate.* Brussels: European Wind Energy Association.

Fagerberg, Jan and Martin Srholec. 2008. "National Innovation Systems, Capabilities, and Economic Development." *Research Policy* 37(9): 1417–1435.

FAO. 2006. *Livestock's Long Shadow: Environmental Issues and Options.* Rome: Food and Agriculture Organization.

Ferguson, Niall. 2006. *The War of the World: Twentieth-Century Conflict and the Descent of the West.* New York: Penguin.

2010. "Complexity and Collapse." *Foreign Affairs* 89(2): 18–32.

2011. *Civilization: The West and the Rest.* New York: Penguin Press.

Fernández de Lis, Santiago and Emilio Ontiveros. 2009. "Towards More Symmetric and Anti-Cyclical Monetary and Financial Policies." http://voxeu.org/index.php?q=search/node/ontiveros (March) (accessed January 1, 2012).

Fielden, S. L. and M. J. Davidson, eds. 2010a. *International Handbook of Women and Small Business Entrepreneurship.* Cheltenham: Edward Elgar.

2010b. *International Research Handbook on Successful Women Entrepreneurs.* Cheltenham: Edward Elgar.

Firebaugh, Glen. 2000. "The Trend in Between-Nation Income Inequality." *Annual Review of Sociology* 26: 323–339.

Florida, Richard. 2005. "The World is Spiky." *The Atlantic Monthly* (October): 48–50.

Floud, Sir Roderick, Robert William Fogel, Bernard Harris, and Sok Chul Hong. 2011. *The Changing Body: Health Nutrition, and Human Development in the Western World since 1700.* Cambridge University Press.

Flyvbjerg, Bent. 2006. "Five Misunderstandings about Case-Study Research." *Qualitative Inquiry* 12(2): 219–245.

Fourcade-Gourinchas, Marion and Sarah L. Babb. 2002. "The Rebirth of the Liberal Creed: Paths to Neoliberalism in Four Countries." *American Journal of Sociology* 107(9): 533–579.

Freedman, Charles, Michael Kumhof, Douglas Laxton, and Jaewood Lee. 2009. "The Case for a Global Fiscal Stimulus." IMF Staff Position Note 09/03, issued March 6. Washington, DC: International Monetary Fund.

Frey, Carl Benedikt and Michael A. Osborne. 2013. "The Future of Employment: How Susceptible Are Jobs to Computerization? Oxford Martin Programme on the Impacts of Future Technology." www.oxfordmartin.ox.ac.uk/down loads/academic/The_Future_of_Employment.pdf (accessed July 9, 2015).

Friedberg, Aaron L. 2011. *A Contest for Supremacy: China, America, and the Struggle for Mastery in Asia*. New York: W. W. Norton.

Friedman, George. 2009. *The Next 100 Years: A Forecast for the 21st Century*. New York: Anchor Books.

Friedman, Thomas L. 2005. *The World Is Flat: A Brief History of the 21st Century*. New York: Farrar, Straus & Giroux.

Fukuyama, Francis. 1989. "The End of History?" *The National Interest* (Summer).

Furman, Jeffrey L., Michael E. Porter, and Scott Stern. 2002. "The Determinants of National Innovative Capacity." *Research Policy* 31(6): 899–933.

Garrett, Geoffrey. 1998. *Partisan Politics in the Global Economy*. Cambridge University Press.

GEM. 2013. *2012 Report on Women and Entrepreneurship*. www.gemconsor tium.org/docs/download/2825 (accessed April 9, 2015).

  2015. *GEM 2014 Global Report*. www.gemconsortium.org/docs/3616/gem-2014-global-report (accessed April 9, 2015).

Gerring, John. 2007. *Case Study Research*. Cambridge University Press.

Ghemawat, Pankaj. 2007. "Why the World Isn't Flat." *Foreign Policy* (March–April): 54–60.

  2011. *World 3.0: Global Prosperity and How to Achieve It*. Boston, MA: Harvard Business Review Press.

Gilpin, Robert. 1981. *War and Change in World Politics*. Cambridge University Press.

  1987. *The Political Economy of International Relations*. Princeton University Press.

  2000. *The Challenge of Global Capitalism*. Princeton University Press.

Gittelman, Michelle. 2006. "National Institutions, Public–Private Knowledge Flows, and Innovation Performance." *Research Policy* 35(7): 1052–1068.

Glavic, Peter and Rebeka Lukman. 2007. "Review of Sustainability Terms and their Definitions." *Journal of Cleaner Production* 15(18): 1875–1885.

Glick, Reuven and Andrew K. Rose. 1999. "Contagion and Trade: Why Are Currency Crises Regional?" *Journal of International Money and Finance* 18(4): 603–617.

Goldemberg, José, Suani Teixeira Coelho, and Patricia Guardabassi. 2008. "The Sustainability of Ethanol Production from Sugarcane." *Energy Policy* 36(6): 2086–2097.

Goldstone, Jack A. 2009. *Why Europe? The Rise of the West in World History, 1500– 1850.* Boston, MA: McGraw-Hill.

2011. "Understanding the Revolutions of 2011: Weakness and Resilience in Middle Eastern Autocracies." *Foreign Affairs* 90(3): 8–16.

2012. "A Theory of Political Demography." In Jack A. Goldstone, Eric P. Kaufmann, and Monica Duffy Toft, eds., *Political Demography: How Population Changes Are Reshaping International Security and National Politics.* Boulder, CO: Paradigm Publishers, pp. 10–28.

Grossbard, Shoshana Amyra and Alfredo Marvao Pereira. 2010. "Will Women Save More than Men? A Theoretical Model of Savings and Marriage." CESifo Working Paper No. 3146. Munich: Ifo Institute for Economic Research.

Guillén, Mauro F. 2001. *The Limits of Convergence: Globalization & Organizational Change in Argentina, South Korea, and Spain.* Princeton University Press.

ed. 2013. *Women Entrepreneurs: Inspiring Stories from Emerging Economies and Developing Countries.* New York: Routledge.

2015. *The Architecture of Collapse: The Global System in the 21st Century.* Oxford University Press.

Guillén, Mauro F. and Esteban García-Canal. 2009. "The American Model of the Multinational Firm and the 'New' Multinationals from Emerging Economies." *Academy of Management Perspectives* 23(2): 23–35.

2010. "How to Conquer New Markets with Old Skills." *Harvard Business Review* 88(11): 118–122.

Guillén, Mauro F. and Sandra L. Suárez. 2005. "Explaining the Global Digital Divide: Economic, Political and Sociological Drivers of Cross-National Internet Use." *Social Forces* 84(2): 681–708.

2010. "The Global Crisis of 2007–2009: Markets, Politics, and Organizations." *Research in the Sociology of Organizations* 30A: 257–279.

Haggard, Stephan. 1990. *Pathways from the Periphery: The Politics of Growth in the Newly Industrializing Countries.* Ithaca, NY: Cornell University Press.

Haggard, Stephan and Robert R. Kaufman. 1995. *The Political Economy of Democratic Transitions*. Princeton University Press.

Hamel, Jacques. 1993. *Case Study Methods*. Newbury Park, CA: Sage.

Hansen, Jim. 2006. "The Tipping Point?" *New York Review of Books* (January 12).

Harley, Sharon. 2007. *Women's Labor in the Global Economy: Speaking in Multiple Voices*. New Brunswick, NJ: Rutgers University Press.

Harrison, Ann and Margaret McMillan. 2007. "Outlining a Research Agenda on the Links between Globalization and Poverty." *Journal of Economic Inequality* 5(1): 123–134.

Henisz, Witold J., Bennet A. Zelner, and Mauro F. Guillén. 2005. "Market-Oriented Infrastructure Reforms, 1977–1999." *American Sociological Review* 70(6): 871–897.

Hillebrand, Evan. 2008. "The Global Distribution of Income in 2050." *World Development* 36(5): 727–740.

Hobsbawm, Eric. 1994. *The Age of Extremes: A History of the World, 1914–1991*. London: Michael Joseph.

Howe, Neil and Richard Jackson. 2012. "Demography and Geopolitics." In Jack A. Goldstone, Eric P. Kaufmann, and Monica Duffy Toft, eds., *Political Demography: How Population Changes Are Reshaping International Security and National Politics*. Boulder, CO: Paradigm Publishers, pp. 31–48.

Hu Angang. 2011. *China in 2020: A New Type of Superpower*. Washington, DC: Brookings Institution Press.

Huntington, Samuel P. 1993. "The Clash of Civilizations?" *Foreign Affairs* 72(3): 22–49.

Hymer, Stephen. 1976 [1960]. *The International Operations of National Firms: A Study of Direct Foreign Investment*. Cambridge, MA: MIT Press.

IEA. 2010. *World Energy Outlook*. Paris: International Energy Agency.

Ikenberry, G. John. 2006. *Liberal Order and Imperial Ambition: Essays on American Power and World Politics*. Cambridge, MA: Polity Press.

  2011. "The Future of the Liberal World Order." *Foreign Affairs* 90(3): 56–68.

ILO. 2009. *Global Employment Trends for Women*. Geneva: International Labor Office.

IMF. 2007a. "Globalization and Inequality." In *World Economic Outlook*, pp. 31–65. Washington, DC: International Monetary Fund.

  2007b. "The Globalization of Labor." In *World Economic Outlook*, Chapter 5. Washington, DC: International Monetary Fund.

  2009. *Global Financial Stability Report*. Washington, DC: International Monetary Fund.

2010. *Long-Term Trends in Public Finances in the G-7 Economies.* Washington, DC: International Monetary Fund.

2011. *World Economic Outlook: Tensions from the Two-Speed Recovery: Unemployment, Commodities, and Capital Flows.* Washington, DC: International Monetary Fund.

2015. *World Economic Outlook: Uneven Growth.* Washington, DC: International Monetary Fund.

Jacques, Martin. 2009. *When China Rules the World: The Rise of the Middle Kingdom and the End of the Western World.* New York: Allen Lane.

Jakab, Zoltan and Michael Kumhof. 2015. "Banks Are Not Intermediaries of Loanable Funds – and Why this Matters." Working Paper No. 529. London: Bank of England.

Jaquette, Jane S. and Kathleen Staudt. 2006. "Women, Gender, and Development." In Jane S. Jaquette and Gale Summerfield, eds., *Women and Gender Equity in Development Theory and Practice.* Durham, NC: Duke University Press, pp. 17–52.

Johnson, Malcolm L., ed. 2005. *The Cambridge Handbook of Age and Aging.* Cambridge University Press.

Kaid, Lynda Lee. 2009. "Changing and Staying the Same: Communication in Campaign 2008." *Journalism Studies* 10(3): 417–423.

Kapstein, Ethan B. and Nathan Converse. 2008. *The Fate of New Democracies.* Cambridge University Press.

Kennedy, Paul. 1987. *The Rise and Fall of the Great Powers.* New York: Vintage.

Keohane, Robert O. 1984. *After Hegemony: Cooperation and Discord in the World Political Economy.* Princeton University Press.

Khanna, Ayesha and Parag Khanna. 2014. "Disciplining the Sharing Economy." Project Syndicate, 25 September. www.project-syndicate.org/commentary/ayesha-khanna-and-parag-khanna-on-why-smart-regulation-will-bring-the-best-out-of-the-sharing-economy#VmvABMa3PEd0rHer.99 (accessed July 9, 2015).

Kharas, Homi. 2010. "The Emerging Middle Class in Developing Countries." OECD Working Paper No. 285. Paris: OECD.

Kissinger, Henry. 2011. *On China.* New York: Penguin Press.

Klapper, Leora, Raphael S. Amit, and Mauro F. Guillén. 2010. "Entrepreneurship and Firm Formation across Countries." In Josh Lerner and Antoinette Schoar, eds., *International Differences in Entrepreneurship.* University of Chicago Press and National Bureau of Economic Research, pp. 129–158.

Kokubun, Ryosei and Jisi Wang, eds. 2004. *The Rise of China and a Changing East Asian Order.* Tokyo: Japan Center for International Exchange.

Kristinsson, Kari and Rekha Rao. 2008. "Interactive Learning or Technology Transfer as a Way to Catch-Up? Analysing the Wind Energy Industry in Denmark and India." *Industry and Innovation* 15(3): 297–320.

Krugman, Paul. 1994. "Competitiveness: A Dangerous Obsession." *Foreign Affairs* 73(2): 28–44.

Kumhof, Michael and Romain Ranciere. 2010. "Inequality, Leverage, and Crises." IMF Working Paper No. 10/268. Washington, DC: International Monetary Fund.

La Porta, Rafael, Florencio Lopez-de-Silanes, Andrei Shleifer, and Robert W. Vishny. 1998. "Law and Finance." *Journal of Political Economy* 106(6): 113–155.

Laeven, Luc and Fabian Valencia. 2008. "Systemic Banking Crises: A New Database." IMF Working Paper 08/224. Washington, DC: International Monetary Fund.

Lancaster, Chase and Anubhav Raj. 2009. "Rational Lifetime Investment Strategies: Gender Differences in the Allocation of Assets in Retirement Savings Plans." Honors Thesis, Duke University. http://econ.duke.edu/ uploads/media_items/lancaster-chase-raj-anubhav.original.pdf (accessed April 3, 2015).

Landes, David. 1998. *The Wealth and Poverty of Nations: Why Some Are So Rich and Some Are So Poor.* New York: W. W. Norton.

2003. *The Unbound Prometheus: Technological Change 1750 to the Present.* Cambridge University Press.

Lang, Lily, Victoria Ivahina, and Josh Lerner. 2013. "The Disintermediation of Financial Markets: Direct Investing in Private Equity." NBER Working Paper No. 19299. Cambridge, MA: National Bureau of Economic Research.

Lèbre La Rovere, Emilio, André Santos Pereira, and André Felipe Simões. 2011. "Biofuels and Sustainable Energy Development in Brazil." *World Development* 39(6): 1026–1036.

Lema, Adrian and Kristian Ruby. 2007. "Between Fragmented Authoritarianism and Policy Coordination: Creating a Chinese Market for Wind Energy." *Energy Policy* 35: 3879–3890.

Lewis, Patricia. 2006. "The Quest for Invisibility: Female Entrepreneurs and the Masculine Norm of Entrepreneurship." *Gender, Work and Organization* 13(5): 453–469.

Lin, Justin Yifu. 2012. *Demystifying the Chinese Economy.* Cambridge University Press.

Lior, Noam. 2008. "Energy Resources and Use: The Present Situation and Possible Paths to the Future." *Energy* 33(6): 842–857.

Lipset, Martin Seymour. 1959. "Some Social Requisites of Democracy: Economic Development and Political Legitimacy." *American Political Science Review* 53(1): 69–105.

Liu, Xielin and Steven White. 2001. "Comparing Innovation Systems." *Research Policy* 30: 1091–1114.

Lloyd-Sherlock, Peter. 2010. *Population Ageing and International Development*. Bristol: Policy Press.

Lupu, Noam and Jonas Pontusson. 2011. "The Structure of Inequality and the Politics of Redistribution." *American Political Science Review* 105(2): 316–336.

Lusardi, Annamaria and Olivia S. Mitchell. 2014. "The Economic Importance of Financial Literacy: Theory and Evidence." *Journal of Economic Literature* 52(1): 1–40.

Mansfield, Edward D. and Helen V. Milner. 1999. "The New Wave of Regionalism." *International Organization* 53(3): 589–627.

Martinez, Alonso and Ronald Haddock. 2007. "The Flatbread Factor." *strategy +business*. www.strategy-business.com/article/07106?pg=all (accessed March 25, 2015).

Matthew, Richard. 2012. "Demography, Climate Change, and Conflict." In Jack A. Goldstone, Eric P. Kaufmann, and Monica Duffy Toft, eds., *Political Demography: How Population Changes Are Reshaping International Security and National Politics*. Boulder, CO: Paradigm Publishers, pp. 133–146.

Matthiessen, Christian Wichmann, Annette Winkel Schwarz, and Søren Find. 2006. "World Cities of Knowledge." *Journal of Knowledge Management* 10(5): 14–25.

McGillivray, Mark and Norab Markova. 2010. "Global Inequality in Well-Being Dimensions." *Journal of Development Studies* 46(2): 371–378.

McKinsey Global Institute. 2015. *The Internet of Things: Mapping the Value Beyond the Hype*. Chicago, IL: McKinsey Global Institute.

McNeill, William H. 1963. *The Rise of the West: A History of the Human Community*. University of Chicago Press.

Megginson, William L. and Jeffry M. Netter. 2001. "From State to Market: A Survey of Empirical Studies on Privatization." *Journal of Economic Literature* 39(2): 321–389.

Merrill Lynch. 2012. *Affluent Insights Survey 2012*. New York: Merrill Lynch.

Meyer, John W., John Boli, George M. Thomas, and Francisco O. Ramirez. 1997. "World Society and the Nation-State." *American Journal of Sociology* 103(1): 144–181.

Milanovic, Branko. 2009. "Global Inequality Recalculated: The Effect of New 2005 PPP Estimates on Global Inequality." Policy Research Working Paper 5061. Washington, DC: World Bank.

Mirchandani, Kiran. 1999. "Feminist Insight on Gendered Work: New Directions in Research on Women and Entrepreneurship." *Gender, Work and Organization* 6(4): 224–235.

Moore, Barrington. 1966. *Social Origins of Dictatorship and Democracy: Lord and Peasant in the Making of the Modern World.* Boston, MA: Beacon Press.

Moran, Theodore H. 1977. *Multinational Corporations and the Politics of Dependence: Copper in Chile.* Princeton University Press.

Morris, Ian. 2010. *Why the West Rules – For Now: The Patterns of History, and What They Reveal about the Future.* New York: Farrar, Straus & Giroux.

Munck, Gerardo L. 2003. "Measures of Democracy, Governance and Rule of Law: An Overview of Cross-National Data Sets." Los Angeles: School of International Relations, University of Southern California. http://sitere sources.worldbank.org/INTMOVOUTPOV/Resources/2104215–114806336 3276/071503_Munck.pdf (accessed August 24, 2011).

Murphy, Kevin M., Andrei Shleifer, and Robert Vishny. 1989. "Income Distribution, Market Size, and Industrialization." *Quarterly Journal of Economics* 104(3): 537–564.

Nathan, Andrew J. 2011. *America's Challenge: Engaging a Rising China in the Twenty-First Century.* Washington, DC: Carnegie Endowment for International Peace.

Naudé, Wim. 2010. "Entrepreneurship Is Not a Binding Constraint on Growth and Development in the Poorest Countries." *World Development* 39(1): 33–44.

Neiva de Figueiredo, João and Mauro F. Guillén, eds. 2011. *Green Products: Perspectives of Innovation and Adoption.* New York: Productivity Press.

Nichter, Simeon and Lara Goldmark. 2009. "Small Firm Growth in Developing Countries." *World Development* 37(9): 1453–1464.

Nidumolu, Ram, C. K. Prahalad, and M. R. Rangaswami. 2009. "Why Sustainability Is Now the Key Driver of Innovation." *Harvard Business Review* 87(9): 56–64.

Nomura. 2009. "China: A Secular Shift." *Asian Bank Reflections,* Volume 3.

Nordhaus, William and Edward Kokkelenberg, eds. 1999. *Nature's Numbers: Expanding the National Economic Accounts to Include the Environment.* Washington, DC: National Academies Press.

North, Douglass C. 1990. *Institutions, Institutional Change, and Economic Performance.* Cambridge University Press.

   1991. "Institutions." *Journal of Economic Perspectives* 5(1): 97–112.

   1997. "Understanding Economic Change." In Joan M. Nelson, Charles Tilly, and Lee Walker, eds., *Tranforming Post-Communist Political Economies.* Washington, DC: National Academy Press, pp. 13–18.

Nye, Joseph S., Jr. 1990. *Bound to Lead: The Changing Nature of American Power.* New York: Basic Books.

   2004. *Soft Power: The Means to Success in World Politics.* New York: Public Affairs.

   2010. "The Future of American Power: Dominance and Decline in Perspective." *Foreign Affairs* 89(6): 2–12.

   2011. *The Future of Power.* New York: Public Affairs.

Nye, Joseph S., Jr. and Jisi Wang. 2009. "Hard Decisions on Soft Power: Opportunities and Difficulties for Chinese Soft Power." *Harvard International Review* 31(2): 18–22.

OECD. 2004. *Women's Entrepreneurship: Issues and Policies.* Paris: Organisation for Economic Co-operation and Development.

   2008. *The Seoul Declaration for the Future of the Internet Economy.* Paris: OECD. www.oecd.org/internet/consumer/40839436.pdf (accessed October 8, 2015).

   2011a. *Towards Green Growth.* Paris: Organisation for Economic Cooperation and Development.

   2011b. "Greening Growth." www.oecd.org/document/25/0,3746,en_2649_201185_48443289_1_1_1_1,00.html (accessed September 7, 2011).

   2011c. *Divided We Stand: Why Inequality Keeps Rising.* Paris: OECD Publishing. http://dx.doi.org/10.1787/9789264119536-en (accessed January 1, 2012).

   2013. "Measuring the Internet Economy: A Contribution to the Research Agenda." OECD Digital Economy Papers, No. 226. Paris: OECD Publishing. http://dx.doi.org/10.1787/5k43gjg6r8jf-en (accessed July 9, 2015).

   2014a. *Measuring the Digital Economy: A New Perspective.* Paris: OECD Publishing.

   2014b. "Skills and Jobs in the Internet Economy." OECD Digital Economy Papers, No. 242. Paris: OECD Publishing. http://dx.doi.org/10.1787/5jxvbrjm9bns-en (accessed July 9, 2015).

Olson, Mancur. 1982. *The Rise and Decline of Nations: Economic Growth, Stagflation, and Social Rigidities.* New Haven, CT: Yale University Press.

Oneal, John R. 1992. "The Affinity of Foreign Investors for Authoritarian Regimes." *Political Research Quarterly* 47(3): 565–588.

O'Neill, Jim. 2011. *The Growth Map: Economic Opportunity in the BRICs and Beyond*. New York: Penguin.

Ontiveros, Emilio. 2000. *La Economía en la Red: Nueva Economía, Nuevas Finanzas*. Madrid: Taurus.

      2015. "Treinta años después: evidencias e interrogantes." *Telos* 100 (April).

Ontiveros, Emilio and Santiago Fernández de Lis. 2010. "Euroland Put to the Test: Can European Monetary Union Still Be Saved?" *International Policy Analysis* (Friedrich Ebert Stiftung) (May): 19–23.

Ontiveros, Emilio, Ignacio Rodríguez Teubal, and Álvaro Martín Enríquez. 2008. "EU–Mercosur Business Cooperation: ICTs and the Information Society. Working Group on EU–Mercosur Negotiations. Reviving the EU-Mercosur Trade Talks." *Fecomercio* (July): 236–264.

Philippon, Thomas and Ariell Reshef. 2013. "An International Look at the Growth of Modern Finance." *Journal of Economic Perspectives* 27(2): 73–96.

Polanyi, Karl. 1957 [1944]. *The Great Transformation*. Boston, MA: Beacon Press.

Polillo, Simone and Mauro F. Guillén. 2005. "Globalization Pressures and the State: The Global Spread of Central Bank Independence." *American Journal of Sociology* 110(6): 1764–1802.

Pomeranz, Kenneth. 2000. *The Great Divergence: China, Europe, and the Making of the Modern World Economy*. Princeton University Press.

Rajan, Raghuram. 2005. "Has Financial Development Made the World Riskier?" Kansas City: Federal Reserve Bank of Kansas City, August. www.kansasci tyfed.org/PUBLICAT/SYMPOS/2005/PDF/Rajan2005.pdf (accessed July 9, 2015).

Ramo, Joshua Cooper. 2009. *The Age of the Unthinkable: Why the New World Disorder Constantly Surprises Us and What We Can Do About It*. New York: Little, Brown.

Reddy, Sudhakar and Jyoti Painuly. 2004. "Diffusion of Renewable Energy Technologies: Barriers and Stakeholders' Perspectives." *Renewable Energy* 29(9): 1431–1447.

Reinhardt, Carmen M. and Kenneth S. Rogoff. 2009. *This Time Is Different: Eight Centuries of Financial Folly*. Princeton University Press.

Reinhardt, Forest L. 2008. "Environmental Product Differentiation: Implications for Corporate Strategy." In Michael V. Russo, ed., *Environmental Management: Readings and Cases*. Thousand Oaks, CA: Sage, pp. 205–227.

Roberts, Paul. 2004. *The End of Oil: On the Edge of a Perilous New World.* Boston, MA: Houghton Mifflin.

Robertson, Roland. 1992. *Globalization: Social Theory and Global Culture.* London: Sage.

Rodrik, Dani. 2006. "Goodbye Washington Consensus, Hello Washington Confusion?" *Journal of Economic Literature* 44(4): 973–987.

Rothbard, Nancy P. and Jeanne M. Brett. 2000. "Promote Equal Opportunity by Recognizing Gender Differences in the Experience of Work and Family." In E. A. Locke, ed., *The Blackwell Handbook of Principles of Organizational Behavior.* Oxford: Blackwell, pp. 389–403.

Rozanov, Andrew. 2005. "Who Holds the Wealth of Nations?" *Central Banking Journal* 15(4): 52–57.

Rueschemeyer, Dietrich, Evelyn Huber Stephens, and John D. Stephens. 1992. *Capitalist Development and Democracy.* University of Chicago Press.

Schmidt, Eric and Jared Cohen. 2013. *The New Digital Age: Reshaping the Future of People, Nations, and Business.* New York: Knopf.

Schumpeter, Joseph A. 1934. *The Theory of Economic Development.* Cambridge, MA: Harvard University Press.

　　1975. *Capitalism, Socialism and Democracy.* New York: Harper.

Sciubba, Jennifer Dabbs. 2012. "A New Framework for Aging and Security." In Jack A. Goldstone, Eric P. Kaufmann, and Monica Duffy Toft, eds., *Political Demography: How Population Changes Are Reshaping International Security and National Politics.* Boulder, CO: Paradigm Publishers, pp. 63–77.

Sebai, Saber. 2014. "Further Evidence on Gender Differences and their Impact on Risk Aversion." *Journal of Business Studies Quarterly* 6(1): 308–319.

Semenov, Mikhail A. and Peter R. Shewry. 2011. "Modeling Predicts that Heat Stress, Not Drought, Will Increase Vulnerability of Wheat in Europe." *Scientific Reports* 1: article number 66. www.nature.com/srep/2011/110818/srep00066/full/srep00066.html?WT.ec_Id=SREP-20110823 (accessed September 6, 2011).

Sen, Amartya. 1992. *Inequality Re-Examined.* Cambridge, MA: Harvard University Press.

Setser, Brad W. and Rachel Ziemba. 2009. *GCC Sovereign Funds: Reversal of Fortune.* New York: Council on Foreign Relations Press.

Shen Dingli. 2009. "Sino-American Relations: Mutual Accommodation." *International Studies* 1. www.cas.fudan.edu.cn/view.en.php?id=1563.

Shleifer, Andrei S., Rafael La Porta, and Florencio Lopez-de-Silanes. 2008. "The Economic Consequences of Legal Origins." *Journal of Economic Literature* 46(2):285–332.

Snyder, Margaret. 2000. *Women in African Economies: From Burning Sun to Boardroom*. Kampala, Uganda: Fountain Publishers.

Sovacool, Benjamin. 2008. "Renewable Energy: Economically Sound, Politically Difficult." *The Electricity Journal* 21(5): 18–29.

Spence, Michael. 2011. "The Impact of Globalization on Income and Employment: The Downside of Integrating Markets." *Foreign Affairs* 90(4): 28–41.

Spengler, Oswald. 1932 [1918–1923]. *The Decline of the West*. New York: Alfred A. Knopf.

Stern, Nicholas. 2007. *The Economics of Climate Change: Stern Review*. Cambridge University Press.

Stiglitz, Joseph E. 2002. *Globalization and Its Discontents*. New York: W. W. Norton.

Strange, Susan. 1996. *The Retreat of the State: The Diffusion of Power in the World Economy*. Cambridge University Press.

Suárez, Sandra L. 2006. "Mobile Democracy: Text Messages, Voter Turnout, and the 2004 Spanish General Election." *Representation* 42(2): 117–128.

   2014. "Symbolic Politics and the Regulation of Executive Compensation: A Comparison of the Great Depression and Great Recession." *Politics & Society* 42(1): 73–105.

Subramanian, Arvind. 2011. *Eclipse: Living in the Shadow of China's Economic Dominance*. Washington, DC: Peterson Institute for International Economics.

Sundén, A. and B. Surette. 1998. "Gender Differences in the Allocation of Assets in Retirement Savings Plans." *American Economic Review Papers and Proceedings* 88(2): 207–211.

Swaine, Michael D. 2011. *America's Challenge: Engaging a Rising China in the Twenty-first Century*. Washington, DC: Carnegie Endowment for International Peace.

Sydorovych, Olha and Ada Wossink. 2008. "The Meaning of Agricultural Sustainability: Evidence from a Conjoint Choice Survey." *Agricultural Systems* 98(1): 10–20.

Tarrow, Sidney. 2001. "Transnational Politics: Contention and Institutions in International Politics." *Annual Review of Political Science* 4: 1–20.

Taylor, Philip. 2008. *Ageing Labour Forces*. Cheltenham: Edward Elgar.

Thomson Reuters. 2013. *Building BRICKs*. New York: Thomson Reuters.

Toynbee, Arnold Joseph. 1934–1961. *A Study of History*, 12 vols. New York University Press.

Treisman, Daniel. 2007. "What Have We Learned about the Causes of Corruption from Ten Years of Cross-National Empirical Research?" *Annual Review of Political Science* 10: 211–244.

TrendLab. 2011. *Global Risk: New Perspectives and Opportunities*. Philadelphia, PA: Knowledge@Wharton.

Truman, Edwin M. 2008. *A Blueprint for Sovereign Wealth Fund Best Practices*. Washington, DC: Peterson Institute for International Economics.

2010. *Sovereign Wealth Funds: Threat or Salvation?* Washington, DC: Peterson Institute for International Economics.

UN. 2010. *2009 Global Trends: Refugees, Asylum-Seekers, Returnees, Internally Displaced and Stateless Persons*. New York: United Nations High Commissioner for Refugees.

UNCTAD. 2010. *World Investment Report 2010*. New York: United Nations Conference on Trade and Development.

2011. *World Investment Report 2011*. New York: United Nations Conference on Trade and Development.

2014. *World Investment Report 2014*. New York: United Nations Conference on Trade and Development.

2015. *World Investment Report 2015*. New York: United Nations Conference on Trade and Development.

UNESCO. 2009. *Water in a Changing World*. Paris: United Nations Educational, Scientific and Cultural Organization.

UNIFEM. 2005. *Progress of the World's Women 2005*. New York: United Nations Development Fund for Women.

2010. *Annual Report 2009–2010*. New York: United Nations Development Fund for Women.

Urdal, Henrik. 2012. "Youth Bulges and Violence." In Jack A. Goldstone, Eric P. Kaufmann, and Monica Duffy Toft, eds., *Political Demography: How Population Changes Are Reshaping International Security and National Politics*. Boulder, CO: Paradigm Publishers, pp. 117–132.

Van Agtmael, Antoine. 2007. *The Emerging Markets Century: How a New Breed of World-Class Companies is Overtaking the World*. New York: Free Press.

Vernon, Raymond. 1971. *Sovereignty at Bay: The Multinational Spread of US Enterprises*. New York: Basic Books.

Véron, Nicolas and B. Wolff Guntram. 2015. *Capital Markets Union: A Vision for the Long Term*. Bruegel Policy Contribution. http://bruegel.org/2015/04/capital-markets-union-a-vision-for-the-long-term/ (accessed October 8, 2015).

Victor, David G. and Kassia Yanosek. 2011. "The Crisis in Clean Energy." *Foreign Affairs* 90(4): 112–120.

Wallerstein, Immanuel. 1974. *The Modern World-System: Capitalist Agriculture and the Origins of the European World-Economy in the Sixteenth Century.* New York: Academic Press.

Walter, Carl E. and Fraser J. T. Howie. 2011. *Red Capitalism: The Fragile Financial Foundation of China's Extraordinary Rise.* Singapore: John Wiley.

Wang Jisi. 2011. "China's Search for a Grand Strategy." *Foreign Affairs* 90(2): 68–79.

Waughray, Dominic, ed. 2011. *Water Security: The Water–Food–Energy–Climate Nexus.* Washington, DC: Island Press/World Economic Forum.

Weber, Klaus, Gerald F. Davis, and Michael Lounsbury. 2009. "Policy as Myth and Ceremony: The Global Spread of Stock Exchanges, 1980–2005." *Academy of Management Journal* 52(6): 1319–1347.

Weber, Max. 1978. *Economy and Society.* Berkeley, CA: University of California Press.

WEF. 2011. *The Global Gender Gap Report.* Geneva: World Economic Forum.
    2015. *The Role of Financial Services in Society: Statement in Support of Macroprudential Policies.* Geneva: World Economic Forum.

Willenbockel, Dirk. 2011. *Exploring Food Prices: Scenarios Towards 2030 with a Global Multi-Region Model. Oxfam Research Reports.* Institute of Development Studies at the University of Sussex.

World Bank. 2001. *Engendering Development through Gender Equality in Rights, Resources, and Voice.* Washington, DC: World Bank.
    2009. *Doing Business: Women in Africa.* Washington, DC: World Bank.
    2010a. *Women, Business, and the Law.* Washington, DC: World Bank.
    2010b. "About Doing Business." www.doingbusiness.org/reports (accessed 16 August, 2010).
    2010c. "Indicators of Governance and Institutional Quality." http://sitere sources.worldbank.org/INTLAWJUSTINST/Resources/IndicatorsGovernan ceandInstitutionalQuality.pdf.
    2011a. *World Development Indictors.* Washington, DC: World Bank.
    2011b. *Multipolarity: The New Global Economy.* Washington, DC: World Bank.
    2014. *Doing Business 2015: Going Beyond Efficiency.* Washington, DC: World Bank.

WWF. 2010. *Living Planet Report 2010: Biodiversity, Biocapacity, and Development.* Gland, Switzerland: World Wide Fund for Nature.

Yin, Robert K. 2003. *Case Study Research: Design and Methods*, 3rd edition. Thousand Oaks, CA: Sage.

Zhu Feng. 2008. "China's Rise Will Be Peaceful: How Unipolarity Matters." In Robert S. Ross and Zhu Feng, *China's Ascent: Power, Security, and the Future of International Politics*. Ithaca, NY: Cornell University Press, pp. 34–54.

Zingales, Luigi. 2015. "Does Finance Benefit Society?" NBER Working Paper No. 20894. Cambridge, MA: National Bureau of Economic Research.

Index

3D printing, 113
9/11, 1

Abu Dhabi Investment Authority, 31–2
Accenture, 12
Acer, 26
Afghanistan
    state failure in, 5
Africa
    Chinese and Indian investments in,
        33
    mobile phone use in, 27
aging, 39, 52–5
    impact on women, 87
AIDS, 81
AiG, 153
Alexander the Great, 69
anocracies. see failed states
Arab Spring, 56, 89, 193
Arcor, 26
authoritarian regimes. see dictatorship

banks. see financial services
Barclays, 32
Bharti Airtel, 27
Bimbo, 26
biofuels, 53, 140
Blackstone, 32
Boserup, Ester, 129
Boston Consulting Group, 36
Brazil, 14, 17, 22, 26–7, 36, 53, 81, 90, 98,
        117
    growth model, 2
    population age structure in, 53
    R&D in, 22
Bremmer, Ian, 36, 65–6, 182–3
Bretton Woods, 11
BRICs (Brazil, Russia, India, China),
        12, 22
British Petroleum, 31

British riots, 89
Brundtland Commission, 139
business
    and sustainability, 94
BYD, 26

Carlyle Group, 32
Castells, Manuel, 8
Cemex, 26–7
Center for Systemic Peace, 67
Chaparral Steel, 27
Cheney, Dick, 182
Chernobyl, 137, 166
Chile, 27
    coup of 1973, 36
China. see also renminbi
    and its Asian neighbors, 172
    and its demographic decline, 168–73
    and its view on its own ascendancy,
        179–81
    and reserve currencies, 178
    and sustainability, 92
    as global power, 160, 162–75, 177,
        179–83
    as world's largest economy, 1
    economic and financial rise, 1
    entry into the WTO, 1
    gender imbalance in, 42
    growth model, 2
    inequality in, 77, 79
    poverty in, 83
    R&D in, 22
    wind turbine manufacturers in, 22
Citigroup, 32
climate change. see warming, global
clothing industry, 52
    and footwear combined, 53
Club of Rome, 137
CNOOC, 27
collaborative economy, 113–14

Cold War, 3
competitiveness
    and sustainability, 147–8
complexity, 3, 184, 186, 189–91
conflict, 70–2
    as a consequence of inequality, 87, 89–91
Corus Group, 27
crises
    currency, 15
crisis, financial, 1–3
crowd funding, 156

Decade for Women, 129
democracy
    transition to, 61–2, 64
demography
    global trends and turning points, 39–44,
        48, 51–5, 57–9
Diamond, Jared, 167
dictatorship
    and economic performance, 64
    and transition to democracy, 61–2, 64
DP World, 26, 31

Easterly, William, 84
Economist (magazine), 91
ecumene, 181
Embraer, 26
emerging economies, ix, 1–2
    accumulation of foreign exchange
        reserves by, 8
    and sustainability, 94
    R&D in, 21
emerging-market multinationals. *see*
    multinational firms
energy, 142–4
entrepreneurship, 123–35
    women in, 128–35
environment. *see* sustainability
Esping-Andersen, Gøsta, 129
Eurasia Group, 36, 66
Euromonitor, 48
Europe
    economic and financial crisis in, 16–17,
        92
European Union, 11, 17

Facebook, 65, 156
failed states, 68–70
    definition of, 60
families
    and demographic changes, 55
family structures, and population aging,
    55–6
Federal Reserve, 15
Ferguson, Niall, 71, 166
fertility, 40
    and women's education, 42
    in poor countries, 42
financial markets, 149–59, 194–5
financial services, 19–20, 149–59
    and shadow banking, 157
Financial Services Authority, 153
food, 139–41
Food and Agriculture Organization (FAO),
    140
Ford Motor Co., 101–2
foreign direct investment, 25–6
Fortune Global 500, 25
Franco, General, 60
Fraser Institute, 67
Freedom House, 67
Friedberg, Aaron, 182
Friedman, George, 172
Friedman, Thomas, 14
Fudan University, 181
Fukuyama, Francis, 59, 64

G7, 19, 21
G20, 21, 97
Gazprom, 26
GE Plastics, 27
gender. *see also* women
    and inequality, 85–7, 89, 104–7
General Motors, 38
geopolitics, 164–73, *see also* power
    and population size, 169–70
    and size of the economy, 169–71
    and wealth, 164–8
Gerdau, 27
Ghemawat, Pankaj, 10
Gilpin, Robert, 8
Global Institute for Tomorrow (GIFT), 146

global powers. *see also* geopolitics
  definition of, 164
Goldstone, Jack, 44
Google, 66
governance, 66–8
government, quality of. *see* governance
Great Depression, 17
green products and services, 148
Gulf Cooperation Council, 147
Gulf War of 1990–1991, 71
G-Zero, 183

Hansen, Jim, 138
Heritage Foundation, 124
high net worth individuals, 103–7
  female, 104–7
Hobsbawm, Eric, 59
Hu Angang, 179–80
Hu Jintao, 180
Huntington, Samuel, 59

IBM, 12
ICT (Information and Communications
  Technology), 111–13
  and employment, 114–15
  and government, 115–16
Ikenberry, John, 182
imbalances, global, 8–12, 14, 16–17, 19–22
IMF (International Monetary Fund), 17, 19,
  22, 35, 64, 79, 84, 110, 120, 195
India
  growth model, 2
  inequality in, 79, 84
  poverty in, 83
  R&D in, 22
Industrial and Commercial Bank, 27
inequality, 77, 79, 81–2
  and conflict, 87, 90
  and economic growth, 81
  and gender, 85–7, 89
  and poverty, 83–5
  and trade, 86
  consequences of, 87, 89–91
  defined, 77
  in wealth, 76
  within and across countries, 80–1

Infosys, 26
institutional domains, 191–4
institutional gearbox
  defined, 191–4
institutions 120–8. *see also* institutional
  gearbox
International Energy Agency, 142, 144
international system of states
  as institutional gearbox, 192
Internet
  and political mobilization, 64–6
iPhone, 172
ITT, 36

Jacques, Martin, 168
Jaguar, 27
Japan, 1
  fiscal problems in, 20

Kennedy, Paul, 166
Keohane, Robert, 166
Keynesian policies, 11
Kissinger, Henry, 160
Krugman, Paul, 181
Kuwait Investment Authority, 31
Kyoto Protocol, 137

labor market
  as institutional gearbox, 191
Land Rover, 27
Latin America
  mobile phone use in, 12
Lenovo, 26
life expectancy, 40
Lin, Justin Yifu, 179
London Stock Exchange, 31
long arc of instability, 62
Lucas paradox, 17

Malthus, Thomas R., 137
Marxism Today, 168
McKinsey and Co., 113
McNeill, William, 181
Mercosur, 11
Merrill Lynch, 32
MGM Mirage, 31

middle class, 92–102
  as consumer, 99–102
  definition, 94–5
migration, international, 39
MINTSs (Mexico, Indonesia, Nigeria, Turkey, South Africa), 12
mobile phones
  and political mobilization, 64–6
Model T Ford, 101
Moore's Law, 11
Morgan Stanley, 32
Morris, Ian, 167
Mubarak, Gamal, 61
Mubarak, Hosni, 61
multinational firms
  and national sovereignty, 37
  owned by the state, 36
multipolarity. see poly-centric world

Nair, Chandran, 146
Napoleon, 166
NASA, 138
National Academy of Sciences, 137
Nazi Germany, 166
Nigerian National Petroleum Corp, 33
North American Free Trade Agreement (NAFTA), 11
North Korea, 48, 60
Norwegian Government Pension Fund-Global, 32
Nye, Joseph, 66

O'Neill, Jim, 22
Obama, Barack, 65
obesity, 39, 48
occupy movement, 90, 193, 196
OECD (Organisation for Economic Co-operation and Development), 81, 83, 112

P&O, 31
Park, General, 60
Patten, Chris, 169
Peking University, 180
pensions, 20, 52
Polanyi, Karl, 87

political mobilization
  and new media, 64–6
political regimes, definition of, 60
political representation system
  as institutional gearbox, 192
poly-centric world, 37, 183
polygamy
  in Siberia, 42
population
  projections of world's total, 57
population growth, and geopolitical power, 44
Population Reference Bureau, 42
poverty, 5, 76–7, 83–4
power
  geopolitical, 35–7
  smart, 173
  soft, 172–3
power and multinational firms, 34
power, global balance of, 3, 6, 66
Prahalad, C.K., 148

Rajan, Raghuram, 149
rating agencies, 152
refugees, 70
regulation, financial, 154–5
regulation of sustainability. see sustainability
renminbi, 17
  as reserve currency, 169
Repsol YPF Brasil, 27
research and development (R&D), 21, 117
Research In Motion, 66
resource curse, 75
Rinker, 27
rise and decline of nations, 165–70, 172–3
  theories of, 168–70
Roberts, Paul, 139
Robertson, Ronald, 8
Robinson, Joan, 17
Roubini, Nouriel, 183

SABIC, 27
Sainsbury, 31
Samsung Electronics, 34
SARS, 3, 64

Saudi Arabia, 27
Schumpeter, Joseph, 21
Sen, Amartya, 81
Shen Dingli, 181
Silk Road, 69
Singapore Investment Corporation, 32
Sinopec, 27
skills gap, 79
smart power, 173
soft power, 172–3
Somalia, 5, 51
    state failure in, 60
South Korea, 30
Sovereign Wealth Fund Institute, 31
Sovereign wealth funds, 31–2
Soviet Union, 61
Spain, 53
    terrorist attacks, 65
Spence, Michael, 85
Spengler, Oswald, 165
St John, Henry, 165
Standard Bank Group, 27
Standard Chartered, 32
state
    capacity, 5
    capacity and legitimacy, 2
    legitimacy, 59
state apparatus
    as institutional gearbox, 193
state-owned enterprises, 68
Stern, Nicholas, 137
Subramanian, Arvind, 169
sultanistic regimes, 61, 75
    definition of, 61
sustainability, 136–45, 147–8
    and business practices, 148
    and competitiveness, 147–8
    and human behavior, 138
    and incentives, 139
    and regulation, 148
    and technology, 147
    and the economy, 136
    awareness of, 136
    China's role in, 145
    role of emerging economies in, 146–7
swine flu, 3

Tata Communications, 26
Tata Motors, 27, 101
Tata Steel, 27
technology, 108–18
    and banking, 155–6
    and inequality, 76
Tenaris, 26
terrorism, 59, 61
tipping point, 136
Tokyo, 37
Total, 31
Toynbee, Arnold, 165
trade
    and inequality, 87
trade blocs
    emergence of, 11
Transparency International, 67
Tsinghua University, 179
Turner, Lord, 153
turning points
    definition of, 7
    global, 149–59
twenty-first century
    characteristics of, 1–3, 5–7

UBS, 32
uncertainty, 2, 184, 195
United Kingdom, 37
United Nations, 22, 26
United Nations Population Division, 42
United States
    as global power, 117
    financial crisis in, 157
    marriage rates in, 42
Unocal, 27
urbanization, 44
Urdal, Henrik, 56
US Air Force, 72
US Congress
    action against Chinese acquisitions, 27
US Patent & Trademark Office, 34

Vale, 26
Vernon, Raymond, 36

Wang Jisi, 180
warming, global, 137
   and agriculture, 140
   and cities, 145
wars, 65, 70–1
   civil, 59
Washington Post, 90
water, 139, 141–2
wealth, inequality in. *see* inequality
Weber, Max, 67, 93
welfare state, and population aging, 39
Wen, Jiabao, 180
Westphalia, Peace of, 164
WikiLeaks, 65
Wilson, Charles, 38
Wipro, 26
women. *see* also gender
   and entrepreneurship, 128–35

and legal rights, 86
and politics, 87
work, and population aging, 150
World Bank, 21, 67, 76, 86, 102, 117, 120, 124
World Economic Forum, 67, 76, 87
World Trade Organization, 9, 11
World War II
   effect on government budget
      deficits, 9

Xiaoping, Deng, 84, 179

YouTube, 65
Yuan. *see* renminbi

Zain Africa, 27
Zhu Feng, 180